Understanding Psychological Research
An Introduction to Methods

Richard St. Jean
University of Prince Edward Island

with an Appendix by
Daniel J. Wiener

Toronto

Canadian Cataloguing in Publication Data

St. Jean, Richard, 1943-
Understanding psychological research: an introduction to methods
1st ed.
Includes index.
ISBN 0-13-027027-X
1. Psychology—Research—Methodology. 2. Psychology, Experimental.
I. Title.

BF76.5.S24 2001   150'.7'2   C00-932549-2

ISBN 0-13-027027-X

Vice President, Editorial Director: Michael Young
Editor-in-Chief: David Stover
Acquisitions Editor: Jessica Mosher
Marketing Manager: Judith Allen
Signing Representative: Jaycee Jovic
Associate Editor: John Polanszky
Production Editor: Susan Adlam
Copy Editor: Karen Bennett
Production Coordinator: Wendy Moran
Page Layout: Anne Mac Innis
Art Director: Mary Opper
Cover Design: Lisa LaPointe
Cover Image: PhotoDisc
1 2 3 4 5   05 04 03 02 01

Printed and bound in Canada

Prentice
Hall
Canada

For the Three C's - Carrie, Craig, and Connor.

CONTENTS

PREFACE

It is often difficult to find the perfect textbook to suit one's teaching needs. In teaching my research methods classes I tried several very detailed full-length texts that appealed to me, but which my students found tedious and difficult. Part of the problem was that the chapters tended to run long, often including numerous boxed inserts and elaborate research examples. Students sometimes had difficulty identifying and focussing on essential concepts—separating the wheat from the chaff, so to speak. I began searching for a briefer text that I hoped would present the essential concepts in a more concise, yet interesting and readable format. Not finding any that met all my criteria, I was persuaded to try to write my own. It was certainly a more difficult challenge than I imagined, and took longer than I anticipated, but I hope that I have succeeded at least in some small measure.

Although I did not start out to write a Canadian-oriented text, the book seems to have evolved in that direction. In the first place, I found myself including research examples drawn from my own work and that of my students and colleagues. Some, such as the Canadian Study of Health and Aging, reflect national concerns, while others were carried out in Canadian locations, focussed on Canadian populations, or dealt with issues of regional concern. In the second place, it seemed to me that a unit on research ethics intended for Canadian university students would not be very useful without a discussion of the Canadian Psychological Association (CPA) Code of Ethics and the new Tri-Council Policy. In the process of presenting this material I made the happy discovery that the four principles of the CPA Code serve exceptionally well as a central organizing framework for discussing the major ethical issues that occur in psychological research.

The book can be used in many different ways, but is primarily intended as a basic text for the research methods course that is usually required of psychology majors. It shows why (and how) research is the heart of the discipline, the basic tool for building an understanding of psychological processes. Fundamental methods such as observation, self reports, archival and trace research, and experimental and quasi-experimental designs are fully described and illustrated. The chapters have been kept relatively brief, primarily by not including the boxed inserts and sidebars that festoon full-length texts, so that it is usually possible to read each in a single session. Important terms and concepts appear in boldface and are defined in the text as they occur and also in a chapter glossary. Each chapter also has a summary that briefly reviews the main points. Separate appendices present the fundamentals of writing research reports in American Psychological Association (APA) style (including a sample paper) and an introduction to basic statistical concepts. I have presented the chapters in the order that I find most useful in my own teaching, but with few exceptions, they can be easily rearranged to suit different organizations.

ACKNOWLEDGMENTS

A textbook is never a solitary creation. I am fortunate to have received help and encouragement from many sources. Foremost among those due thanks is my department colleague Thomy Nilsson, whose persuasions were responsible for getting me started. Two other department colleagues, Philip Smith and Cathy Ryan, provided valuable advice and guidance regarding important issues in the ethics of research. Our lab instructor, Paul Gray, contributed helpful information on formatting research reports. I am also grateful to Don Gorassini, Maxwell Gwynn, and John Harpur, who furnished careful, detailed reviews of several early chapters. Special thanks to Dan Wiener, a former UPEI colleague (now at Central Connecticut State University), for allowing me to use his class handout on statistics as an appendix.

An important source of input was the written and verbal comments provided by many of the students enrolled in my research methods courses who voluntarily read drafts of chapters placed on library reserve. I was also fortunate to have had the services of several very bright and capable student assistants—Lynette Barrett, Karen Chipman, Kelly Robinson, and Shirliana Sherren—who tracked down references and helped edit preliminary drafts.

The good folks at Pearson Education Canada—acquisitions editors Nicole Lukach and Jessica Mosher, and developmental editors Lise Creurer and John Polanszky—dispensed helpful information and advice throughout and, most importantly, kept me on track and on schedule. I am also grateful to Karen Bennett for her careful copy editing.

Finally, a special word of thanks to my wife Carrie for her continuing love and support, and to our two boys, Craig and Connor, who showed remarkable forbearance and patience, especially in allowing Dad use of the family computer for extended periods of time.

INTRODUCTION TO RESEARCH METHODS

WHY A COURSE ON RESEARCH METHODS?

One popular image of psychologists is that of a Freudian analyst listening to a patient on a couch talk about sexual fantasies. This image is so pervasive that it is sometimes indiscriminately applied to all psychologists. Be prepared for the equivalent of "Oh, you're a psychologist. Are you going to analyze me?" A second popular image is that of a scientist in a lab coat attaching wires to people's heads to figure out how their brains work. This modern, hard science image of psychology may be more appealing to some students, while for others it conjures up a Frankenstein-like suggestion of control and dehumanization.

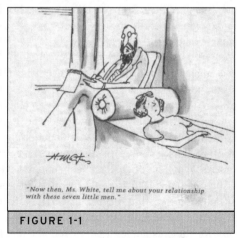

"Now then, Ms. White, tell me about your relationship with these seven little men."

FIGURE 1-1

Of course, neither image is representative of what the vast majority of psychologists do. Yet the two images do reflect a dichotomy in psychology not found to a comparable extent in any other discipline. Psychology is both an applied discipline that offers to help people directly and a basic science that tries to understand human behaviour. Other disciplines such as medicine and physiology seek to meet only one or the other of these objectives. Historically, both applied and basic science objectives have coexisted within the single discipline of psychology. (Although recent efforts to separate them have resulted in rival professional societies, both still employ the name psychology and share the common goal of increasing our understanding of human behaviour.) This dichotomy certainly creates difficulty for beginning students who may expect to be taught therapeutic techniques, but wind up learning about the results of experiments instead. Most students study psychology because they want to better understand themselves and others. At the start, research is far from their minds. A course in research methods is often taken only because it is a requirement for a psychology major or for certain upper-level courses. Therefore, it is not surprising that some students resent this requirement since they have no plans to do research themselves. Disciplines such as physics, biology, or history do not, typically, require undergraduate methods courses. So, why is a course on research methods required at an early stage in your psychology studies?

The Complexity of Behaviour

One reason for this requirement is the complex nature of psychology's subject matter. The complexity arises because there is such a tremendous amount of variability in behaviour. Surely you have noticed that different people encountering the same situation—whether it be a movie, a party, or a university exam—respond in many different ways. At a party, for example, some people mix freely and easily while others hang back at the fringes. To further complicate matters, an individual will behave differently at different times in the same situation. The person who is the life of the party on one occasion may be quiet and withdrawn on another occasion. This degree of variability does not occur in other sciences. For example, it makes no difference in a chemistry lab whether sulfur comes from Nevada, Saskatchewan, or Ethiopia; it reacts the same way every time. Not so in psychology. Variability stemming from genetics, cultural differences, social roles, changes in mood, and many other sources, makes "facts" in psychology much more difficult to establish than in other sciences.

As you proceed in your study of psychology you will discover many controversies and areas of dispute. These arise not only over what the facts mean but, at times, even over what the facts are. For instance, you may be aware of the recently publicized debates over the validity of "recovered" memories of sexual abuse. Some authorities argue that such memories represent actual events, while others are equally adamant that these memories are not genuine, but instead may literally be created by the therapists' suggestions and questions (Pezdek & Banks, 1996). Disagreements even persist over the extent that our everyday memories, even for very recently encountered events, may be subject to distortion. Do factors such as mood, the wording of questions, and the interpretation we place upon the events alter our recall of them (Schachter, Norman & Koustall, 1998)? The fact that questions such as these have not been definitively answered (at least, so far) may be disconcerting for students hoping to discover "the real answers."

The Value of Research Methods

From the outset you need to realize that psychological facts are heavily dependent upon the methods used to produce them. Even if you never do any research of your own, you need to understand the principles of research well enough to know what to believe and what to doubt. I strongly encourage you, whenever you are presented with statements of supposed fact, to ask questions like, "How do they know that?" or, "Is there evidence to support these claims?" You will learn that the research basis for some conclusions is much stronger than for others. For example, there is little reliable evidence to support the common assumption that opposites attract. On the other hand, there is a very strong database supporting the notion that "birds of a feather flock together" (Myers, 1996). Whatever your reasons for studying psychology—whether to prepare for a psychology-related career, to understand and help others, or just because it sounds interesting—you will do better if you have the tools and understanding necessary to distinguish reliable psychological findings from those based on various pseudo-scientific sources. Indeed, there is evidence that taking a course in research methods substantially reduces belief in astrology and the claims for such paranormal phenomena as telepathy, precognition and astral projection (Moirier & Keeports, 1994). One of my major goals in writing this book is to help you become an intelligent, and discriminating, consumer of psychological research.

There is also another way in which research methods should prove valuable to you. Many upper-level psychology courses require students to conduct research projects as a way of gaining a better understanding of the subject matter. Some courses may require you to locate and read journal articles, present summaries of research reports, and evaluate the quality of the evidence supporting various sides of a psychological issue. If you take advanced research courses, or enroll in an honours program, you may be required to design, conduct, analyze, and write up an original research study. The skills learned in a research methods course will prepare you to meet these requirements and should also help you to do well in a wide variety of courses.

What if I Don't Go into a Research Field?

Many students will find employment in fields such as education, business, or government, where there may be little need to conduct research. Others will enter applied fields of psychology such as counselling, social work, or testing, where the main focus is provision of services to clients. Of what possible use will their research training be?

The answer, surprisingly, is that it may be more directly helpful than any of their other courses. One reason is that success in any of today's professions demands that its practitioners keep up with a rapidly changing field. Basic research skills such as locating informational sources, finding relevant articles, reading and evaluating the quality of the information provided, and making informed judgments as to its applicability are critical to the practice of any profession. A second reason is that good job performance often requires a problem-solving approach. For example, as a school psychologist you encounter a child who appears seriously depressed and is unable to concentrate on school work. What can you do to help? Devising a successful intervention requires that you identify the source of the problem. This, in turn, means that you must gather relevant information, judge its applicability, develop a hypothesis as to the cause of the problem, formulate and implement a treatment plan, and, finally, evaluate its success. These steps, in fact, are the same as those involved in carrying out any research project. Keep in mind also that doing research involves collaborating with others, learning to improvise when things don't go as expected, and, of course, communicating one's methods and findings to others.

Hopefully, the message is clear. Learning to use the scientific method, combined with practical research experience, provides invaluable training for performing successfully in a wide range of practical situations, both on the job and in one's daily life.

WHAT IS SCIENCE ANYWAY?

In junior high school, science was a required course. In it, I was taught that science is an organized collection of facts. Thus, biology was a science since it represented a large set of facts about living creatures, organized into categories such as phyla and species. In thinking about this definition, I began to wonder if my collection of baseball cards was also a science. After all, it too represented a large assemblage of facts, such as batting averages, runs batted in, and games played. These facts were also well organized, since players were classified by league, team and position. And, just as in other sciences, when new facts were obtained (new cards acquired via purchase or trading) they could be fitted into the existing collection. There I was, only in the eighth grade and already a bona-fide scientist!

Well, maybe not. Collecting a lot of information and developing a system to organize it can make you an authority on a particular subject. (I was a whiz with baseball facts.) However, it does not make you a scientist. What distinguishes science is how the information is gathered, not the nature of the information or how it's organized. What's so special about the scientific method? For a start, let's consider other sources of knowledge.

Other Sources of Knowledge

Common sense. "Don't you have any common sense?" I recall my mother asking me this question when she caught me playing football in the clothes I was supposed to be wearing to Sunday school. My mother's definition of common sense seemed to focus on things you should know without having to be told—things that should be obvious to everyone.

Unfortunately, the fact that something seems obvious to us at the time does not make it correct, or even obvious to others. For instance, in the early seventies it seemed obvious, to some, that breaking down barriers between people would improve communication and enhance productivity. It was just common sense. As a result, the open-classroom and open-office concept came into vogue. Walls between rooms were removed and large, open spaces were incorporated into new buildings. Everyone could know what anyone else was doing. The nineties, however, saw a return to walls, partitions and private spaces. After all, it's just common sense that people need a feeling of privacy!

Common sense has a way of changing with the social and political climate of the times. Less than 100 years ago, for example, it was common sense that women were too emotional and illogical to profit from a college education or to be allowed to exercise important political responsibilities such as casting a vote. Can you think of any widely held beliefs today that people accept as "just plain common sense"?

Reason. About twenty-four hundred years ago the development of principles of logic by the early Greek philosophers led to the view that the world operated according to universal laws. This prepared the way for deliberately seeking new knowledge using tools such as logic and mathematics. Truth was to be sought by applying the principles of deductive logic as exemplified by the well-known syllogism, "All men are mortal. Socrates is a man. Therefore, Socrates is mortal." Plato developed the view that reason was an innate faculty that could be used to discern ultimate truth. In his famous Allegory of the Cave, Plato compared our use of sensory information to gain knowledge to that of prisoners chained deep inside a cave who can only perceive the outside world through shadows cast on the wall in front of them. Therefore, observations were held to be untrustworthy since, at best, they were but dim reflections of the truth—a truth that could be apprehended only through reason.

Reason plays an important role in science, but by itself it is not science. Scientific facts are derived from direct empirical observation, not from simply thinking or reasoning about them. Once a number of observations have been established, reason is used to organize them into a framework or theory. Logical deduction may be employed to draw out implications of this theory, often in the form of hypotheses that can be tested to help determine the theory's adequacy.

Authority. "You want to know? Ask Joe." Authority has probably always been the most useful source of practical knowledge. Ever since some of our earliest ancestors found ways to persuade fellow tribe members to store food for the winter or hunt according to a group plan, certain individuals have been recognized as having more knowledge than others. Of course, such individuals are of great value to society and are typically accorded special status as leaders, priests, or wise persons. As societies became more organized, such authorities often became sanctified, or even deified, to the extent that it became unthinkable to question their spoken or written word. Inevitably, problems arose when these persons exercised their authority over matters of which they had little knowledge. Aristotle's wisdom was so immensely respected that his view of the physical world was not seriously questioned until the time of Copernicus and Galileo, nearly two thousand years after Aristotle's death.

The tremendous impact of authority, especially its tendency to elicit unstinting obedience, has been documented in a series of dramatic studies by Stanley Milgram (1974)—well known to all students who have taken a social psychology course. As you may recall, Milgram found that when an authority gave orders to research participants to repeatedly deliver what they believed to be very dangerous levels of shocks to other participants, most completely obeyed. The tremendous power of authority to compel assent, even in the search for scientific truth, was vividly illustrated by the ability of the Roman Catholic Church to force Galileo to recant his view that the earth moved around the sun. Knowledge based on authority tends to be dogmatic and highly resistant to change.

Science

How is science different from other sources of knowledge? The key ingredient is observation. Science obtains knowledge by using observation to establish facts. While people have always obtained knowledge informally through looking, listening, and touching, there are two essential characteristics that qualify observations as scientific. First, they are deliberate and systematic rather than incidental or casual. Something that just happens to catch your eye, however interesting or unusual, is not a scientific observation. In order to qualify as scientific, a careful plan for making observations is drawn up in advance and the resulting data are systematically recorded. The second essential characteristic is that scientific observations are publicly verifiable. This means that other scientists, following the same plan, should record essentially the same observations. If observations cannot be verified they cannot serve as the basis of factual knowledge. The fundamental premise of science is that facts obtained by observation take precedence over knowledge based on common sense, logic, or authority.

SCIENCE AND PSYCHOLOGY

In the 1700's, it was far from obvious that psychological knowledge could be obtained using the scientific method. One of the earliest investigations of a psychological nature took place in Paris in 1784. In that year, the King of France established a Royal Commission of renowned scientists, headed by Benjamin Franklin, to investigate a curious phenomenon known as "animal magnetism."

Animal Magnetism

Practised by Franz Anton Mesmer and his disciples, animal magnetism was a form of healing ritual in which the practitioner caused a "magnetic fluid" to be passed through the bodies of patients seeking cures for various diseases. Following the application of this treatment, patients typically experienced bodily convulsions or some other form of crisis and, subsequently, experienced profound relief from their ailments (Laurence & Perry, 1988). Word of these miraculous cures quickly spread, and soon neither Mesmer nor his appointed disciples could keep up with the demand.

In order to make his treatment more widely available, Mesmer developed a group therapy technique. He constructed an apparatus known as the baquet—a large, shallow oaken tub, filled with glass, minerals and water. Iron rods that protruded from the baquet at various angles were grasped by patients as they crowded around. In addition, a cord was passed around the huddled bodies to make certain that all were closely connected. When everything was in readiness, soft music was played to announce the arrival of the magnetizer. Dressed in flowing robes and carrying a large "magnetic" wand, Mesmer would make a dramatic entrance. By fixing someone with his stare, or touching with his wand, a crisis would be precipitated in one patient and then transmitted to the next person. This precipitation of crisis would continue on around the baquet until the magnetism had coursed through everyone. The scene was quickly transformed into a sort of bedlam, in which patients laughed, sobbed, shrieked, thrashed about and fell into convulsions. Those who convulsed most violently were removed to a nearby padded room. Many, if not all, so treated claimed to be relieved of whatever malady had been afflicting them.

The Franklin Commission

The Commission headed by Benjamin Franklin was quite thorough. Rather than relying on Franklin's authority, the commission used the scientific method. First, they examined the baquet. However, with the instruments at their disposal, they were unable to detect any flow of magnetism. Next, the members of the commission subjected themselves to the treatment. To do so, they first prepared themselves mentally to report only those effects that surpassed what might reasonably be ascribed to suggestion. The members reported experiencing no untoward effects. However, when they observed the magnetic sessions directly and interviewed patients, it became apparent that at least some were experiencing strong effects. Learning that patients varied in their susceptibility to the effects, the commission took pains to select and carefully study several of the most responsive individuals. These studies, which constitute one of the earliest known psychological investigations, are remarkable for their systematic nature.

In one series of trials they blindfolded their subjects and persuaded them that they were about to be touched by a magnetic object. They were then touched with some ordinary, nonmagnetized object, such as a stick of wood. The typical result was a full convulsive crisis. In a second series of trials, these same individuals were distracted in some manner and, without their knowing it, were then touched with a "magnetized" rod. The result was nothing—no effect at all. The commissioners concluded, quite reasonably, that magnetic effects could be obtained only when magnetism was expected. In their official report, the Commission stated that animal magnetism did not exist and that whatever effects were observed could be ascribed to the exercise of the imagination (Franklin et al., 1785/1970).

The Lesson

Today it seems a simple matter to have debunked Mesmer's beliefs, but those beliefs were not unreasonable for his time. Within a decade after Galileo, William Gilbert had completed experiments on magnetism which demonstrated its invisible effects at a distance. In 1750, Benjamin Franklin himself published a "fluid theory" of electricity based on his experiments. In 1760, Luigi Galvani found that animals were a source of electricity somehow involved with nerves. Thus, Mesmer's idea of invisible magnetic fluids in animals and people was entirely consistent with the knowledge and authorities of his day.[1]

Mesmer's error was his uncritical assumption that the crises and convulsions he witnessed were caused by ripples in a magnetic fluid. He did not check for other possible causes and, in fact, refused to accept the findings of the Franklin Commission. The great lesson for science and psychology was that controlled observations are essential in establishing claims about the underlying causes of human behaviour.

SCIENTIFIC KNOWLEDGE

We have seen that science is not simply common sense, or reliance on authority, or the application of reason. Instead, science is empirical. It asks questions of nature and relies on direct observation to provide answers. Such observations must be systematically made and be verifiable by others. An area of study is recognized as a science when its practitioners begin to assemble these observations into some organizing framework and to propose underlying principles that tie the observations together. The goal of science is the production of organized, fact-based knowledge. The qualifier "fact-based" differentiates science from forms of knowledge that rely on methods other than observation—for example, religion, intuition, and folk knowledge.

Description

Scientific knowledge exists in several different forms or levels, roughly corresponding to the sophistication of the methods used to produce it. At its most basic level, scientific knowledge consists of **description.** When phenomena have been carefully observed, measured and classified in some way, we have a set of descriptive facts. For example, in her study of wild chimpanzees, Jane Goodall provided us with descriptions of the size of the colony, mating and eating habits, infant care, and responses to outside threats. She added to our existing knowledge of the species by providing detailed descriptions of tool use, something not previously observed in chimpanzees.

Correlation

A more advanced level of knowledge occurs when we are able to establish *relationships* among variables. This requires us to go beyond simply making observations; we must also relate these observations to particular conditions. For example, we can easily provide detailed descriptions of ice—its colour, density, and crystal composition—but we have achieved a more advanced level of knowledge when we can relate its formation to the ambient temperature. Similarly, in psychology we would like not only to describe certain patterns of behaviour—such as parenting, dating, or bullying—but also to relate these patterns to specific factors in the physical or social environment, as well as to mental or physiological processes occurring within the organism.

Correlational research is the term used to describe studies that provide us with knowledge of how psychological variables relate to one another. When a relationship between variables has been established it becomes possible to fulfill a practical aim of science—that of prediction. Knowing the relationship between water and temperature, for example, we can confidently predict when ice will form. Curiously, temperature has also figured into some interesting psychological research. For example, it has been found that aggressive episodes, especially those involving physical assault and attempted murder, are more likely to occur as the mercury soars on summer days (Anderson, Bushman & Groom, 1997). The relationship between temperature and aggression was so strong that the researchers offered the dire prediction that massive outbreaks of violent behaviour will accompany global warming.

Understanding

The highest level of scientific knowledge is **understanding**. Perhaps you are taking courses in psychology to improve your understanding of human behaviour. If so, think for a minute of what it means to understand something. While this question can be answered at varying levels of complexity and sophistication, at its root is the notion of identifying underlying causes. We come to understand important behaviours, such as shyness, aggression, or anxiety attacks, when we can point to factors that have a causal influence on them.

You should appreciate that understanding represents an advance over correlational knowledge. It is possible to predict that flicking a wall switch will be followed by a light turning on without having the slightest understanding of circuits or electricity. For prediction, it is only necessary to know that two events reliably covary—that is, go together. To achieve causal understanding, we must demonstrate that two other conditions have been met. The first of these is a time-order relationship. If X causes Y, then X must precede Y in time. If TV watching causes aggressive behaviour, we must be able to show that the TV watching came first. Otherwise, it may simply be the case that children who are naturally aggressive also enjoy watching aggression on TV. Whenever a causal relationship is claimed, we should check to see that the time-order relationship is satisfied.

There is still another criterion that must be met, and that is that there must be grounds for excluding other plausible causes. Recall the claims that Mesmer was making for animal magnetism. The flow of the magnetic fluid in a person's body was held to be the cause of the convulsive crisis, and the crisis in turn produced the medical cure. The evidence for this connection was that there was a covariation between the application of magnetism and the convulsions—the two clearly went together. As well, a time-order relationship had been established: the magnetism preceded the convulsions. To the casual observer, then, it certainly seemed that magnetism must be the cause. The problem was, of course, that other plausible causes could not be eliminated. The plausible alternative suggested by the Franklin Commission, that the effects were due to expectation and imagination, also fit the initial observations. When controlled observations were made it was the animal magnetism interpretation that was ruled out.

Much of the material covered in later chapters of this book, particularly in the experimental chapters, is directed toward the issue of establishing causation. As we will see, the general way that this is accomplished is through the introduction of control procedures. The general issue of control, along with other fundamental concepts in understanding research, is presented in the next section.

FUNDAMENTAL CONCEPTS

No matter what area of psychology you may choose, there are some essential terms and concepts that you must be familiar with in order to understand the basic findings and conclusions.

Control

In defining the scientific method I equated it with systematic observation. "Systematic" means planned, orderly, and controlled. The concept of control is basic and essential. Controlled observations are those that are made under a very specific set of conditions— a set of conditions where influencing factors can be clearly delineated. This may sound a bit abstract. It will help to look at the concept more specifically in terms of three interrelated meanings.

A very basic way of instituting control is through deliberate **manipulation** of a variable that may influence the phenomenon we are observing. The variable manipulated is called the **independent variable**. In their investigations, the Franklin Commission took pains to manipulate whether the subjects were in contact with a magnetic object. That is, some observations were made with the magnetic object in contact and some without. These observations were critical since they enabled the commission to determine whether the presence of a magnetic object, by itself, produced convulsions. The key ingredient of experimentation is the systematic manipulation of conditions under which the observations are made—a point that I will expand on later.

A second, and related, meaning of control is **constancy.** Whenever the effects of an independent variable are being investigated, it is essential that other influencing factors be ruled out. In the case of animal magnetism there were many **extraneous variables**, other than the presumed critical one of contact with a magnetic object, that could potentially influence the outcome. Among these, we could include individual differences in susceptibility, the nature of the patient's illness, the status and prestige of the magnetizer, and, perhaps most importantly, the subject's beliefs regarding the effects to be expected and the knowledge of when magnetism was being applied. To prevent such extraneous variables from having an influence, we can, where possible, hold them constant. A variable is held constant when we prevent it from changing during the course of an investigation. By blindfolding their participants and, thereby, preventing them from knowing when they were in contact with the magnetic object, the Franklin Commission held constant the critical variable of expectation.

Not all extraneous variables can be held constant. Whenever more than one person is tested, there will be potentially important differences in age, health, background and experience. If different locations or times are employed, these factors, too, may have an impact. Our major concern is with keeping such extraneous variables from having any systematic influence on our observations. If, by some chance, one of these extraneous factors changed systematically along with the independent variable, this would create a serious flaw known as a **confound.** For example, if only those people susceptible to convulsions were treated with magnetism and those not susceptible were not, we would have such a confound. Clearly, we would not know whether to attribute the observed outcome to the presence of magnetism or to the reactions of particular sorts of people.

How can we prevent such a critical flaw from occurring? The answer is, by applying a third means of control known as **balancing.** Balancing means that we deliberately distribute these extraneous factors evenly across the main conditions of observation. For example, we could ensure that people both high and low in susceptibility were tested in both magnetic and nonmagnetic conditions. If we are going to make observations at different locations and at different times we can make certain that these factors are evenly spread across our major conditions of observation. Several different techniques are used to achieve balancing, but discussion of these will be deferred to later chapters.

Independent Variable

I introduced the concept of the independent variable as one of the key ingredients of control. At this point it is important to distinguish two different ways in which this term is used. The first usage has already been introduced—that of a variable that is manipulated in order to determine its effect on some other variable. Thus, for example, we might manipulate the level of lighting in a room to determine its effect on reading speed, or the level of noise to determine its effect on concentration. As we learned in the previous section, manipulating an independent variable while holding constant, or balancing, other extraneous variables is the best way to satisfy the criteria for a causal explanation.

A second use of the term "independent variable" is to designate variables whose levels are **selected** but not manipulated. There are many important variables that cannot be manipulated, either because their nature does not permit manipulation or because of ethical considerations. Variables such as biological characteristics (sex, age, race), social characteristics (family background, socioeconomic status, religious affiliation) and psychological characteristics (intelligence, anxiety, extroversion) obviously cannot be manipulated by the researcher. Yet, clearly, these variables will have an impact on a wide range of human behaviours. In order to study the influence of such variables, the researcher can systematically select particular levels. For example, we could study the relationship of age to memory by selecting samples of twenty-, forty-, and sixty-year-old individuals. In many areas of psychology (especially social behaviour), effects related to gender are of great interest and, accordingly, the researcher will select comparable samples of males and females. In our discussion of animal magnetism, we noted that people differed in their susceptibility to its effects. Modern investigators of animal magnetism (hypnosis) routinely administer tests of susceptibility in order to select samples that represent varied levels of responsiveness.

Thus, the term "independent variable" can refer either to a manipulated or to a selected variable. Whenever you read of a study's independent variable you should ask yourself whether it was selected or manipulated. The distinction is critically important for answering questions of causality. When the independent variable has been manipulated, and the effects of other variables have been controlled, we can reasonably infer a causal influence. If, for example, we have systematically manipulated the level of noise while controlling for other variables, we then are able, with a fair degree of confidence, to determine whether noise influences the ability to concentrate.

Such is not the case, however, if the levels of the independent variable have been selected. Suppose that we had selected two schools that differ in the level of surrounding noise. One school is located in a quiet suburb and the other in a noisy section of the inner city. If we find that the kids in the quiet school concentrate better, can we conclude that this difference is due to the level of noise? As you can probably tell, the answer is "not necessarily." The reason, of course, is that particular characteristics of the schools will differ in many ways—students' individual home environments, quality of the teachers, classroom facilities—and it is possible that the effects we observe could be due to any, or all, of these differences.

As you may recall from our previous discussion, any systematic differences between levels of the independent variable, other than those that the investigator is studying, produce confounds. This is always a major problem in any study in which the levels of the independent variable are selected. We can reduce this problem somewhat by selecting levels in such a way that some of these other factors are balanced or held constant, and thus do not become confounds. However, it is much more difficult to control extraneous variables in this way than it is when the independent variable is manipulated.

Dependent Variable

The **dependent variable** is some measurable aspect of the behaviour being observed. The label "dependent" indicates that its observed level is thought to depend on the level of the independent variable. The dependent variable is sometimes called the outcome variable, since a study's results (or outcomes) are determined by measurements made on it. In the example above, the dependent variable was concentration. Its level was thought to depend on the independent variable of noise. In the Franklin Commission's investigation of animal magnetism, the dependent variable was the occurrence of a convulsive crisis. In any study, one of the most important decisions is choosing an appropriate dependent variable to be studied. Of equal importance is finding an adequate way to measure it.

Operational Definitions

When we initially select variables for a study, these variables exist at a conceptual (or abstract) level. We may wish to study noise and concentration, for instance, and we can indicate in a general way what we mean by these concepts. For example, we may think of noise as a somewhat loud and potentially unpleasant sound. Concentration refers to the application of mental effort to a particular task. So far, so good. However, in order to study the relationship of noise to concentration, we must first turn our conceptual definitions into **operational definitions**. That is, we must specify how the levels of the independent and dependent variables are to be measured or produced.

It may be easier to see the necessity for this in the case of the dependent variable. If we want to know whether concentration is affected by noise, we must be able to measure differences in the level of concentration. There are lots of ways this could be done. For example, we might measure the number of mathematical problems solved in a given time, the score on a comprehension test following the reading of an essay, or performance on a challenging video game. The point, for now, is that we must select a particular operation that will allow us to attach numbers to the dependent variable. Once we have done this, we can then relate these numbers to levels of the independent variable. For example, we might find that in the quiet condition, there was an average of ten math problems completed, compared to only five in the noisy condition.

The levels of the independent variable must also be operationally defined. That is, we must specify the procedure used to measure, or to produce, the levels of noise employed in the study. If the independent variable of noise is to be manipulated, we would specify the levels in terms of volume, pitch, and duration. If the levels are selected, for example a noisy versus a quiet classroom, we should specify as precisely as possible just what these differences are. For example, the selection of the noisy classroom may have been based on the school's location in the flight path of a major airport.

To summarize briefly, whenever you read a study, you should attempt to identify the independent and dependent variables and to specify how each has been operationalized. As you become increasingly familiar with the research process, you will also learn to ask additional questions. In particular, you will want to question whether the results are reliable and the conclusions valid. The answers to these questions, as we shall see, depend largely on the adequacy of the measures.

Reliability

In common parlance, we use the word "reliable" in the sense of being dependable. Do you have a reliable car—one that starts dependably and doesn't break down? A reliable measure is basically the same. It works well; you can depend on it. Usually, in judging the reliability of a measure, we ask about its consistency. Does it give basically the same result each time it is applied? If we decide to use a set of math problems to measure concentration, we would expect this measure to give approximately the same result each time it was applied—as long as the conditions are the same. The major ways of assessing reliability are presented in the chapters on observational and self-report methods.

There is still another meaning of the reliability concept. In asking whether the results are reliable, we are, in a sense, asking whether the results could be due to chance. If the quiet group finished ten problems but the noisy group only five, we should ask whether this might simply have been a chance occurrence. Maybe if we did it again, there would be no difference, or perhaps the noisy group would do better. If you have taken a course in statistics, this should sound familiar. You may have learned how to use tests of statistical inference, such as the t test or F test, to determine the likelihood that a particular difference would occur if chance alone were responsible. If we can say, with a reasonable degree of certainty, that chance was not responsible, the results are said to be statistically significant.

Validity

Even if our results are reliable, they may not be valid. To see why, imagine measuring intelligence by placing a tape measure around the circumference of someone's head and recording to the nearest centimetre. Is this a reliable measure? Certainly, since we will get virtually the same result every time. Is this a valid measure of intelligence? If it were, we could do away with all the fuss and bother of IQ testing and put a quick end to the debates over race and intelligence!

Validity is sometimes thought of as the truthfulness of a measure. Does it indeed measure what it is designed to measure? In other words, validity relates, at least in part, to the adequacy of the operational definition. Is counting the number of math problems a person can complete within a given period of time an adequate way of measuring concentration? Would some other measure be better? We also should ask about the validity of the operational definition of the independent variable. Have we really created substantial, noticeable differences in noise level? Validity is assessed through a number of different procedures, some of which will be presented in later chapters.

Theory and Hypothesis

These terms are used often in science, yet are easily confused with each other. A **theory** is an explanation that is advanced to account for observed facts. An **hypothesis** is a testable prediction that can be evaluated by collecting new data. These terms are closely related since hypotheses are often derived from theories and used to test them.

You may have encountered the use of the term "theory" in murder mysteries. A dead body is found and, after piecing together the available clues, the detective puts forth a theory as to the motive and possible identity of the murderer. As new facts come to light, the first theory may be rejected and a new one advanced. The same occurs in science. We observe some interesting facts—for example, convulsions in Mesmer's patients after being touched with a magnetic wand—and then put forth a theory. Mesmer developed an elaborate theory about a magnetic fluid that permeated the universe. When currents or ripples in this fluid passed through the human body, a convulsive crisis occurred. The observations made by the Franklin Commission were inconsistent with Mesmer's theory, and the commissioners advanced a new theory based on the processes of expectation and imagination.

Over the years, many different theories have been put forth to account for responses to animal magnetism and its successor, hypnosis (Gauld, 1992).

Theories are judged successful when they meet two criteria. First, they must help to organize and explain observations that have already been made. Second, they must be capable of being tested; that is, they must lead to predictions that can be confirmed through making new observations. If a theory is frequently confirmed it becomes increasingly useful and may eventually come to be widely accepted. Such has been the case, for example, with Darwin's theory of evolution in biology and Einstein's theory of relativity in physics. If a theory cannot be confirmed by new data, it is found wanting and may either be revised or, ultimately, discarded.

The process of testing theories requires that hypotheses be derived from them. Recall that we defined a hypothesis as a testable prediction. If the prediction is verified, this lends support to the theory it came from. As an example of this process, consider a theory of hypnosis developed by Sarbin and Coe (1972). Hypnosis is explained in terms of social role taking and role enactment. People who are responsive to hypnosis, according to this view, willingly place themselves in the appropriate role and, by developing accurate expectations and using imagination and imagery skills, they are able to give a convincing hypnotic performance. This is an interesting theory because it contrasts sharply with more traditional theories that view the hypnotic subject as entering an altered state of consciousness and becoming passively responsive to the hypnotist's suggestions.

It has also shown itself to be a useful theory since it has led to a number of testable hypotheses. For example, role theory views responses to posthypnotic suggestions as voluntary, intentional acts (in contrast to the traditional view of posthypnotic behaviour as involuntary and compulsive) that are performed when the participant judges them appropriate to the hypnotic role. This leads to the testable hypothesis that people are more likely to carry out posthypnotic acts when they believe that the hypnotist is watching them closely than when the hypnotist's attention has been directed elsewhere.

To test this hypothesis, a study was conducted in which the independent variable was the presence or absence of the experimenter (St. Jean, 1978). For half the participants, the experimenter was seated next to the subject when the posthypnotic signal was given, but for the other half the experimenter had left the room to attend to an emergency. The results were that more than three times as many participants carried out the response in the experimenter's presence than in his absence, thereby confirming the hypothesis. Since the hypothesis was confirmed, additional support was provided for role theory. And, since role theory has led to a number of predictions that have been confirmed, it has been judged to be a generally useful theory.

Almost all theories, even those that have been successful, are likely to change over time. As research data accumulates, it is often the case that some of the findings run counter to theoretical expectations or are not easily accounted for. In addition, new theories are likely to be formulated that provide alternative accounts of the data. The existence of two or more rival explanations will usually stimulate a surge of new research in an effort to determine which theory does the better job. In hypnosis, for example, neodissociation theory (Hilgard, 1977) has rivaled role theory by presenting a very different account of the observations. Hypnosis is viewed as characterized by divisions in consciousness in which areas of experience become functionally isolated from one another—somewhat akin to multiple personality. The hypnotic participant is thought to experience a sort of double consciousness—one part responsive to the hypnotist's suggestions while the other part remains in contact with the outside world.

In response to this theoretical challenge, modifications have been made to role theory which help it to better account for particular facts, such as the reports of involuntariness that often accompany the hypnotic experience (Coe & Sarbin, 1991). In addition, several new theories of hypnosis have developed based on a general social-cognitive approach to behaviour (Kirsch & Lynn, 1998). One of these, the response set theory of hypnosis (Kirsch, 2000), makes the interesting claim that all behaviour, whether hypnotic or waking, is involuntarily activated by mental response sets, but can be interpreted as either voluntary or involuntary depending on the immediate cues in the situation. The rival neodissociation theory has also given birth to a new version called dissociated controls theory, which claims that hypnosis disrupts the function of the frontal lobes so that behaviour can be directly activated without conscious control (Woody & Bowers, 1994). These developments are exciting because they reveal new ways of understanding the age-old mysteries of hypnosis. The general progress of science can be tracked through the continuous process of revising old theories, or formulating new ones, to better account for research observations. Each new formulation, or revision, has the goal of providing a more comprehensive and useful account of the phenomenon being studied.

The ultimate goal of science is to produce a complete understanding of the phenomena of nature. While this goal may never be reached in a final sense, scientists approach it through the continuous process of developing, testing, and refining theoretical statements. These statements, sometimes called principles or axioms, set forth the fundamental relationships thought to exist among the conceptual variables of interest. Much of the effort that goes into the development of psychology, or any science, is focussed on the construction and testing of these statements.

SUMMARY

Students frequently wonder why a course on research methods is required for a psychology degree. The tremendous variability in people's behaviour makes it more difficult to establish facts in psychology than in other sciences. As a result, the validity or trustworthiness of research findings is heavily dependent on the quality of the methods used to produce them. A knowledge of research methods is essential to becoming an informed consumer of psychological research. This acquired skill is important to your success in both upper-level psychology courses and in the practice of applied psychology.

Science is not simply an organized collection of facts. What distinguishes science from other forms of knowledge is the method used to acquire information. In everyday life we often rely on common sense, reason, or authority as sources of information. While useful, each of these sources is prone to error. The key ingredient in science is systematic observation that is verifiable by others. The fundamental premise of science is that facts obtained by observation take precedence over knowledge based on common sense, logic, or authority.

A landmark study conducted in 1784 helped establish that psychological knowledge could be acquired through the scientific method. The French Royal Commission, headed by Benjamin Franklin, investigated Franz Anton Mesmer's unusual therapeutic practice involving animal magnetism. Employing systematic observation, and basic controls for expectancy, the Commission concluded that animal magnetism produced no effects by itself. Instead, the mere belief that magnetism was being practised was responsible for the results obtained.

Scientific knowledge exists in several different forms or levels. At its most basic level, scientific knowledge consists of careful description of natural phenomena. A more advanced level, correlational knowledge, involves finding relations among variables, thus enabling us to predict the value of one variable from knowledge of another. The highest level of scientific knowledge is understanding, achieved when we are able to establish a cause (or causes) for the phenomena studied. In addition to covariation, a time-order relationship and the exclusion of other plausible causes are necessary for a causal explanation.

A key concept in understanding research is control—the process of establishing particular sets of conditions under which observations are made. Control is achieved through manipulating potential causal variables and through holding constant, or balancing, any extraneous variables that could influence the observations being made. The levels of an independent variable are produced by direct manipulation or are selected from among naturally existing levels. The dependent variable is the outcome variable in a study, thought to depend directly on the independent variable. Operational definitions of independent and dependent variables specify precisely how these variables are measured or produced. It is important that measures be both reliable (consistent) and valid (truthful) in order for trustworthy facts to established. A theory is an explanation put forward to account for established facts. Theories are evaluated by testing hypotheses derived from them. On the basis of a number of such tests, theories may be supported, revised, or ultimately discarded.

KEY TERMS

balancing: The process of distributing extraneous variables evenly across the conditions of observation.

constancy: A basic control technique that involves holding the levels of one or more variables at a fixed level.

correlational research: Research that provides knowledge about the naturally occurring relationships among variables.

confound: A condition that occurs when the levels of an extraneous variable changes systematically with the level of an independent variable; a serious flaw that threatens the internal validity of an experiment.

control: A basic process in science involving identifying and accounting for variables that have, or potentially could have, an influence on the phenomena being studied.

dependent variable: Some aspect of the behaviour being observed; its observed level depends on the level of the independent variable; the outcome variable.

description: The process of observing, classifying, and measuring natural phenomena; the most basic level of scientific knowledge.

extraneous variables: Any variables, other than the one of interest, that could potentially influence the phenomena being investigated.

hypothesis: A testable prediction, often derived from a theory.

independent variable: A variable whose potential effect on the phenomena of interest is being investigated; can be either manipulated or selected.

manipulation: Systematically changing the level of an independent variable; varying the conditions under which observations are made.

manipulated independent variable: A variable that is manipulated in order to determine its effect on some other variable.

operational definition: A definition of a variable based on the actual procedures used to measure or produce it.

reliability: The consistency of a measure; the extent to which the same, or similar, observations are made when the measuring operations are repeated.

selected independent variable: A variable whose levels are selected from naturally occurring levels (such a gender or age) in order to determine its relationship to some other variable.

theory: An explanation that is advanced to account for observed facts.

understanding: The highest level of scientific knowledge, established by the process of identifying a cause, or causes, of the phenomena under investigation. This level of knowledge is usually expressed in the form of theoretical principles.

validity: The truthfulness of a measure; the extent to which differences in the levels of an operationally defined variable reflect differences in the conceptual variable.

ENDNOTE

1. In fact, in a curious way, Mesmer's ideas may have found a modern incarnation. Recent neurological research (Ziemann, Corwell, & Cohen, 1998) has employed an external wire coil (a wand?) to induce changes in the magnetic field of the brain. This is thought to increase brain plasticity—the ability to reorganize—which, in turn, may help in recovery from epilepsy, strokes, and other brain traumas.

chapter two

OBSERVATIONAL METHODS

Observation is the heart of research. In order to find out things—to make discoveries or to answer questions—we begin by making and recording observations. Sometimes these observations are made in laboratory settings under rigorously controlled conditions; other times we make them in the field under less controlled but more natural conditions. Laboratory methods will be discussed later in the book, in the experimental chapters. We will begin our coverage of psychological research by looking at methods that are used outside of the laboratory, in "natural" settings.

TYPES OF OBSERVATIONAL METHODS

Observational methods fall into two categories: (1) those in which the observer tries to avoid any intrusion into the setting, and (2) those in which the observer deliberately intervenes in some fashion. Each has advantages and drawbacks.

Natural Observation

Making observations in a natural, or nonlaboratory, setting, without any intervention on the part of the researcher is called simply, "**natural observation**." This method is preferred when you want to discover what normally happens in a situation—that is, when no observers or recording instruments appear to be present. We know from casual observation, as well as from research on surveillance effects (e.g., St. Jean, 1978), that we often act differently if we feel others are watching. This presents us with a dilemma, however, since we can't know what is happening unless we actually do make some observations. The solution, if we can manage it, is to make the observations so unobtrusively that a person's behaviour is not affected. For example, as part of a class project, my students observed whether people washed their hands after using the facilities in public washrooms. Almost all of them did when it was obvious that there were others present. However, many did not when they felt themselves to be alone. (The student observers sat in toilet stalls with their feet pulled up and listened for the sound of running water!)

The method of natural observation is quite familiar. We use it every day—for example, when we sit in a mall or other public place and take note of what people are doing, the clothes they are wearing, and who they are with. Of course, observations of this nature are often made quite haphazardly. To qualify as scientific the observations must be planned in advance and then carried out and recorded in a systematic fashion.

A good example of this method is Jane Goodall's studies of chimpanzees in the wild. Her basic method was to establish herself unobtrusively near a chimp colony, often partially concealed by bushes or rocks. Typically, she would take up her position before daybreak, while the chimps were still sleeping, in order to avoid any intrusion into their daily routine. By identifying individual chimps and carefully monitoring the activities of each over an extended stretch of time, Goodall was able to provide a much more detailed account of chimpanzee behaviour than had previously existed. For example, her research revealed that chimps are carnivorous, make and use tools, engage in group warfare, transfer adolescent females from one tribe to another, adopt infants who have been orphaned, and seek out and eat medicinal plants when ill. Such patient observation over a span of nearly four decades has revealed that chimpanzees are remarkably like humans (Miller, 1995).

Using Intervention

The method of natural observation is not always feasible or practical. One problem is that interesting events or behaviour may occur infrequently, or sporadically. We may be interested in studying how people respond to emergency situations, such as earthquakes or floods, as well as to nonemergency situations, such as meeting an attractive stranger. If we knew about these situations ahead of time we could plan to be on hand with our clipboards or video cameras. But how could we possibly know? Sometimes we may have advance warning, as in announcements from the weather office regarding the expected track of a hurricane, and can arrange to have an observer in place. In other cases we may be able to produce the events ourselves, as in staging a shoplifting incident in view of unsuspecting shoppers in a department store. In the latter case we have used an intervention strategy to facilitate the observations we want to make.

Staging the Event. A common tactic of some researchers, especially those interested in social behaviour, is to stage an event in the context of some everyday situation. For example, to study responses to frustration, Doob and Gross (1968) arranged to have an accomplice drive to an intersection with a traffic light, stop for a red light and, when the light changed to green, remain stationary rather than proceed through the intersection. The reactions of drivers in cars directly behind the experimental vehicle (for example, horn honking, shouts, and gestures) were noted and recorded. The important point is that the intervention appeared to be a naturally occurring event and was responded to as such.

As ethical researchers we must take care to produce minimal interference in people's lives. In this case, the intervention constituted a delay of less than half a minute. How far researchers can ethically go in such interventions is governed by codes of ethics and may often be determined by a human ethics committee before the research is approved. (See Chapter 9 for a full discussion of ethics in research.)

Field Experiments. In some cases the sole purpose of the intervention is simply to create a situation that is likely to produce the behaviour we want to observe—horn honking, helping responses, interpersonal attraction, or whatever. In other cases, we may wish to do more than simply set the stage for behaviour; we may want to create a situation in which we can systematically observe the effects of certain variables on that behaviour. This is accomplished by manipulating an independent variable within a natural context, producing a study that is usually called a **field experiment.** For example, Doob and Gross (1968) arranged their traffic light study in order to study the effects that high- and low-status frustrators, manipulated by alternating trials using late-model expensive cars and older junk heaps, would have on the expression of aggression. They found considerably more horn honking and fist waving in response to the low-status (older) vehicle. Other follow-up studies (e.g., Turner, Layton, & Simons, 1975) used this situation to investigate variables such as the presence of aggressive cues (shotgun racked in the rear window) and anonymity of the driver (visible or not visible). Can you think of any other variables that might have an effect on driver aggression?

A field experiment focussing on a very different form of behaviour was conducted in the natural setting of a provincial park—Capilano Canyon, in British Columbia. One of the features of this park is a long, wobbly 230-foot high suspension bridge that crosses a rocky chasm. Male hikers crossing this bridge were approached by an attractive female confederate (or in some cases a male confederate) who asked their help with a class psychology project. The project involved responding to a short questionnaire on response to scenic attractions and writing a short story based on a picture of a young woman they were shown. Following the man's participation the interviewer said she would like to explain the project in more detail when she had time and provided her telephone number in case he would like to talk further. In comparison to men who crossed a safe, sturdy bridge (or who were approached by a male interviewer), approximately three times as many attempted a follow-up contact with the attractive interviewer. Moreover, the stories they wrote contained more sexual imagery than those of males who met the same interviewer on the safe bridge. Apparently the arousal generated by the shaky bridge was transformed into sexual arousal in the presence of the attractive female interviewer (Dutton & Aron, 1974).

Participant Observation. A very different form of intervention is the method of **participant observation**. Basically this involves having the researcher in place to begin with and, therefore, in a position to observe the events and behaviours of interest. The observer is not hidden as in the case of natural observation. Instead, the researcher is accepted as part of the social context and may even be a full-fledged member of the social group that is being studied.

A fascinating example of participant observation was provided by Canadian researcher

Daniel Wolf (1991), who for three years rode, drank, and fought as a member of a biker gang in Edmonton, Alberta. Drawing on his personal experiences and firsthand observations Wolf furnished a detailed insider view of biker life, including conflicts with police and other gangs, initiation and disciplining of gang members, territorial behaviour, and the effect of the gang on members' attitudes, emotions, and actions. Wolf draws a compelling picture of the gang as a tightly knit brotherhood that cares for and protects its members while drawing a clear dividing line between itself and the rest of society.

A classic study of religious cults using the method of participant observation was carried out by Festinger, Riecken and Schachter (1956). They provided a detailed account of the inner dynamics of a small religious cult that had predicted the world would soon end in a flood sent by God. What made this case particularly interesting is that an exact date and time had been specified. The researchers arranged to join the cult and participated in group activities for several months leading up to the predicted day of doom. They discovered that a number of the members were heavily committed to belief in the prophecy—in some cases, having quit jobs and given away all worldly possessions. The question the researchers wanted to answer was how these strongly committed cult members would react when the appointed day came and the world did not end. Several interesting responses were noted. At first, some members seized on an interpretation provided by their leader that helped justify and explain their behaviour—that God was so moved by their faith that he had, at the last minute, decided to give the human race a second chance. Later, the group held public press conferences and made active attempts to recruit new members. These efforts to convince others of the rightness of their cause were interpreted as attempts to reduce dissonance by gathering social support to help bolster threatened beliefs.

The method of participant observation is attractive in that it provides access to events and behaviours that would otherwise be hard to observe. The danger, of course, is that by the act of participating the observer may influence the course of events. Festinger and his colleagues were aware of this and tried to be as unobtrusive as possible. However, their mere presence could easily have had an influence, perhaps by conveying the impression that the cult's beliefs must be very important if outsiders had come so far to join. This is an example of a larger class of problems that may prove troublesome when observational methods are used. We'll examine these concerns more closely later in the chapter.

GATHERING OBSERVATIONAL DATA

What to Observe

Continuous Records. Researchers involved in making field observations, especially in a new area of study, may feel that they should try to record everything that happens. This approach seems sensible since we may not yet know what the critical variables are and we don't want to miss anything important. With the aid of audio and video equipment, supplemented by computer technology, producing such a **continuous record** would appear to be a plausible goal. For example, a researcher interested in children's schoolyard behaviour may elect to videorecord the entire 20-minute recess period. A moment's reflection should make clear, however, that even videotaping does not provide a complete record of events. What is recorded depends on camera placement and lens angle, and may also be subject to time limitations. There is always the possibility that events of special interest may occur outside the camera frame or time frame.

There are practical limitations as well. Eventually the researcher has to extract quantitative data (numbers) from the recordings. Going over the records to code them and obtain the critical data needed for analysis usually takes much more time than it did to record the observations in the first place. And it can be an exceptionally tedious task. For example, each 10-second clip of the tape may need to be played, and replayed, to determine whether it contains an act meeting the definitional crtieria for physical or verbal aggression. In this approach, more data are typically collected, sometimes at considerable cost, than researchers subsequently find time to analyze. An alternative is to record only the events of interest as they occur and keep the continuous record as a safeguard to fill in cases that may have been missed, or to enable an independent observer to provide a reliability check. Nevertheless, certain types of events, such as sequences of verbal behaviours, or changes in bodily postures or gestures, may be difficult to measure as they occur, leaving continuous records, which can be examined minutely, as the best way to record the data.

Selective Records. **Selective records** involve recording only certain behaviours or certain aspects of the behaviours. Decisions about what to record must, of course, be made prior to the start of the study. The investigator designs a data form that indicates what is to be observed, along with a format for recording the pertinent data. One type of form that is frequently used is the **checklist**. It contains a list of the behaviours, events, and participant characteristics that are of interest and can be used by simply placing a checkmark beside each category that is noted in the situation being observed. For example, in a study of petty theft, student observers positioned themselves near the bulk candy aisle in a supermarket. Each observer was provided with a checklist that contained spaces for recording data on passing shoppers—approximate age, sex, whether alone or in a group, and, most critically, whether candy was stolen. Their (perhaps not too surprising) finding was that the majority of candy thievery was perpetrated by teenagers in groups. Since the observations made are entirely defined by the checklist categories, other potentially interesting information (for example, the dress, demeanour, and nonverbal behaviours of the shoppers) may be missed or only sporadically recorded.

Alternatively, the selective record may involve quantitative measures, rather than simply categories. **Rating scales** may be employed to record the degree or intensity of particular behaviours—for example, how aggressive, or sociable, or cooperative it is. Numerical ratings from 1 to 5 (or occasionally 1 to 10) are used for each behaviour rated. Such scales are often accompanied by guideline definitions of some, or all, of the numerical points, and observers typically receive training sessions in their use.

Other quantitative measures, such as measuring the speed or frequency of particular behaviours, may also be employed. For example, in a series of interesting studies, Levine (1997) has measured the walking speed of pedestrians in various-sized cities around the world. These measures, along with observations of talking speed and the rate at which simple transactions, such as buying a postage stamp, take place, have been used as indicators of the pace of life in various North American cities and countries around the world. Among other interesting findings Levine has reported that pace of life is positively correlated with the incidence of coronary heart disease. It may be that a faster pace of life is indicative of greater overall stress. Expanding Levine's observations by recording the frequency with which pedestrians make eye contact or stop to glance at their reflections in store windows would make a fascinating class project.

Interobserver Reliability. As we have seen, observations may be continuous or selective, and either qualitative or quantitative. Whatever the form of the gathered data, though, they must be shown to be reliable before conclusions can be based on them. In particular, we need to show that independent observers will record the same (or highly similar) data. This is the requirement of **interobserver reliability**. It can be met by having two (or more) separate, and noncommunicating, observers record the same behavioural episodes and checking the extent to which their records are in agreement. If checklist categories are used we can determine the percentage of cases in which the same categories are checked. (A general rule of thumb is that anything less than 85% is considered unacceptable.) If the data are quantitative, reliability can be checked by computing correlation coefficients. (See Appendix B for a discussion of the nature of correlation coefficients.) Usually reliability coefficients are expected to be .80 or higher. If the reliability is unacceptably low this may mean that the categories or rating scales are too vague to be useful and that new, or better, measures are needed. For this reason it is generally recommended that pilot studies, or pretests, using a small number of participants be carried out before undertaking a major research project.

Whom to Observe

Whom you observe usually depends on the research topic and the particular question being asked. Observational research is often done to compare the behaviour of different groups of people in a particular situation. For example, do males and females differ in their response to a frustrating situation, such as someone butting into line ahead of them? Alternatively, we may wish to examine how people in general behave in different situations. To further our understanding of response to line butting we might observe responses in different types of lines (perhaps nightclub versus course registration lineups) and in different locations within the line (near the front versus near the back).

No matter what the purpose of the study, it is almost never possible to observe all persons of interest. Selecting the sample to be observed involves several considerations.

How Many Observations Are Needed? Usually the number of observations required is greater than one would imagine. Statistical calculations typically require a minimum of four to six independent measurements. However, any study that employed so few observations would have such little power as to not be worth doing. **Power** is the ability to detect whatever effect the independent variable has.[1] The power of any study depends directly on the number of observations made, as well as on the size of the **treatment effect** (the amount of difference the treatments make) and the amount of variability. We can estimate the number of observations needed to produce a desired level of power if we are willing to make assumptions about effect size and variability (Keppel, 1991). For example, assuming an effect of average size we would need approximately 60 observations per condition to produce a study with a power level of 80% (one that would be successful four times out of five in detecting the effect of the independent variable). While this number may appear daunting it is certainly preferable to design a study with a sufficient number of observations than to fail to come up with a finding merely because the sample size was too small.

Controlling Factors to Reduce Variability. One way to reduce variability, and hence increase power without an increase in sample size, is to employ a **homogeneous** sample—that is, composed of people who are similar to one another on the basis of age, sex, education, skills, social status, and other identifiable factors. The particular factors to be controlled will depend on what you are measuring. For example, willingness to help a stranger probably does not depend on a person's handedness or eye colour, but may well depend on gender, time of day, and the size of the city. Figuring out what factors are relevant is part of the skill a researcher develops through experience and knowledge of previous research in the area. However, there are drawbacks to being very selective about the sample chosen. One is that the researcher may have difficulty finding enough people who meet the criterion. A second is that the study's findings may pertain to such a narrow range of conditions and persons that they will be of little general interest.

An important characteristic of good research is that its results can be *generalized* (broadly applied) to persons and conditions beyond those included in the study. This characteristic contributes to a study's **external validity** (discussed in greater detail in Chapter 5). In order to generalize, the particular persons you observe, and the circumstances you observe them under, must be *representative*. That is, they must adequately reflect the range of persons and circumstances that you want your conclusions to apply to. For example, conclusions about the causes, or consequences, of aggression based on a study of adolescent boys in the inner city may not apply very well to boys and girls growing up in a small rural community.

An unfortunate fact of research is that efforts to improve the external validity of a study are, at the same time, likely to decrease the sensitivity of the study. This is so because including a wide variety of persons and settings will increase variability and thereby make it harder to detect the influence of the independent variable. For example, we could detect the effects of TV viewing on aggression most clearly by observing children of identical age, sex, social status, and religious upbringing. The only factor, ideally, that would change would be the amount, or type, of TV viewing, and we could then easily determine whether this change had an effect. However, if we study a wide variety of children, of both sexes, of different ages, from different socioeconomic levels and social settings, then each of these factors will have some influence on the data. Even if we are somehow able to balance these factors across conditions they will still create so much **error variance** (or background noise) that it will be difficult to detect the effect of the one factor we are interested in. (This is explained more fully in Chapter 5 when we look at the logic underlying analysis of variance.)

Avoiding Confounded Effects. In addition to the problems created by the increased level of noise there is also a greater chance that one or more of these factors may become **confounded** with the variable of interest. As described in Chapter 1, a confounding factor is one that changes systematically with the levels of the variable you are studying. For example, suppose that in the TV and aggression study we had decided to show a violent cartoon to one fourth-grade class and a nonviolent cartoon to another fourth-grade class. The problem is that there are bound to be differences between the classes to begin with. It is rarely the case that children are randomly assigned to classes. If a teacher has developed a reputation for working well with discipline problems then he or she is likely to be assigned a disproportionate share of the children who have been held back, or who have displayed aggressive or unruly behaviour. Another teacher might work best with shy, sensitive children and generally be assigned a quieter class. If the first teacher's class were assigned the violent cartoon while the second class saw the nonviolent cartoon it would be easy to see that we have a problem. Any differences in level of aggression could be due to pre-existing differences in the temperament and attitude of the children observed, rather than to the violence level of the cartoon. When such confounding exists it is impossible to tell what effect, if any, the independent variable had.

The best way to keep variables from being confounded is to hold them constant. Thus, for example, we might select just those children who are very much alike to begin with— perhaps 10-year-old boys who have had no previous history of discipline problems. Even if we were to use such a restricted sample we could not be certain that other potentially important variables had been held constant. The boys may vary in family background, parenting, number of siblings, place of residence, or amount of TV watching.

When relevant factors cannot be held constant, you can avoid letting them confound your results by **balancing** them across the levels of the independent variable. (While this increases the generalizability of your results, don't forget that it also increases the variability.) For example, you might test an equal number of boys and girls, with and without a history of discipline problems, from both single and two-parent families. What variables you choose to balance will depend on your judgment (based on common sense and a knowledge of past research) of which factors are likely to be particularly relevant. Obviously, you cannot deliberately balance all potentially relevant factors; there are simply too many of them. As well, successful balancing requires a large population base of potential participants. These concerns are elaborated on in Chapter 5.

Balancing can also be achieved indirectly by making a large number of observations and relying on the process of **randomization**. If you had a fairly large population of fourth-grade children to draw upon you could simply flip a coin, or use a table of random numbers (Appendix C), to determine whether each child is assigned to the violent or nonviolent cartoon. When the numbers are large enough, all of the extraneous factors tend to balance out so that the two groups are roughly the same to begin with. Deliberate balancing and randomization can also be combined, for example by randomly assigning equal numbers of girls and boys to each of the two test conditions. This is a very common research practice and, in fact, constitutes a specific research strategy known as a *factorial design* (covered in Chapter 7).

PROBLEMS WITH OBSERVATIONAL METHODS

Peoples' Reactions to Being Observed

Have you ever suddenly discovered that someone was watching you when you didn't expect it? If so, did it make you feel a bit uneasy and cause you to quickly check your recent behaviour—was I scratching myself, picking my nose, staring at an erotic photo? As noted in the washroom study, the presence of others tends to remind us of social norms. It is also often the case that people become uncomfortable when they feel they are being closely observed and may even seek to escape the situation. **Reactivity** is the general name that is given to effects that are entirely, or largely, attributable to the awareness of being observed. In virtually every psychological study we need to ask ourselves whether, and to what extent, the results are due to reactivity.

Psychologists first became aware of this problem through a series of studies carried out many years ago at the Hawthorne industrial plant in Illinois (Roethlisberger & Dickson, 1939). The researchers there wanted to learn what factors would improve worker productivity. They selected a particular group of workers and isolated them in a special room set up for the study. Over a six-month period, a series of modifications was made to the workers' environment and schedule. The lighting was changed, work breaks rescheduled, and hours rearranged, to name just a few of the alterations. The curious finding was that every time a change was made, the workers' productivity increased. It soon became apparent that it wasn't the particular nature of the change that mattered. All that mattered was that the workers knew that *some* change had been made and that they would be closely examined to determine their reaction. Researchers often speak of the **Hawthorne effect** when referring to behavioural changes that occur in response to interested attention from researchers. In fact, the Hawthorne effect is such a striking example of reactivity that the two terms are sometimes used interchangeably. Strictly speaking, however, the Hawthorne effect is only one of several forms reactivity can take.

Being helpful and cooperative. Like the Hawthorne workers, people in general are usually helpful and motivated to cooperate. Because an appreciation of the value of science is widespread in our society, people are often willing to go out of their way to try to help researchers. This is especially so when participants have been actively recruited to serve in a study, but may occur even when they are not. The desire to help frequently leads participants to behave in ways they think the researcher is looking for, rather than in ways they would normally behave. Thus, most participants are responsive to the **demand characteristics** (Orne, 1962) of the research setting. Demand characteristics are any cues in the situation that tend to convey to the participant some notion of what the hypothesis is, or what behaviour is expected.

Looking good. It is natural to want others to think well of us, to approve of our actions and, in general, to think of us as good people. Therefore we make an effort to behave in more ideal, socially acceptable, or ego-enhancing ways when others are watching. This is especially so if the observers are admired and respected members of society. The desire to look good is so strong that if there is a choice between helping the experimenter by confirming the hypothesis, on the one hand, or appearing healthy, normal or "cool," on the other hand, most research participants will choose the latter course of action (Sigall, Aronson, & Van Hoose, 1970). In most cases, however, there is no conflict between the desire to be helpful and the desire to look good; both motives are likely to lead to cooperative behaviour.

Anxiety and arousal. We have all experienced the apprehension of performing before an audience; we may have even witnessed cases of "stage fright" so severe that the performer has fainted or "frozen up." The knowledge that one is being observed can be severely inhibiting, leading to safe or conservative responses. For example, participants who respond to word association tests (where the experimenter presents a word such as "table" and the person responds with the first word thought of) in public are especially likely to respond with trite or common associates, such as "chair" in response to "table" (Allport, 1924). There is ample evidence that awareness of being observed increases general arousal level (Cottrell, Wack, Sekarak, & Rittle, 1968). This leads to an enhancement of dominant physical responses such as running or exerting physical force, but to a decrement in performance that requires thinking or decision making. Thus, for example, students often have more difficulty in writing exam answers when they feel they are being closely watched by the instructor.

Antagonism. Sometimes the effect of being observed is to engender a feeling that we are being intruded upon, that our privacy is being invaded. No one likes the feeling of being put under a microscope. In fact, a number of studies suggest that being stared at produces negative emotions and aversive responses (e.g., Ellsworth & Carlsmith, 1973). A few people seem to develop particularly hostile attitudes to research and may attempt to undermine it by behaving in a manner opposite to what they believe is expected. This has sometimes been called the "screw you" effect (Masling, 1966).

Minimizing Reactivity. An obvious way to avoid these problems is, simply, to avoid being obvious. If people are unaware that they are being observed they will behave in their usual manner. Thus, researchers sometimes go to great lengths to disguise the process of making observations. If you have ever seen the TV show *Candid Camera* you are aware of the hidden camera trick! In addition, researchers may sometimes hide in toilet stalls (Middlemist, Knowles, & Matter, 1976), employ observers who are part of the natural situation (St. Jean, 1978), or even completely change their identities (e.g., Humphreys, 1975) in order to observe behaviour that would otherwise be inaccessible.

As you may have surmised, in some cases these solutions may lead to serious ethical complications (see Chapter 9 for a full discussion). Spying on people's private behaviour is an invasion of privacy. As a general guide, observing behaviour that is public does not present an ethical problem, provided that **anonymity** is preserved. This means that no identifying information pertaining to the people observed are included in any report of the study's findings. When the behaviour is not public it is ethically mandatory that **informed consent** be obtained beforehand. This means that potential participants must be apprised of the nature of the study, including the types of observations that will be made, and give their free consent before the study can commence. While obtaining such consent may introduce some reactivity, there usually is no ethical alternative. Remaining inconspicuous and assuring participants that their anonymity will be respected can help reduce some problems of awareness. Another solution, explored earlier in the chapter, is participant observation. When the observer is accepted as part of the social context or general background, the problem of reactivity is less likely to arise.

There is, however, one approach available to researchers that completely eliminates reactivity. This method involves studying behaviour only after it has occurred. Chapter 4 presents two forms of such *ex post facto* (after the fact) research that do not depend on making live observations.

Observer Objectivity

Why It's Hard to be Objective. When researchers invest a great deal of effort into a project it is with the hope and expectation that the results will justify it. Scientists are human, after all, and they certainly want to produce valuable research findings that will be recognized by others. They may even yearn for international acclaim and dream of winning the Nobel prize! At a more mundane level, scientists are aware that continued financial support depends on their track record of publications in recognized journals. It's entirely natural then for even the most objective researchers to hope for impressive results.

Despite these strong career motivations, deliberate cheating is fairly rare. Scientists know that once results are published others will check those results and find any mistakes. Even unintentional mistakes, whether due to carelessness or honest error, may damage a researcher's reputation. If, however, the results are shown to be fabricated or plagiarized, the researcher's career will be irreparably damaged. The real problem with observer objectivity, then, is not intentional cheating or misrepresentation, but rather with errors that occur unintentionally.

Sometimes these errors are random and don't affect a study's basic findings (although they may create undesirable "noise" that can sometimes obscure a finding). When errors are not random, however, but are consistently in a particular direction, then what happens is that basically invalid (untrue) findings are created. Constant errors of this sort may be a direct result of the researcher's expectancies. In other words, what the researcher believes will occur may influence the actual observations that are made.

Many examples of observer bias have been documented in the psychological literature. Among the most striking are those that are created by the expectancy (or belief) that certain events will take place. A well-known example is Rosenthal and Jacobson's (1968) study of expectancy in the classroom. These researchers tested children in fifth grade classrooms and informed the teachers that certain students had scored very high on a test of academic potential. These students, the researchers said, had been performing at no better than an average level so far, but could be expected to "bloom" in the future. In fact, however, the names given to the teachers of these "potential academic bloomers" were selected at random from the class lists. When the researchers returned to the school nine months later, they discovered that these students had indeed bloomed. They were earning better grades, enjoying school more, and were even scoring higher on standard IQ tests. These dramatic changes appeared to be a direct result of changes in the teachers' expectancies.

Such findings, of course, are of tremendous practical consequence for teaching and other interpersonal activities, but they also pose a special problem for psychological researchers. How can we ever be sure that our results aren't simply due to our beliefs?

Striving for Objectivity. The first step, of course, is to become aware of the potential for bias. This awareness should lead the researcher to carefully check all procedures for possible subjectivity. Operationalizing independent and dependent variables, as well as carefully controlling extraneous variables (as discussed in Chapter 1), are the frontline defence against the threat of bias. In addition, special procedures have evolved for the specific purpose of guarding against observer bias.

Standardizing observations. In recording observations we are continually making classification decisions. For example, in observing schoolyard aggression we must determine whether a particular action qualifies as a punch, a kick, a slap, a shove, or some other form of aggression. There are bound to be ambiguous cases. Was that elbow in the ribs an accidental brush or a real attempt to hurt? A researcher should determine ahead of time where ambiguities are likely to occur and make rules for dealing with them in a consistent manner. An important safeguard is to hold training sessions for observers who will be recording the data. Maintaining consistency is vital. As discussed earlier, it is important to check that several independent observers will record essentially the same observations, thereby establishing interobserver reliability (see Chapter 1). This ensures that even if there is some bias in how events are classified it will be the same in all conditions of observation. A bias that occurs only in some conditions, but not in others, completely undermines the study's validity. (This is a form of confounding, discussed earlier in the chapter and also in Chapter 1.)

Automated recording methods. Computers are unbiased recorders that can register and store responses without the need for human intervention. Their use is rapidly increasing, as evidenced by the growing tendency to collect data from on-line experiments. However, there are important limits to what they can accomplish. These procedures are best suited to recording verbal data, such as responses to survey questions or judgments of visually presented stimuli. At present, they are not well suited to recording personal or social behaviour. (However, this may change as the use of surveillance cameras in workplaces, shopping malls and recreation areas continues to grow.)

Employing "blind" controls. If the individual making the observations is unaware of the researcher's expectations then the potential for bias is reduced. It is not completely elimi-nated, however, for the observers may form their own expectations based on initial obser-vations, or what they know of the study's purpose. A better safeguard, when feasible, is to keep the observer blind to the particular condition under which observations are being made. For example, in studying factors that influence aggression in schoolchildren we might wish to test the hypothesis that the viewing of violent content on TV increases the tendency to behave aggressively. Accordingly, we arrange to have children view either a violent or nonviolent cartoon and then to be observed during a free play period. While it might be possible to keep the observers unaware of the hypothesis, a much better safeguard is to keep them blind to the study's condition. That is, they should not be able to identify whether a particular child was exposed to the violent or nonviolent cartoon. The same holds true for the person doing the computer data entry or analysis. Using a code for the conditions known only by a third party, data may be summarized and analyzed without any biassing expectations about how the results should turn out.

In addition to keeping the observer blind, some studies also use procedures that keep the participants blind to the identity of the treatment they have received. These procedures are discussed further in Chapter 5 under the heading of placebo controls. When controls are employed to keep both observers and participants blind, the design is called **double blind**. Such double-blind controls, where feasible, are probably the best possible safe-guards since they eliminate, or at least greatly reduce, bias stemming from both observer expectancy and participant reactivity.

SUMMARY

Observation is the heart of science. The process of making observations utilizes either the method of natural observation or methods that employ some form of intervention. Natural observation is the process of gathering data in natural settings without any interference from the researcher. More often, the researcher uses some form of intervention in order to set the stage for particular behaviour to occur, to conduct a field experiment in which an independent variable is manipulated in a natural setting, or to place a researcher in a particular social setting to collect data through participant observation.

Gathering observational data requires that decisions be made on both what to observe and whom to observe. Data collection may employ either continuous records, in which an attempt is made to record everything of interest, or selective records, in which particular aspects are chosen. Selective records include checklists, rating scales, and various quantitative measures such as speed or frequency. Regardless of the recording method used, the data should meet the criterion of interobserver reliability (agreement between two or more independent observers).

Decisions as to whom to observe involve considerations of sampling, representativeness, and sample size. Control procedures, such as the selection of a homogeneous sample, may be introduced to reduce variability. However, such procedures tend also to reduce external validity. Usually, the most important concern is the avoidance of confounded effects. This may be achieved through using basic control procedures such as holding variables constant or balancing them across conditions of observation.

Two major problems tend to occur with observational methods. One involves people's reactions to being observed. "Reactivity" is any change in behaviour that occurs as a result of awareness that one is being observed. These changes include cooperativeness, concern with looking good, arousal and anxiety, and, occasionally, antagonism. Efforts to minimize reactivity include disguised observations and indirect measures. Ethical considerations demand that privacy be protected and anonymity preserved. Closer, or more detailed observation, should be carried out only with participants' informed consent.

The second problem is the potential for observer bias. Factors such as anticipated outcomes and the desire for professional recognition and advancement combine to produce strongly held expectancies for particular outcomes. Unless preventive steps are taken such expectancies may influence the actual data obtained. Important controls include standardization of procedures, automated recording, and the use of blind and double-blind procedures.

KEY TERMS

anonymity: A condition ensuring that no identifying information pertaining to the people observed are included in any report of the study's findings.

balancing: The process of distributing extraneous variables evenly across the conditions of observation.

checklist: A record of observations obtained by noting the presence or absence of predefined categories of behaviours and events.

confounded: A study is said to be confounded when the level of an extraneous variable changes systematically with the independent variable. As a result the study's validity is seriously compromised.

continuous record: A recording of behaviour and events that attempts to be inclusive, to encompass everything of potential interest.

demand characteristics: The total set of cues in an observational condition or setting that tend to convey to the participant information about the study's hypothesis or purposes.

double blind: A control procedure that ensures that neither the participants nor the observers can identify the conditions of observation.

error variance: The amount of variability in a set of scores that is not related to the treatment.

external validity: Extent to which a study's findings are apt to generalize beyond the conditions obtained in the original investigation.

field experiment: A study in which an independent variable is manipulated in a natural setting.

Hawthorne effect: Changes in behaviour that occur in response to interested attention from researchers.

homogeneous: A term used to describe a sample whose members have very similar characteristics.

informed consent: The process of informing potential participants of the nature of the observations to be made and gaining their consent as a prior requisite to carrying out the study.

interobserver reliability: The extent to which independent observers agree in recording the same behaviours and events.

natural observation: The method of making observations in natural (real-life) settings without any intervention on the part of the researcher.

participant observation: A study in which the observer is a part of the natural situation or plays a role in the social process being observed.

power: The ability of a study to detect the effect of the independent variable under investigation.

randomization: The process of assigning participants to observation conditions on the basis of chance.

rating scale: A numerically graded scale used to rate the intensity or degree of particular behaviours.

reactivity: Changes in a person's behaviour that are attributable to awareness of being observed.

selective record: A recording of behaviour and events that focuses only on certain predefined aspects.

treatment effect: The amount of impact the independent variable has on the dependent variable; how much difference a particular treatment makes.

ENDNOTE

1. You may have encountered the concept of power in a statistics course where it was defined as the probability of correctly rejecting a false null hypothesis (that is, of not committing a type 2 error).

chapter three

SELF-REPORT METHODS

We have said that observation is the heart of science. In the previous chapter we covered ways of directly observing and recording behaviour—for example, through creating a continuous record or by measuring the frequency or duration of a particular behaviour. There is, however, an alternative way to study behaviour. Rather than directly observing behaviour as it occurs we can, instead, simply ask people questions and record their answers. In a sense, we can classify this approach as a form of structured observation. Asking questions is an intervention, one that sets the stage for a particular type of behaviour (a self report) to occur. In fact, this approach has become such a specialized form of studying behaviour that it is usually regarded as an entirely separate methodological approach.

Almost every study in psychology can be classified as either a behavioural observation study or some form of self-report study. To oversimplify things a bit, the researcher can typically choose to either watch what people are doing or to ask people questions. If our primary interest is in what people do we would typically choose an observational procedure; if, however, we are interested in what people think (or say) we would choose a self-report procedure.

The focus of this chapter is self-report methods. In the sections that follow we will examine what is probably the most widely-used form of self-report method—survey research.

PURPOSE OF SURVEYS

In Chapter 1 we discussed the main goals of science: description, correlation/prediction, and understanding. Surveys are especially useful in serving the first goal. When appropriately carried out they provide an accurate description of the thoughts, beliefs, or experiences of a particular population. As an example, consider Mazer and Percival's (1989) survey of university students' experiences of sexual harassment. Their purpose was to provide an accurate and comprehensive description of the frequency with which students had encountered various forms of sexual harassment. They found that some forms of sexual harassment (for example, sexually suggestive looks or gestures) were frequently encountered, while others (for example, coercive pressure to engage in sexual intercourse) were fairly rare. In attempting to understand, and deal with, sexual harassment, a necessary first step is a thorough documentation of its occurrence.

The second goal of science, correlation and prediction, may also be served by surveys. By collecting demographic information from survey respondents, and by categorizing incidents by setting and perpetrators, Mazer and Percival (1989) were able to establish important relationships between sexual harassment and various social and personal variables. For example, students reported that harassment experiences were far more likely to occur with other students than with faculty or staff. In addition, third- and fourth-year students were more likely to have experienced harassment than those in their first or second year. In this way, surveys often yield information about what variables are correlated and this information, in turn, may serve as the basis for making predictions.

The third goal of science, understanding, is not as well served by surveys. Understanding involves establishing causal relationships, and this requires more than just the covariation information provided by correlational data. A time-order relationship and the elimination of alternative plausible causes are also necessary. Although surveys can often show how variables are correlated (covariation) they are rarely able to reveal time-order relationships and are not well suited to eliminating alternative causes. Experimental research, introduced in Chapter 5, is the method best suited to establishing causal relationships.

What Is a Survey?

A survey is defined by the presence of two primary ingredients. The first is a predetermined set of questions administered in a standardized fashion. Mazer and Percival (1989) presented written descriptions of 36 incidents that could, potentially, be construed as sexual harassment. Each description was followed by a set of four questions. For example, one of the incidents was "Students receive unwanted deliberate touching or physical closeness from faculty." The set of questions that followed asked respondents to indicate whether they regarded this as sexual harassment, how often they had experienced it, how many other students they believed had experienced it and how serious they felt the incident to be. All 36 incidents, each with its attendant four questions, were presented in standardized written form in a fixed order. This standardization made it possible to meaningfully compare various categories of respondents—males with females, fourth-year with first-year students, and arts with science majors.

The second ingredient is the use of **sampling**. Surveys are rarely, if ever, responded to by the entire set of persons we are interested in. Instead a subset (sample) of a larger population is selected to provide data. The process of sampling is so intimately associated with surveys that the entire method is sometimes called a sample survey.

Sampling Concepts

Surveys are typically administered to only a small subset of the **population** of individuals we are studying. A population is the total set of cases that interest us. Mazer and Percival defined their population as all full-time and part-time students enrolled at the University of Prince Edward Island at the time the study was carried out. In surveys such as the Gallup poll the population may be defined as all eligible voters residing in the United States.

In order to sample from a population we must first develop a **sampling frame**. A sampling frame is, basically, a list of all the elements, or members, of a particular population. In an important sense, a sampling frame serves as the operational definition of the population. The sampling frame employed by Mazer and Percival was a list of names of students who had officially registered for one or more courses. It's important to note that the sampling frame may not be a completely accurate reflection of the actual population. Some students who had registered may have dropped out; others may have been attending classes and studying but not have officially registered.

The sample drawn for study is usually a small subset of the total population. Approximately 25 percent of the student population was selected to receive the sexual harassment survey. Each person, or case, selected for the sample is called a single **element**. A sample is said to be **representative** of its population when the characteristics of the elements included in the sample match those of the larger population. The sample of students who responded to the sexual harassment survey contained a slightly higher proportion of female and upper-level students than in the total university population, but in other respects was quite similar. A sample's representativeness is critically important in establishing the **external validity** of the study. As you may recall from our mention of this concept in Chapter 2, external validity refers to the extent to which a study's findings can be generalized beyond the particular conditions of observation. In the context of survey research we are usually interested in generalizing the results from our sample to the population as a whole.

Approaches to Sampling

In general, sampling can be classified as either probability or non-probability. **Probability sampling** is done in such a fashion that we can specify the exact probability of any population element being included in the sample that is drawn. **Nonprobability sampling** is carried out without being able to specify each element's chance of inclusion.

Nonprobability sampling. One form of nonprobability sampling is called **accidental sampling**. An accidental sample is one formed on the basis of convenience or happenstance. Most student surveys employ accidental sampling. Questionnaires may be handed out in the library, to students leaving class, or in residence hallways. Usually, the representativeness of such samples is highly questionable. The composition is probably determined by factors such as class schedule, faculty of study, and whether the researchers personally know the students. Often large segments of the student population, such as those who live off campus or don't study in the library, will be excluded.

Although student samples are typically accidental, so are those in some published studies. For example, Ruback and Juieng (1997) asked a sample of shoppers at a mall how they would respond to a driver waiting to take a parking spot that they were about to vacate. In particular, they were asked whether they would speed up their departure to accommodate the waiting car. One of the aims of the study was to compare stated opinions with actual observations of such occurrences in the mall parking lot. Their sample was (apparently) obtained by approaching shoppers in a mall until 100 had agreed to participate. This is certainly a practical way to obtain the data they wanted, but it does have some drawbacks. Although the researchers did describe some of the characteristics of the sample they obtained (sex, race, and age) we have no way of judging whether the respondents are representative of drivers in general, or even of those persons who happened to be in the mall at the time.

A second type of nonprobability sample is the **purposive sample**. In a purposive sample the elements are handpicked. For particular purposes a sample that is intentionally (purposively) selected may be judged more useful than one whose selection is left to chance. During election campaigns, for example, the news media may focus on a few key electoral districts, or selected races, feeling that these are critical in determining the overall outcome. When important local news breaks the media may solicit reactions from selected community leaders thought to represent popular opinion. A few years ago when our psychology department did a curriculum review a purposive sample, composed of recent graduates known to be enrolled in various graduate and professional programs, was selected to provide feedback on their undergraduate course work. Purposely selecting such an expert sample can be critical to achieving the goals of a particular research study or, in our case, program review.

Probability samples. In a probability sample we can specify in advance the chance of any particular population element being included in the sample that is drawn. The most common form is the **simple random sample.** The defining criterion is that all elements have an equal chance of being included. The exact probability of inclusion is determined by dividing the population size by the sample size. Thus, if the population has 2000 members and a sample of 100 is to be drawn, each element has a 1 in 20 chance of being selected. The selection process is critical in ensuring that randomness is established. The usual procedure is to number each element of the sampling frame and then enter a table of random numbers (see Appendix C). If the first number encountered matches one of the element numbers then that element is selected. Continuing to read numbers in any direction, the matching process is carried out until the desired sample size in reached. An alternative procedure is to divide the population size by the sample size to get a number referred to as k. (In the above example k is 20). We then choose a random number between 1 and k (by using a table of random numbers) to select the first element from the sampling frame list and then every kth element following the first is also selected. Mazer and Percival (1989) selected the sample for their sexual harassment survey in this manner. They selected every fourth person on an alphabetized list of names received from the registrar's office.

When we draw a random sample we are relying entirely on chance. If our sample is relatively large and if the population it's drawn from is relatively *homogeneous* (composed of similar elements), then the unbiased selection procedure based on chance should provide a representative sample. However, if the population is *heterogeneous* (composed of diverse elements) and if the sample is not especially large there is a good possibility that random sampling will not produce a representative sample. Let's see how this could come about. Mazer and Percival (1989) selected a large sample of more than 600 students, but suppose their sample had been much smaller—100, say. The university population is fairly diverse, containing both full- and part-time students, married students and single students, science students and arts students, mature students as well as younger students. A small random sample could over-represent some groups while under-representing others. It may, by chance, contain a disproportionately large number of female arts majors living in campus residences. Their experiences with sexual harassment may be much different from, say, mature male veterinary students living off campus. If at the start of the survey we know of important groupings in the population that are likely to affect responses we can take this into account in our sampling procedure.

The way to do this is through a procedure called **stratified random sampling**. We begin by dividing the population into strata (or categories). In the sexual harassment study we might decide that sex and years in college are particularly important factors. The population is then stratified along these lines—female underclass, female upperclass, male underclass, and male upperclass. Our approach would to be sample randomly from within each of these four strata—perhaps drawing 25 from each to make up our total sample of 100. We could draw either equal-sized samples, as in this example, or, more typically, samples that are proportionate in size to each stratum—thus, if female underclass students represented 35% of the university population we would select 35 for our sample of 100. If the population is large and diverse a stratified random sample will be more representative than a simple random sample.

Sample Size and Error

"How many people do I need to include in my survey?" This question is typically asked by students who are administering a questionnaire as part of a class research project. (It's also a question asked by professional researchers.) A simple answer is, "The more the better." Other things being equal the larger the sample the more representative of the population it is likely to be and the smaller the sampling error will be. Of course, other things are not always equal. Student surveys usually employ accidental samples which have little hope of being representative, no matter how large.[1] Other important factors include the heterogeneity of the population (the extent to which it is composed of distinct subgroups) and the expected response rate.

Perhaps the most important factor in determining sample size is the desired amount of **sampling error**. You may recall from introductory statistics that the mean of a random sample is the best estimate of the mean of the population from which the sample was drawn. The key word is *estimate*. We don't expect the sample mean to be exactly the same as the population mean. If we were to draw additional samples from the population we would find some variation among the sample means. We would expect some to be above the actual population mean and some below it. This variation in sample means (or response percentages) constitutes sampling error. The size of the sampling error depends partly on the variability (or heterogeneity) of the parent population and partly on the size of the population and the size of the sample drawn. The only practical way the researcher can control sampling error is by adjusting sample size. In practice, researchers begin by specifying a tolerable sampling error—for example, plus or minus three percent with a 95% confidence interval. (This means that 95% of the same-sized samples drawn from a given population would produce a result within 3% of the reported result). Then, they consult tables in specialized survey texts or manuals (e.g. Salant & Dillman, 1994) that present sample sizes for different degrees of sampling error for various-sized populations. Interestingly, once the population size reaches 25,000, or larger, a sampling error of 3% can be attained with only a little over 1,000 respondents. Thus, the results of most Gallup polls, and other professional surveys of a national scope, are typically based on about 1,000 to 1,200 respondents. Of course, not everyone contacted will respond and the surveyor must take into account the probable response rate. As we will see in the next section, response rates vary considerably with method of survey administration.

ADMINISTERING SURVEYS

Traditionally, surveys are administered in one of three ways—by mail, through a personal interview, or over the phone. Recently, a fourth method, online Web site surveys, has emerged. Each method has its strengths and weaknesses.

Mail Surveys

Mazer and Percival (1989) obtained mailing addresses for everyone in their sample and sent each of the potential participants the sexual harassment survey, along with an explanatory cover letter and a postpaid return envelope. One of the chief advantages of the **mail survey** is that it provides the respondent complete anonymity. The questions can be answered in private and the survey returned without any personally identifying information. This is an especially important consideration when the issue dealt with is a sensitive one or has the potential to cause pain or embarrassment. The fact that the survey questionnaire is self-administered reduces costs and eliminates concerns of potential interviewer bias.

Unfortunately, there are disadvantages as well. Most surveys that are mailed out will never be returned. Response rates average about 30%. Mazer and Percival reported a total return of 36.7%. One concern then is that the initial sample size shrinks tremendously. A much bigger concern is that **response bias** is likely to greatly reduce the extent to which the final sample is representative of the larger population. This happens because those who take the time and trouble to complete the survey are likely to differ in many ways from those who do not. Those who completed the sexual harassment survey may have had a special interest, and perhaps more personal experience with, sexual harassment then those who did not. Mail surveys, in general, because they rely on literacy and verbal skills, are more likely to be responded to by a more highly educated segment of the population (Salant & Dillman, 1994). Mazer and Percival reported that even within their university sample, third- and fourth-year students responded more frequently than did those in their first or second year.

Interviews

One alternative to the mail survey is the **personal interview**. Here, respondents are contacted in person by an interviewer who presents the questions and records the responses.

For example, the ongoing Canadian Study of Health and Aging (1994)—aimed at assessing the health and cognitive functioning of the over-65 population—employs this approach. Trained interviewers contact prospective participants who have been selected at random from social insurance registration lists, and, upon receiving their consent, arrange a personal interview conducted in the participant's residence. The interviewers then administer a standardized questionnaire which covers personal background information, activities of daily living, past and present health problems, and an assessment of cognitive skills. By repeating this procedure with the same respondents at regular intervals the study is able to track changes in functioning that occur with age.

You can probably appreciate some of the advantages that this approach provides. Since interviewers present the questions, and provide clarification where needed, problems with literacy and comprehension are less of a concern than would be the case in a mail survey. The face-to-face approach is also likely to produce higher levels of motivation and interest. In fact, response rates are typically much higher (often around 80%) than are found with mail surveys.

Can you think of any disadvantages? Expense is clearly one. Interviewers must be recruited, trained, and paid a reasonable wage. As a result, budgets for such studies must be much larger than for a comparably sized mail survey. Another concern is the possibility of interviewer bias. Although interviewers are trained to administer the questions and record responses according to a standardized procedure, the data that is recorded relies, at least to some extent, on the interviewers' judgment. Research on experimenter expectancy effects (Rosenthal, 1966) indicates that even unconscious expectations may exert an influence on the data that are gathered. For example, a researcher interviewing a wealthy senior citizen living in her own home in an affluent neighbourhood may expect to find a higher level of cognitive functioning and general health than when interviewing a resident of a county nursing home. The most effective control for such potential bias, keeping the investigator blind to such background or situational factors, is not usually possible in interview studies. The best that can be done is to alert interviewers to the possibility of bias and to standardize the interview procedure as much as possible.

Telephone Surveys

A third alternative is to survey people over the telephone. In the not-so-distant past a **telephone survey** would not have resulted in a representative sample of the general population since it would have excluded lower-income families and individuals. Now, however, virtually every household has telephone service and, as you are doubtless aware, phone surveys have become annoyingly common. The various Gallup polls and political polls that you see reported in the daily news are conducted over the phone. Even people with unlisted numbers can be easily reached with random-digit-dialling techniques.

There are some obvious advantages to phone surveys. A large random sample can be contacted in a fairly short period of time. The response rate, while not as high as personal interviews, is considerably higher than for mail surveys. Although interviewers must be hired and trained, the phone survey is much less time-intensive than the personal interview. It is relatively easy for a supervisor to oversee a number of interviewers and ensure that procedures are standardized.

However, anyone who has been contacted for a phone survey can probably cite some disadvantages. Nowadays, there is such a large volume of solicitation phone calls, from various telemarketing and charitable organizations, that survey contacts are typically regarded as just another bothersome intrusion. Many respondents refuse to be interviewed or terminate the interview early. Complicating matters further, a number of telemarketers have adopted a fake survey approach as part of their sales gimmick (Lavarakas, 1993). In addition, the recent adoption of new phone technologies, such as caller ID and message minders, makes it easier to screen incoming calls and to simply not respond to calls from unknown sources. As a result, response rates appear to be generally declining. Furthermore, it is becoming increasingly likely that those who do respond will have different characteristics than those who don't—perhaps being lonelier, less busy, or simply more politely acquiescent. And, of course, phone surveys are not usually well suited to long, in-depth interviews or those that touch on very personal matters.

Online Surveys

The tremendous growth of the Internet has spawned a new method of data collection. **Online surveys** can now compile tens of thousands of responses more quickly, and far more cheaply, than can be accomplished by telephone or mail. It seems that almost every Web site you turn to, whether commercial, news, sports, entertainment, or special-interest, is making use of this opportunity to sample opinions (e.g., should Pete Rose be in the Baseball Hall of Fame?), product preferences (e.g., which antihistamine works best for you?) and political viewpoints (e.g., what party has the best chance of forming the next government?). In fact, as soon as you register your opinion you can view the up-to-the moment results. (As I write, for instance, 76% of those who responded to a CNNSI online poll answered yes to the question of whether Pete Rose should be admitted to the Hall of Fame.)

Of course, the main concern is whether such polling procedures are valid. Are they representative of the broader population or only those who click onto a particular Web site? This question was recently addressed by the Pew Research Centre (1999) in a study that compared online and telephone poll responses to questions concerning the Bill Clinton-Monica Lewinsky scandal. The online poll, administered by America Online, compiled over 118,000 responses, of which 52% favoured Clinton's resignation. However, three national telephone surveys, each sampling between 500 and 1000 respondents, reported large majorities saying Clinton should *not resign*. Which method should we trust? In this case, the clear answer is the telephone polls. Despite their much smaller samples, the telephone polls have the advantage of employing random sampling methods and, as a result, are more likely to paint a representative picture of the population as a whole.

Can you see the problems with online surveys? There are several. First, of course, many households do not have computers and of those who do, not all are connected to the Internet. Those who are connected are likely to be younger, better educated, and more affluent than the population as a whole. The second problem is that those who respond to the survey are self-selected (rather than randomly selected) and are therefore likely to not be representative of the population of Internet users, or even of visitors to a particular Web site. As you might guess, respondents to online political polls pay more attention to national news and are likely to have stronger opinions on the issues at question than those who don't respond.

Still, Internet polling is viewed as an attractive, low-cost option and, consequently, efforts are underway to improve the representativeness of this method. One such effort involves compiling an e-mail population base, sampling from this known population, and then statistically adjusting for sample-population discrepancies. However, until such methods are fully developed and evaluated it is probably safer to rely on the more traditional polling procedures.

SURVEY DESIGNS

Survey studies can be designed, or arranged, in various ways to answer different questions. This topic is similar to that of experimental designs, which we explore in considerable detail in chapters 5, 6, and 7.

Cross-Sectional Designs

Most survey studies employ the **cross-sectional design**. The defining feature is that the survey is administered to a selected sample on a single occasion. The purpose is to provide a description of a particular population at a particular point in time. Mazer and Percival's (1989) sexual harassment survey is a good example. Their study yielded a detailed description of the reported experiences of a university population at a particular time in history. There is no way of knowing, from this study alone, whether sexual harassment was as prevalent at the University of Prince Edward Island in the sixties or the seventies as it was in the late eighties.

An interesting application of the cross-sectional design is provided by Maticka-Tyndale and Herold (1999), who surveyed Canadian university students with respect to condom usage while on spring break in Daytona Beach, Florida. Several methods of recruitment were used, including direct on-site and bus-ride-home contact and also via a mailed questionnaire to those who had recently returned from break. Site recruitment employed a form of convenience sampling, resulting in what we have termed an accidental sample. Potential respondents were recruited from those found on beaches and pool decks between the hours of 11 a.m. and 4 p.m., from Wednesday to Saturday. This time frame helped ensure a sample that was reasonably sober (serious drinking did not usually begin until late afternoon!) and had been in the area for at least several days so that, presumably, there had been at least some opportunity for sexual activity. Those who agreed to participate privately completed a brief questionnaire that asked about sexual history, previous spring break experiences, expectations regarding the likelihood of sexual activity, intentions to use condoms, and participation in various spring break activities including sexual interaction.

Among the interesting findings was that, despite the sexual milieu, only 25% of the students reported having had sexual intercourse since spring break began. Of those who did have intercourse, 73% reported that the experience took place with a new partner. Of these, almost all (97%) reported intentions to use condoms. Actual use was somewhat related to intentions, but even more strongly related to facilitating conditions such as the availability of condoms and partners' desire for condom use. Surprisingly, alcohol consumption and sexualized spring break activities, such as "dirty dancing," were not related to usage. A somewhat curious finding, in the light of past research on the topic, is that respondents' gender was not related to either reported sexual activity or condom use.

Perhaps there was something about the Florida sunshine, or the nature of the spring break experience, that helped to create gender equity in this regard!

Successive-Independent Samples

When the same survey is administered at different points in time to the same population we are using the successive independent sample design. This adds to the information available from the cross-sectional design since we can now document changes over time. For example, surveys of student drug use have been conducted in the province of Prince Edward Island on six separate occasions, beginning in 1972 (Van Til, MacMillan, & Poulin, 1998). This makes it possible to determine the extent to which the frequency of usage of particular drugs has changed over that time period. It would certainly be interesting to learn how drug usage patterns of the current high school generation compares to their parents' generation. The data indicate that alcohol has maintained a steady and high level of usage over the generations. Tobacco use, on the other hand, reached a high-water mark in the early eighties and has steadily declined since. The use of cannabis has increased somewhat over the years and is now almost as prevalent as tobacco. All other drugs surveyed (LSD, cocaine, heroin, etc.) show sporadic but generally low rates of usage over the entire survey period.

In interpreting such studies we need to be cautious in several areas. First, changes are only interpretable if the successive samples are representative of the same population. If one sample were composed of mainly rural high schools and a second of mainly city high schools we could not directly compare the results. Any differences that were found could just as well reflect urban vs. rural influences, as the passage of time. (The stratified random sampling procedures used in the successive student drug surveys appear to rule out this possibility.) We also need to be cautious not to attribute trends to individuals having changed over time. Successive samples are composed of different sets of individuals and are unable to reveal whether individual respondents have changed. For example, the reduction in rate of tobacco usage suggests that fewer students are taking up smoking than was the case in past survey years, but cannot tell us whether previous smokers have quit.

Longitudinal Design

Changes in individual respondents over time can only be assessed by means of a longitudinal design. The strategy here is to repeatedly measure the same sample. A good example is the Canadian Study of Health and Aging (1994), mentioned earlier in the chapter. This is an ongoing study that attempts to track changes in physical health and cognitive capacity in a representative sample of senior citizens as they grow older. As the data from this study are collected over the years it should become possible to provide detailed answers to questions such as the rate at which various abilities decline and whether age-related declines depend on factors such as gender, diet, exercise, living conditions, education, income level, and specific disease conditions. For example, one recent report (Hogan, Ebly & Fung, 1999) revealed a much greater incidence of functional disability in the very old (85+) than in younger seniors (65-84), even in the absence of underlying disease factors. Another analysis, focussing on life expectancy and dementia, found that the over-65 life expectancy of women with dementia, or living in institutions, was more than twice as great as that for men (Hill, Forbes, & Lindsay, 1997).

A longitudinal design was also employed by MacDonald and Ross (1999) in an interesting study which looked at the accuracy of predictions about dating relationships. Canadian university students were asked to rate the quality of their dating relationships and also to make predictions about how long the relationships would last. The students' roommates and parents were also contacted and asked to provide their assessments of the quality of the relationships and to forecast future longevity. Follow-up interviews were conducted at six-month and one-year intervals. Who do you think made the most accurate predictions? Despite the fact that the students were more confident in their predictions, their roommates and parents were considerably more accurate in forecasting the future of the relationship. Interestingly, the students' assessments of relationship quality were more strongly related to actual outcome than either their explicit predictions or those of their roommates and parents. In other words, the best predictor of the future was their current ratings of the strengths and weaknesses of the relationship. Apparently, however, when making their predictions the students generally ignored any negative aspects of the present relationship and, instead, optimistically forecasted that everything would work out!

The chief advantage of the longitudinal design is that it enables us to study individual change, as opposed to cultural or social change. The chief disadvantage is respondent mortality. In the course of repeated testing it is almost inevitable that some of the original respondents will have moved, will be unwilling to continue participating, or will have died. As the original sample shrinks in size it tends to become progressively less representative of the population it was drawn from. In the Canadian Health and Aging Study the deaths of some of the starting participants leaves us with a group of people who, in all probability, were sturdier and healthier to begin with than were those participants who died within the first few years of the study.

There are also several concerns that stem from repeated testing. One of these is **pretest sensitization**, an awareness of the focus of the survey that develops from exposure to the first administration. Such sensitization may result in participants paying more attention to certain matters or concerns, for example personal health issues, than they would otherwise. The problem with this is that any change that does occur may do so partly, or wholly, because of this sensitization. For example, a longitudinal survey aimed at assessing how political and social attitudes change during the course of one's lifetime may itself create changes, through increased awareness of social issues, that otherwise would not have taken place. This concern may have a familiar ring to it. In fact, it is a special case of the more general problem of reactivity discussed in Chapter 2.

The reactivity caused by repeated testing may sometimes create seemingly the opposite effect. If you learned that you were going to be surveyed on a topic at regular intervals you might, in order to present yourself favourably, decide to be as consistent as possible in your answers. Without the intrusion of the survey, and its arousal of a consistency motive, your opinions may have changed over time without your even being particularly aware of it. In fact, studies have shown that when attitude change takes place most people have difficulty recalling what their former attitudes and behaviours were, or even that there was any change at all (Bem & McConnell, 1970; Ross, McFarland & Fletcher, 1981). The problem, then, with both pretest sensitization and arousal of the consistency motive is that the results obtained from the repeated surveys of longitudinal studies may not generalize to those in the population who were not included in the sample and, therefore, were not subject to these influences.

VALIDITY OF SELF REPORTS

You may recall from our discussion in Chapter 1 that the concept of validity refers to the truthfulness or genuineness of a measure. With respect to surveys the important question is whether self-report data do, in fact, accurately reflect the feelings, thoughts, and behaviours of the respondents. One would think, for example, that there should be a close correspondence between self reports of behaviour and behavioural observations. However, a great deal of research in social psychology has shown that this is often not the case. In a classic study, LaPierre (1934) mailed questionnaires to a variety of innkeepers, restaurant owners, and tavern operators, asking whether they would serve Chinese customers. Of those responding, over 90% said that they would not. Sadly, this was not surprising. What was surprising was that LaPierre had just completed a cross-country auto trip in the company of a Chinese couple, had stopped at the very same establishments included in the survey, and on only a single occasion was the Chinese couple refused service. Clearly, the survey responses were not a valid indicator of actual behaviour.[2]

Social psychologists have documented a large number of situations in which reports of predicted or intended behaviour have been dramatically incorrect. When participants are asked to predict their (or others') behaviour in Milgram's obedience experiments (Milgram, 1974), almost everyone predicts he or she would disobey; in the actual situation, of course, most participants completely obeyed. Similarly, when asked how they would respond in the Asch (1951) conformity experiment or in one of Latané and Darley's (1970) bystander intervention studies, participants are nearly unanimous in reporting that they would not conform, but would indeed provide help to an innocent victim. As a class project some student researchers asked fellow students how they would respond to an encounter with a lost child who tearfully begged for assistance in locating her mother. All would help. Later, some students participated in an experiment which required that they hurry as quickly as possible to another location on campus. En route, they encountered the lost tearful child asking for help. Only one in ten stopped to help; the rest (90%) hurried to keep their appointment.

Findings such as these appear to create doubt about the validity of surveys. However, the fact that people cannot accurately predict, or sometimes even recall, their behaviour does not necessarily undermine the validity of surveys. It may be that the survey provides a perfectly valid assessment of people's opinions and beliefs. The fact that beliefs and behaviours are sometimes quite different may be due to the fact that, in many cases, they are controlled by different variables (Nisbett and Wilson, 1977). Indeed, we would run into the same concerns if we were to rely solely on observational studies to reveal people's thoughts and feelings. For example, observing soldiers in boot camp repeatedly running obstacle courses and performing forced marches would not give us a valid assessment of the soldiers' feelings about these activities. Nor should it cause us to question the validity of observational studies. In general, if you want to know what people do, you should observe. If you want to know what people feel, or think, you should ask.

Does the Question Shape the Answer?

A major threat to survey validity comes from a somewhat unexpected source—the wording and format of the questions asked (Schwarz, 1999). For example, one study asked respondents what they considered "the most important thing for children to prepare them for life." (Think for a moment of how you would answer.) When choosing from among alternatives offered on a list, over 60% chose "To think for themselves." However, fewer than 5% came up with the same, or similar, answer when no list was offered (Schuman & Presser, 1981). What can we conclude, then, about what people really think?

This question is considered in detail by Schwarz (1999) in a recent article in *American Psychologist*. Research clearly shows that answers to survey questions can change dramatically depending on response options, the ways in which rating scales are labelled and arranged, and the order in which questions are presented. Yet, Schwarz argues that the situation is not hopeless. Attitudes that are strongly held and personal behaviours that are well represented in memory (for example, whether you have ever been to Australia or acted in a stage play) are not likely to be distorted by the form of the question. Rather, it is the more mundane or vague memories and beliefs that are particularly susceptible to distortion. For example, how much TV do you watch in an average day, how healthy is your general diet, how satisfactory are your relationships with others? These sorts of judgments are context-dependent; they will hinge on what we've recently been thinking about and on information that we've recently been exposed to. For instance, in judging whether our marital relationships are generally satisfactory we are likely to be influenced by recent events (for example, whether we have recently had a fight with our spouse or, perhaps, have just returned from a romantic getaway) and by what we might have recently learned about the relationships of other couples. Most real-life judgments are formed in this manner. Schwarz argues that the same is true of survey responses and concludes by noting that "questionnaires are also a source of information that respondents draw on in order to determine their task and to arrive at a useful and informative answer" (p. 103). Guidelines for wording questions and constructing response formats have been developed to help standardize the respondents' interpretations and thereby minimize some of these concerns (Sudman & Bradburn, 1982; Sudman, Bradburn & Schwarz, 1996).

Honesty of Self Reports

A further concern is whether respondents are trying to provide honest answers. We noted in Chapter 2 that study participants are generally inclined to be helpful and cooperative, but are also quite concerned with presenting themselves in a favourable light. Both tendencies may compromise the validity of self reports. The tendency to say yes or to agree, known as the **acquiescence tendency,** is generally recognized as a threat to validity. Fortunately, this bias can be anticipated, and neutralized, by asking questions that don't require an agree or disagree response, or by asking the same question several times with the wording reversed.

The **social desirability bias** is a tendency to select response options that are socially approved, or that put the respondent in a favourable light. This would be the case, for example, if on a TV survey respondents over-reported the number of times they had watched the national news and under-reported viewings of *Baywatch* or the World Wrestling

Federation. This bias can sometimes be neutralized by emphasizing and ensuring anonymity of responses, stressing the importance of accurate reporting, and attempting to present various response options as equally socially desirable (DeMaio, 1984).

SUMMARY

Self-report methods represent a specialized, but widely used, form of structured observation. Most studies in psychology employ either a self-report procedure, a direct observational procedure or, in some cases, both. Common forms of self-report include survey questionnaires, interviews, psychological tests, and self-rating scales.

Surveys, the most widely employed self-report procedure, are primarily used to describe or characterize the population of interest. Surveys may also be used to provide correlational data. A survey consists of a predetermined set of questions administered to a sample selected from a particular population. Elements, or members, of the population are represented by a list called a sampling frame. In probability sampling elements are sampled from this frame in such a manner that the likelihood of any element's selection can be specified in advance. Simple random sampling and stratified random sampling are the two main forms of probability sampling. Two forms of nonprobability samples, in which the likelihood of an element's selection cannot be specified, are accidental samples and purposive samples. Probability samples are more likely to be representative of the population than are nonprobability samples. In addition, they allow the researcher to calculate the amount of sampling error, the extent to which means or percentages are likely to vary from population values. The larger the sample size the smaller the sampling error will be.

Surveys are typically administered in one of four ways. Mail surveys provide anonymity and the convenience of self-administration, but typically have a low and potentially unrepresentative return. Personal interviews have the advantage of a much higher return and the opportunity to clarify meaning, but are expensive, time-consuming, and potentially subject to interviewer bias. Telephone surveys reach large representative, samples quickly and inexpensively, but are increasingly viewed as an unwelcome intrusion so that response rates are dropping. Online surveys have a very short history, but their use is proliferating. They are able to reach very large samples very rapidly, but respondents are self-selected and drawn from such specialized segments of the population that sample representativeness is questionable.

Surveys may be designed in several different ways, depending on their purpose. Cross-sectional designs, intended to describe a population at a single point in time, involve administering a survey to a selected sample on a single occasion. The successive-independent samples design, aimed at measuring social or cultural change, involves administering the same survey on separate occasions to different samples selected from the same population. The longitudinal design, used to measure individual change, involves administering the same survey on repeated occasions to the same respondents.

The validity of surveys may be questioned on several grounds. Self-report data may be quite inconsistent with observational data. In some cases the inconsistency is due to the fact that self-reports reflect thoughts and feelings, which do not always correspond to behaviours. However, inconsistency also arises due to the form of the question, which may have a determining influence on the answers given. In addition, the honesty of self-reports may be compromised by factors such as the acquiescence tendency and social desirability bias.

KEY TERMS

accidental sample: A sample formed on the basis of convenience or happenstance.

acquiescence tendency: The tendency to say yes or to agree when responding to survey questions.

cross-sectional design: A survey design in which a questionnaire is administered to a selected sample on a single occasion.

element: A single member (person or case) of the population of interest.

external validity: extent to which a survey's findings are apt to generalize beyond the original sample and apply to the population as a whole.

mail survey: A form of survey administration in which questionnaires are mailed to prospective respondents with instructions for self administration.

nonprobability sample: A sample for which we cannot determine the probability of including individual population elements.

online survey: A form of survey administration in which online computer users respond to questions posted on a Web site.

personal interview: A form of survey administration in which potential respondents are contacted in person and asked to respond verbally to questions presented by an interviewer.

population: The total set of cases of interest.

pretest sensitization: An awareness of the focus, or purpose, of a survey study that develops as a result of initial exposure to the survey. This awareness may result in changes in behaviours, or attitudes, that in turn influence responses to subsequent survey administrations.

probability sample: A sample drawn in such a manner that the probability of inclusion of each population element can be specified in advance.

purposive sample: A sample in which the elements are handpicked.

representativeness: The extent to which characteristics of elements included in the sample match those of the larger population.

response bias: The bias that is introduced into survey results when those who respond to a given survey differ in some systematic way from those who do not respond.

sampling: Collecting data from a subset of the population in order to draw conclusions about the population as a whole.

sampling error: The expected variation in means, or percentages, among samples independently drawn from the same population.

sampling frame: A list of the individual elements comprising a particular population.

simple random sample: A sample drawn in such a manner that all population elements have an equal chance of being included.

social desirability bias: A tendency to select response options that are socially approved or place the respondent in a favourable light.

stratified random sampling: A sampling procedure in which the population is first divided into strata (categories or subsets) and a random sample is selected from each stratum.

telephone survey: A form of survey administration in which potential respondents are contacted by telephone by an interviewer who reads the questions and records the answers.

ENDNOTES

1. This does not mean that such surveys are worthless. They often make useful class projects because they directly engage the students with the material and provide a useful exercise in questionnaire design and data analysis. It is also possible that meaningful comparisons can be made among sub-groups of respondents. I usually advise students to try to obtain anywhere from 10 to 20 respondents in each of the subgroups they wish to compare.

2. This study took place at the height of the Great Depression, when anti-Oriental sentiment was particularly strong.

chapter four

EX-POST-FACTO RESEARCH

A scientist's work is similar to that of a detective. Scientific data are comparable to the clues and pieces of evidence that are gathered in a criminal investigation. There are often gaps in the information available to scientist and detective alike, requiring the investigator to put forth an educated guess, a tentative theory, as to the underlying structure that ties everything together. Determining whether this guesswork is correct, or at least on the right track, usually requires additional digging (research) to produce the facts needed to check the theory.

Police investigations are almost always **ex post facto** (after the fact) in nature. The evidence that is turned up—the fingerprints, bloodstains, bullet holes or threatening letters—consists of what has been left behind after the crime has occurred. Psychological research may also rely on ex-post-facto information. Rather than making new observations, the researcher may choose instead to examine traces or records of behaviour that has occurred in the past.

Why might a researcher wish to dig up the past rather than study the present? There are several good reasons for this. One is that the topic of interest may be one that is difficult or impossible to observe at first hand. A good example is the violence and atrocities that sometimes develop out of mob behaviour. Not only are such occasions difficult to anticipate but even if a researcher did happen to be on the scene it might well be under life-threatening circumstances! Mullen (1986) bypassed these problems by studying newspaper and eyewitness accounts of lynch mobs. He was able to show that the larger the mob the greater the likelihood that atrocities such as burning, lacerating, and dismembering the victims would occur.

A second reason for selecting the ex-post-facto approach is that it eliminates a problem that plagues observational and survey research. Reactivity, as you will recall from our discussion in Chapter 2, is the tendency for people to respond differently when they are aware that they are being observed. This problem clearly does not occur when the behaviour that is being studied has already taken place. This advantage is such a strong one that ex-post-facto methods are sometimes discussed under the heading of nonreactive (or unobtrusive) measures.

Two major strategies of ex-post-facto research are discussed below, followed by an evaluation of their usefulness in psychological research.

EXAMINATION OF PHYSICAL TRACES

Physical traces are observable changes in the physical nature of objects that are caused by particular forms of human activity. Think for a minute of some of the traces left behind by your own actions. Perhaps there is a heart with initials carved into a tree trunk, gum that still remains stuck beneath a grade-school desk, or a message written on a washroom wall. It is not unreasonable to think that by studying such remnants we could learn something useful about human behaviour.

Most physical traces reflect either the process of **erosion** or the process of **accretion** (Webb, Campbell, Schwartz, Sechrest, & Grove, 1981). Erosion refers to a wearing away of some substance. The soles of shoes, for example, gradually become worn with continued use. The pattern of such wear could be potentially informative with respect to the wearer's size and characteristic gait. (Joggers can examine the soles of old running shoes to learn about their running style, for example whether they have a tendency to overpronate.) A frequently cited research example is that the tiles around some museum exhibits were found to be much more worn than those around others, presumably a reflection of relative popularity (Webb et al., 1981).

Accretion traces are those in which physical material has built up over a period of time. Examples are easy to find—dust on a bookshelf, fingerprints on a pane of glass, graffiti on washroom walls, or litter along the side of the road. As an example of how an accretion measure could be used in research, think of what students typically do when studying a textbook. They often underline (or highlight) important sentences or phrases, sometimes make notes in the margins, and occasionally leave finger smudges or coffee stains. It is not unreasonable then to think that the number of markings per page, or chapter, may reflect how intensively that section has been studied. (At the very least a student has to open to a chapter before marking in it!) We could easily design a study in which the amount of marking is measured (perhaps during a final exam when books must be left in a designated area outside of the examination room) and then correlated with the grade earned in the course. What do you think we would find? Would there be a relation between the amount of textbook marking and final mark in a course?

A third type of physical trace measure consists of manufactured **products** or their remains. Based on surviving physical evidence, such as pottery shards or flint scrapers, archeologists are able to create surprisingly detailed descriptions of ancient cultures.

Indeed, modern products such as computers, fax machines, satellite dishes, and videotapes probably reveal a good deal about contemporary life styles. What might future archeologists conclude about our culture from the artifacts and remnants that survive us? In a fascinating book, *The Motel of the Mysteries* (Macaulay, 1979), the author suggests a number of humorous but plausible interpretations—for example, that common plumbing fixtures such as sinks and toilets were used in private religious ceremonies and that TV sets served as central communal altars.

An exciting challenge for researchers is to find psychologically meaningful ways of studying product use. One such possibility is to make use of products intended to display a message, such as bumper stickers or T-shirts. These products frequently present statements of belief, allegiance, or social attitude. We could conceivably study whether particular attitudes or values vary with socioeconomic status by comparing the message displays of bumper stickers attached to high-priced luxury automobiles with those affixed to older, less expensive vehicles. What do you think might be found?

An interesting example of research focussing on products that indicate allegiance was reported by Cialdini and his colleagues (Cialdini, Borden, Thorne, Walker, Freeman, & Sloan, 1976). They were interested in a phenomenon called "basking in reflected glory" that occurs when people attempt to publicly associate themselves with successful others, even when they have done nothing themselves to contribute to this success. In North American society this tendency seems to especially manifest itself in the area of sports, as evidenced by the profusion of bumper stickers, caps, T-shirts, and other apparel that bear the logo of university or professional teams. According to the researchers' hypothesis, this "basking" phenomenon should be revealed by an increase in the frequency of wearing team apparel whenever the team was victorious. This hypothesis was tested by observing the apparel of students in classes on the Monday following a weekend football game at seven large universities in the U.S. As the researchers predicted, it was consistently found that the proportion of students wearing school-affiliated apparel was higher following a victory than a defeat.

USE OF ARCHIVAL MATERIALS

A vast, and virtually untapped, reservoir of information is available to researchers for the taking. **Archival material** consists of all forms of narrative information that have been preserved in some manner. Archival sources include newspapers, books, organizational records and files, letters, movies, TV shows, musical recordings, photographs, and works of art. Although these works were created for purposes other than research they contain a wealth of information that can be mined by psychological researchers. For instance, differences in the ways our society views men and women have been studied by examining photographs in popular magazines and newspapers. Photographs of men were found to focus on the head area, but those of women were likely to also include the torso (Archer, Iritani, Kimes, & Barrios, 1983). As the researchers suggest, perhaps the underlying message is that men are to be judged by the shape of their thoughts, but women by the shape of their bodies!

Making effective use of archival material requires, as do all research studies, systematic planning and preparation. The first step is to identify a source of material relevant to the topic being studied. Three general categories of sources have been identified (Judd, Smith, & Kidder, 1991). **Statistical records** include data compiled by government agencies and both private and public institutions. Information regarding traffic accidents, crime rates, hospital admissions, employment, income levels, and other social statistics are included. A second category, **survey archives**, has recently been developed, especially for the benefit of researchers. Government agencies like Statistics Canada, as well as private organizations such as the Pew Research Centre, make available to researchers data files developed from a wide variety of large-scale surveys. Statistics Canada (**www.statcan.ca**), for example, provides survey data in areas such as the economy, the environment, education, employment, health, crime, and tourism. The third category, **narrative records**, consists of all written and pictorial works, whether public or private, that have been preserved in some fashion. Anything from ancient hieroglyphics to the lyrics of modern rap songs, from private diaries and letters to the *Encyclopaedia Britannica*, is a narrative record that can be analyzed in some fashion.

After selecting an appropriate source, the next step is to draw a **representative sample** of material for analysis. Consider a case where a researcher wants to study the communications of males and females seeking dating partners. A good source would be the personal advertisement sections carried by many newspapers and, in some cities, on local cable channels. So far, so good. However, which of the thousands of newspapers published (or cable channels broadcast) across North America should be selected and what time periods should be covered? The answer depends on the goals of the study. If, as in survey research, the goal is to accurately describe the characteristics of a particular population, then some form of probability sampling should be used. A stratified sampling method might be selected to ensure that different geographic regions are adequately represented. If the goal is to chart changes over time then a longitudinal approach should be chosen, sampling the same source repeatedly over particular intervals of time.

Once the sample has been selected and the material assembled, the researcher must code it in a way that meets the goals of the study. When the source is a narrative record the method of coding usually involves **content analysis**. This is "any technique for making inferences by systematically and objectively identifying specified characteristics of messages" (Holsti, 1969, p. 601). Applying this technique requires that the researcher define the characteristics of interest and develop a strategy for identifying the occurrence of these characteristics. In studying personal advertisements placed in newspapers, for example, we might decide to focus on descriptive phrases such as "attractive," "fun-loving," "sophisticated," or "athletic" that are used to describe either the person placing the ad or desired qualities sought in a partner. Rather than simply listing each and every descriptive phrase, it is generally more useful to define a small number of categories that the phrases might fit.

As an illustration of this process we will consider a study of personal ads placed in the *Vancouver Sun* (Davis, 1990). The author described 13 attributes that could be used to code the descriptive phrases found in such ads: *attractive, physique, sex, picture, profession, employed, financial, education, intelligence, honest, humour, commitment,* and *emotion* (pp. 45-46). The contents of each ad were coded for the presence or absence of each of these attributes. The data obtained from this coding enabled Davis to make quantitative comparisons between male and female advertisers. He found that men were more likely than women to specify attractiveness and physique as desired qualities, to indicate a desire for sex, and to specifically request a photo. On the other hand, women were more likely than men to indicate a desire for an employed or professional man, or to specify financial considerations. Women were also more likely than men to mention education or intelligence as desired qualities. The author concluded that, on the whole, personal ads reflected traditional sex-role stereotypes of women as sex objects and men as success objects.

The entire process of doing archival research is well illustrated by McClelland's (1961) landmark studies of achievement motivation in society. In one such study McClelland sought to determine the extent to which different countries around the world varied in the emphasis that was placed on achievement motivation and, more importantly, whether such variation was related to economic success. How can the value placed on achievement be measured? McClelland reasoned that the more achievement was valued, the more it would be emphasized in examples provided to children, especially in stories included in school readers. Accordingly, he selected the reading primers used in elementary grades as an appropriate archival source. Samples of readers were selected from two time periods—1925 and 1950. Within each reader, stories to be coded were randomly selected. The coding involved a form of content analysis in which raters were asked to identify whether the paragraph contained an achievement-related theme. Based on this analysis, McClelland was able to isolate one group of countries whose school readers, at a particular period of time, placed a high emphasis on achievement and to compare them with a second group of countries whose readers placed much less emphasis on achievement. To measure economic success, McClelland collected statistics such as per-capita income and electrical output from appropriate government sources. One of the major findings was that a high emphasis on achievement motivation in grade school was followed, over the succeeding period of time, by a high rate of economic growth. It appeared that lessons learned during grade school were being applied as the country's citizens entered their productive work years in their twenties and thirties.

EVALUATION OF EX-POST-FACTO RESEARCH

Advantages

The major advantage of ex-post-facto research is its nonreactive nature. This helps to boost internal validity since it removes a major source of bias, the knowledge that one is being studied and the consequent belief that a particular form of response is desired or expected. We have seen how powerful the effects of reactivity can be, both in Mesmer's patients who convulsed when they believed magnetism was being applied (Chapter 1) and in the Hawthorne study where every change in working conditions was followed by an increase in productivity (Chapter 2). When we remove the reactive influence stemming from awareness of an observer's attention we greatly improve our ability to assess the uncontaminated influence of a study's independent variable. Since trace and archival data represent behaviour that has occurred in the past such data cannot be influenced by the attention, or expectations, of current researchers. The productivity of nations and the content of grade-school readers, for example, could not be altered by the interests of McClelland's research team. Nor could the content of personal ads be influenced by Davis's interest in sexual stereotyping. While this is an important advantage we must be aware that the absence of reactive influences from current investigators is no guarantee that there were no reactive influences at the time the data was deposited. Statistics relating to economic productivity, for instance, may have been shaped to some extent by government policies, the expectations of particular officials, and, perhaps, the desire to paint a favourable picture of the country's economy. The researcher who uses ex-post-facto data should try to become aware of factors that may have influenced the original data.

The use of ex-post-facto data may also strengthen a study's external validity. One reason for this is that the data source may derive from the entire population of interest rather than from a single sample. Thus, the readers that were coded for achievement themes were those used by nearly all children in that nation's schools. Similarly, the productivity data came not just from one or two regions of the country, or industrial sectors, but instead were aggregated over all regions and sectors. Ex-post-facto data may also cover relatively long intervals of time and thus facilitate generalizations across time periods. The fact that the achievement study extended over a long time span increases our confidence in the durability of the relationship between early exposure to achievement themes and adult productivity. The sheer fact that archival data are used, however, does not automatically confer external validity. Some forms of archival data may be quite limited in the populations, locales, and time periods they represent.

A third advantage of ex-post-facto research is economy. In many research studies the major expense incurred relates to the cost of data collection. Observational and survey studies typically require the hiring and training of observers or interviewers, as well as travel and equipment costs. In many ex-post-facto studies the data have already been collected and, as in various statistical sources or institutional records, may be readily available for use. Some archival or trace data, however, may require substantial effort and expense to put into usable form. For example, archeologists may need to invest enormous resources of time and effort to develop workable translations of hieroglyphic records. Again, as with the claims for internal and external validity, everything depends on the nature of the particular data source.

Disadvantages

These advantages, however, tend to be balanced out by a corresponding set of disadvantages. Perhaps the biggest disadvantage is that ex-post-facto data, when used in isolation, are almost always subject to **alternative interpretations**. Recall, for example, that the wear on tiles in front of particular museum exhibits was taken as an index of relative popularity. It is also possible, however, that the extra wear may simply be due to a particular exhibit's placement, near the entranceway or along a high-traffic corridor. Perhaps it occurred to you that underlinings and notes on textbook pages may simply indicate that a used, rather than a new, book was purchased. While grade-school readers may indeed reflect themes prevalent in a particular culture at a particular time there are also the possibilities that these books may not have been revised for decades or may even have been imported from other countries. Similarly, those who place personal ads undoubtedly represent a very select portion of the population, perhaps overrepresenting people who have not been successful in obtaining partners by more conventional means or who are preoccupied by fantasies of the ideal mate. This susceptibility to alternative interpretations reflects the complete lack of investigator control that is part and parcel of ex-post-facto data. In some studies investigators may be able to anticipate specific rival hypotheses, such as exhibit placement, and select data that are not subject to them. However, compared to other methodological approaches, there is much less leeway for such control in ex-post-facto studies.

A second disadvantage relates to issues of reliability. Depending on the source, both trace and archival data are likely to contain gaps and inconsistencies. One problem is that such data may be haphazardly or selectively deposited. For example, suicide notes may be gathered and analyzed to uncover the motivations behind such extreme actions. However, notes are found in only about one-fourth of suicide cases, and it is unclear whether such messages represent the motives of those who don't leave notes (Webb et al., 1981). A further problem is that even though data have been deposited they may not survive. When the famed library at Alexandria, in ancient Egypt, burned, a great many scientific and cultural texts of the classical world were lost forever. The survival rate of trace data is particularly problematical. Footprints are washed away, fingerprints obliterated, tiles replaced, tombs robbed, files misplaced or stolen, and tapes mysteriously erased or recorded over. Even computerized data may be lost when the system crashes or a virus invades. Whatever the cause, when substantial portions of the data record are missing the reliability of the surviving information may be open to question.

The Multimethod Approach

Every method of research has its strengths and weaknesses. Observational data, as we have seen, are subject to reactivity and observer bias. Survey data may be compromised by question wording and the social desirability bias. Perhaps the best way of overcoming a particular method's disadvantages is to supplement its use with that of other methods. Often the strengths of one method will compensate for the weaknesses of another. Thus, ex-post-facto data may be most useful when used in conjunction with other approaches such as surveys, observational studies, and experiments.

A good example of the multimethod approach is Levine's (1997) research on pace of life, discussed briefly in Chapter 2. He was able to supplement his observational studies of walking speed by making use of certain types of trace and archival data. The time displays of bank clocks (a trace measure) were found to be more accurate in countries that had a more rapid walking pace, suggesting that the underlying cause might be cultural differences in the emphasis placed on time urgency. In addition, Levine was able to use an archival source, public health records in the U.S., to demonstrate a relationship between coronary heart disease and various observational measures of the pace of life (Levine, Lynch, Miyake, & Lucia, 1989). Cities with a faster pace of life suffered a higher death rate from coronary illness, a finding that suggests a connection between stress and time urgency. Such correspondence between data drawn from very different sources strengthens the validity of the study's findings.

SUMMARY

Ex-post-facto research is research that takes place after the fact—that is, after the behaviour of interest has occurred. It is similar to police investigations in that it examines the evidence that has been left behind and then suggests a possible interpretation to account for it. One reason for pursuing such research is that we cannot always anticipate when events of interest might occur, but we can, at least, study their aftereffects. A second reason is to avoid the problems of reactivity that can plague observational and survey research.

One form of ex-post-facto research involves the examination of physical traces of behaviour, changes in the physical nature of objects caused by various sorts of human activity. Most physical traces can be categorized as either erosion or accretion. Erosion is a wearing away of material, such as a scuffed shoe or a worn floorboard. Accretion is an accumulation of material over time, such as dust on a bookshelf or litter alongside a road. A third type of physical trace consists of manufactured products or their remains.

A second form of ex-post-facto research utilizes archival material—any form of narrative information that has been preserved in some fashion. Conducting an archival study involves locating an appropriate source for study, drawing a representative sample from this source, and then coding the material in some systematic fashion. Coding often entails content analysis—identifying specific characteristics of messages and tabulating the frequency with which they occur.

The major advantage of archival research is its nonreactive nature—the fact that the data cannot be influenced by the attentions or expectations of current researchers. A second advantage is that the use of such data may strengthen a study's external validity by virtue of representing the entire population of interest or extending across time periods. A third advantage is that such research is often less costly than observational or survey studies. The major disadvantage is that ex-post-facto data are subject to a variety of alternative interpretations. Since the behaviour has already occurred it is not possible to employ the usual sorts of controls (manipulation, constancy, balancing) that would help to rule out rival explanations. A second problem is that ex-post-facto data may be unreliable due to gaps or inconsistencies in the data record. Every method of investigation has strengths and weaknesses. The best way of overcoming the weaknesses of a particular method is to employ the multimethod approach of combining several different methods of data collection in the study of a particular problem.

KEY TERMS

accretion: A building up of material over a period of time. Accretion patterns may give evidence of particular forms of use or disuse.

archival material: Any form of narrative information that has been preserved in some form.

alternative interpretations: Different ways of explaining or understanding the same set of data.

content analysis: A process of identifying particular characteristics of messages so that they may be systematically analyzed and conclusions drawn.

erosion: A wearing away of some substance. Erosion patterns may give evidence of particular forms of use or disuse.

ex post facto: After the fact; characterizes research that examines traces or records of behaviour that has already taken place.

multimethod approach: An approach to doing research that employs several different methods in the investigation of a particular problem. The multimethod approach strengthens the validity of a study's conclusions.

narrative record: Any body of writing or pictorial representation that has been preserved in some fashion.

products: Manufactured items or their remains. The study of products may yield evidence about behaviour associated with their use.

representative sample: A sample that accurately reflects the population that the researcher wants to draw conclusions about.

statistical records: Collections of quantitative data that may record a wide variety of events—for example, births, deaths, marriages, traffic accidents, hospital admissions, criminal convictions, etc.

survey archives: Data files drawn from large-scale surveys that are made available to interested researchers.

chapter five

BETWEEN-SUBJECTS EXPERIMENTS

The most powerful tool in science is the experiment. It is superior to any other method in its ability to uncover causal relationships, thereby serving the scientific goal of understanding (see Chapter 1). In this chapter we will explore the basic structure of the experiment and show how it is utilized in psychological research. Then, in the following chapters, we will extend this structure in several important ways.

HISTORICAL EXAMPLE

No one knows when the first experiment was conducted. Our early hominid ancestors no doubt performed many experiments as they tried to find ever more effective ways of keeping warm and securing food. We can be certain that there were countless experiments in flint knapping, tool production, fire making, and shelter construction. The results of successful experiments would gradually become incorporated into the customs and folkways of the clan or tribe and preserved for future generations.

One of the earliest experiments that we have knowledge of was performed in ancient Egypt (Jones, 1964). When Egyptian armies returned home with prisoners of war their practice was to publicly execute them. Apparently, the preferred method of execution was lethal injection delivered by snakebite (perhaps employing the Egyptian asp made famous by Cleopatra in her celebrated suicide). On one particular occasion, however, this usually reliable procedure did not work. Several prisoners, despite being bitten, managed to survive. The investigating official learned that some of the prisoners had eaten citrons (a lemon-like fruit) just prior to entering the execution area. Could this have something to do with their survival? To find out, the official arranged for a simple test. When the next group of prisoners was brought in they were thoroughly searched and any food they had was confiscated. They were then secured in a separate area and, for several days, fed the same diet. On the day of execution the prisoners were separated into two groups. Those in one group were each given a citron to eat, while those in the second group received nothing. All of the prisoners were then carefully monitored to assure that each was, in fact, bitten. The identities of those prisoners who immediately succumbed, as well as those who did not, were carefully noted. The result, we are told, was that those without the citron died immediately, but that those who ate it survived, at least for a period of time. With this information in hand the authorities were able to make the appropriate revisions to their execution procedures.

THE ANATOMY OF AN EXPERIMENT

In its root form the word "experiment" simply means to try something different. In fact, all of us perform experiments in our daily lives. We try a new route to our workplace, modify some aspect of our exercise routine, change our grip on the tennis racquet, or add a new ingredient to a favourite recipe. What we hope to accomplish, of course, is to discover what effect this something different will have. Will the alternate route take less time, or the new recipe have a zestier flavour? Essentially, the same is true of a scientific experiment. The only difference between our personal experiments and their scientific counterparts is that the latter are carried out in a more rigorous fashion—under controlled conditions and using carefully specified procedures that may be followed by others.

In a nutshell, an experiment consists of three basic elements: (1) An independent variable is manipulated, (2) A dependent variable is measured, and (3) The influences of other (extraneous) variables are controlled.

Manipulation of an Independent Variable

The first element represents the essential defining criterion of the experiment. The critical feature is the manipulation of an **independent variable**, the trying of something different. What was the independent variable in the citron experiment? It was just that—the citron. It was manipulated by creating two different levels— citron vs. no citron. To carry out any experiment, at least two different levels of the independent variable must be created. This provides us with the essential contrast, the comparison between outcomes in different conditions, that gives the experiment its analytic power. Testing only one level alone (either the citron or the no-citron condition by itself) tells us nothing. The effect of the independent variable is revealed by the *difference* in outcomes between levels. What we want to learn is what difference the citron (or whatever treatment we are investigating) made.

We are, of course, not limited to only two levels of the independent variable. Any number of levels could potentially be included. For example, a third level could be added to the citron experiment by creating another group in which only half a citron is given to each prisoner. The number of levels included, as well as their particular nature, depends on the questions that are being asked. The answers to these questions are given by examining the differences in outcomes among the various levels.

Measurement of a Dependent Variable

What was the **dependent variable** in the citron experiment? The critical observation was whether the prisoner lived or died. Some dependent variables, like this one, can be very simply measured by determining whether an observation is best placed in one category or another. Categorical (or nominal scale) data such as these are usually summarized in terms of percentages. Once we have determined the percentage in each group that survived the snakebite (and calculated the difference) we have given the basic result of the study.

In many cases, though, the dependent variable is measured quantitatively. That is, we measure the extent or degree to which something takes place and express this measurement in numbers. Suppose, for example, that all the prisoners died eventually, but that there was considerable variability in how long this took—some expiring immediately and others holding on for many hours. An appropriate measurement of the dependent variable in this case would be in time units such as minutes and hours (or perhaps the passage of a shadow on a sundial). When the measure is quantitative we usually summarize the results by presenting numerical averages. For example, we might determine that the average time to death was 18.5 minutes in the citron group, but only 1.2 minutes in the no-citron group. Along with such averages we would also include statistics that represent the variability within each group. More on this later.

Control of Extraneous Variables

Were there any controls in this experiment? We mentioned at least one—the standard diet the prisoners were fed. You might recall from Chapter 1 that this is an example of the control technique of **constancy**. Wherever possible we would like to deal with extraneous variables, such as diet, by holding their influences constant. When variables are held constant they remain at the same level and cannot, therefore, influence the outcome of the experiment. Can you think of any other variables that could have influenced the outcome? Before reading further it might be fun to make a quick list. Look at the variables on your list and try to decide if it would be possible, or practical, to hold each of them constant.

Perhaps your list includes factors such as age, health, and body weight. These would certainly be relevant. Other variables relating to the procedure might also be important— size or age of the snake, how often a particular snake has been used, depth and location of the bite, etc. It may be that some of these variables, such as size of snake or number of previous uses, could be held constant. In the case of personal characteristics, such as health or weight, however, there is a danger that one of more of these could become **confounded** with the levels of the independent variable. Unless we are willing to restrict ourselves to a very tiny portion of the prisoner population it will not be possible to hold such variables constant.

Roughly speaking, we can classify extraneous variables as falling into one of two major categories. The first category is *procedural* variables and includes details pertaining to the conduct of the experiment—for example, the diet the prisoners are fed, the size of the snake, location of bite, time of day and other such factors. The second category is *individual-difference* variables (or personal attributes), which includes all the various ways that experimental participants might differ from one another—for example, height, weight, health, age, personal history, emotional makeup, and intelligence, to name but a few. Typically, different control procedures are applied to these two sources of extraneous, or error, variance. In the case of procedural variables, it is critically important to hold them constant in order to avoid potential confounding. We clearly don't want prisoners in the citron group fed a different diet, or bitten by a different-sized snake, than those in the no-citron group. In the case of individual-difference variables we also want to prevent potential confounding, as would occur, for example, if all of the healthy prisoners ended up in one group and the unhealthy prisoners in the other group. But, since we can't usually hold health or other individual difference variables constant, we attempt to prevent confounding through the control technique of **balancing**. That is, we try to form groups in such a manner that they are approximately equal in average health, weight, age, and other individual characteristics. As we will see, there are several different ways of accomplishing this.

WHAT ARE BETWEEN-SUBJECTS EXPERIMENTS?

The title of this chapter, as I hope you may have noticed, is **between-subjects** experiments. Thus far, we have discussed the basic nature of an experiment without specifying what this qualifying term, between subjects, means. Basically, it refers to the way in which participants (or subjects)[1] are placed into conditions—that is, assigned to particular levels of the independent variable. In a between-subjects experiment a *different* group of participants is tested in each condition of the experiment. In contrast, a **within-subjects** experiment involves testing the *same* participants in all conditions. It should be apparent that the citron experiment was between-subjects, one group tested with citron and a second, different, group without citron. A within-subjects experiment would not have been possible here as, given the nature of the treatment, participants could not be tested twice! Since the between-subjects design is a bit easier to understand than the within-subjects design we use it as a model for presenting the basic features of an experiment. The within-subjects design is reserved for the next chapter.

CHARACTERISTICS OF A SOUND EXPERIMENT

A great deal of time, effort, and money are invested in scientific research. This investment is wasted if experiments are carelessly planned or poorly executed. The essential characteristics of good experimental research are presented in this section. I encourage you to think of these as checklist items whenever you are evaluating the quality of a psychological experiment—whether your own or someone else's.

Does the Experiment Possess Internal Validity?

This is the first checklist item and the most important. Validity, as you may recall from Chapter 1, is related to the concept of truthfulness. We saw that a valid measure is one that really does measure the concept it was designed to measure. The **internal validity** of an experiment is also a question of truthfulness. In this case, it's the extent to which the data reveal the true relationship between the independent and dependent variables. The reason any experiment is done is to show this relationship as clearly as possible. We want to know the nature of the relationship between citron and immunity, TV and aggression, magnetism and convulsions. An experiment that is high in internal validity reveals this relationship clearly; one that is low in internal validity leaves the relationship in doubt.

How, then, is high internal validity achieved? Basically, it is accomplished by preventing extraneous variables from becoming confounded with the independent variable. If we are successful, then, we have created a situation in which only the independent variable changes. As a result, any corresponding changes that take place in the dependent variable can clearly be linked to the independent variable. On the other hand, if one or more extraneous variables do change with the independent variable then the nature of the linkage between independent and dependent variable remains obscure. If only the healthy prisoners got citron, as we saw above, we could not be certain about the cause of the immunity. To remove this uncertainty and achieve a high degree of internal validity, our first concern is with ways of avoiding confounding.

As discussed earlier in this chapter, there are two basic techniques for accomplishing this. We can hold variables constant, or we can balance them across levels of the independent variable. There is little more we can say about the first technique except to note that the more variables we are able to hold constant the more clearly we are able to see the effect of the independent variable. And, as indicated earlier, it is especially important to hold procedural variables constant. On the other hand, it is very difficult, if not impossible, to hold individual-difference variables constant. If we are to achieve internal validity, then, we must find some way of balancing out the influences of those variables we cannot keep constant.

Randomized assignment. The usual technique of balancing in the between-subjects design is through **randomized assignment** of participants to conditions. Think again of the citron experiment. What was the method of determining who was in the citron group and who wasn't? The actual answer is lost in antiquity, but we can at least imagine some possibilities. Perhaps volunteers were called for. Or, maybe the official in charge made the decision personally, perhaps placing the more likable of the prisoners in the citron group. Then again, it may simply have been based on time of arrival—the first five prisoners being given the citron and the next five no citron. What method do you think would be the best? Hopefully, you can see the flaws in each of the ones mentioned.

Assuming that the official wanted a truthful (internally valid) answer about the effects of citron, the prisoners should have been assigned to treatment conditions randomly—that is, entirely on the basis of chance. The defining quality of random assignment is that each participant have an equal chance of placement in any particular experimental condition. If this were done then any special characteristics of the prisoners that might affect their response, such as health, weight, or age, should be spread more or less evenly across the two groups. Any initial differences between the groups are entirely due to chance and, based on statistical theory, we can calculate the likelihood of differences of various sizes occurring. Practically speaking, the larger the sample size the more effective random assignment is in balancing these extraneous variables.

Using a table of random numbers. How is random assignment accomplished? Flipping a coin or drawing numbers from a hat are reasonable possibilities, as long as we can be certain that the process is carried out without bias. To make certain that bias is avoided researchers often employ a table of random numbers, such as the one found in the back of this book (Appendix C). If there are only two conditions to assign participants to, as in the citron experiment, we can let the even numbers stand for one condition and the odd numbers for the other. To follow this procedure we need to first make a list of available participants. With the list in hand, open to the table and point your finger at any number. Reading in any direction you would pair the first number with the first name on the list, the second with the second name, and so on until all participants have a number assigned. Then those with even numbers are assigned to one of the conditions and those with odd numbers to the other. We can easily modify this procedure to accommodate three different conditions by allowing the numerals 1, 2 and 3 to represent the first condition, 4, 5 and 6 the second, and 7, 8 and 9 the third. Or, more simply, we could use only the numerals 1, 2 and 3, assigning one to each condition, and ignore any other number that happens to turn up.

Block randomization. The simple randomization process outlined above works fine in theory. However, several practical difficulties with its use have led researchers to a variation called **block randomization**. One such problem is that it could easily result in unequal sample sizes—perhaps giving us ten participants in one treatment group but only four in another. This reduces the power of statistical analysis. A second problem is that it requires us to have a complete list of participants before we begin the experiment. This is frequently not the case; instead we often recruit participants over a period of time, such as an academic semester. Both problems can be solved by using block randomization.

In this procedure the various treatment conditions (levels of the independent variable) are arranged into blocks. Each block contains the total number of conditions, ordered in some random sequence. For example, with three treatment conditions the first block might be [3, 1, 2]. This means that the first person recruited would be assigned to condition 3, the second to condition 1 and the third to condition 2. Thus, we run one participant in each treatment condition before any condition is repeated. If the second block were [2, 3, 1] then the fourth person would be assigned to condition 2, the fifth to condition 3, and the sixth to condition 1. All of the blocks are constructed in advance to accommodate the number of participants anticipated. This process assures equal sample sizes in our treatment conditions. More importantly, it keeps variables associated with time, or place of recruitment, from becoming confounded with the independent variables. For example, student participants who are recruited later in the semester may differ in motivation, or in academic competence, from those recruited earlier. Similarly, students recruited from sociology or biology classes may differ from those in psychology classes. Block randomization ensures that any such differences are equally balanced across treatment conditions.

Computer-assisted randomization. A very easy way to accomplish either simple random assignment or block randomization is to use a computer program such as the Research Randomizer (**www.randomizer.org**). It asks you some basic questions and your responses cause the program to generate one or more sets of random numbers that allow you to select a random sample from a population, to randomly assign participants to conditions, or to randomly order a set of conditions for experimental presentation. I used this program to generate the random number table in Appendix C.

Matching. Between-subject experiments that employ randomization techniques to balance extraneous variables are called **randomized-groups designs**. The main alternative to randomized groups is the **matched-groups design**. The approach here is to attempt to create balance by purposely assigning particular participants to particular treatment groups. This method is most likely to be used when the number of available participants is small, or when there is some particularly important extraneous variable that the researcher wants to be certain is controlled. Both considerations might apply to the citron experiment. If the total number of participants were ten (five per group) we might be concerned that randomized assignment would fail to equalize the two groups. And, if the groups are not equalized, there is a danger that differences in important variables such as body weight or physical health could become confounded with treatment conditions.

The first step in applying the matched groups design is to choose an appropriate matching variable. The variable chosen should be one that (a) is likely, if left uncontrolled, to have a large impact on the dependent variable and (b) can easily be measured. In the citron experiment, body weight meets both criteria. We want to assign participants in such a way that we have approximately the same average weight in each group. One way to accomplish this is to list the weights in ascending or descending order, then take the first two weights on the list and randomly assign one to each group. The same procedure would be followed for each successive pair of weights. It is important that the decision as to which member of each pair is assigned to a particular group should be made by using some randomizing technique, such as the flip of a coin. This makes certain that any systematic bias (for example, always assigning the heavier of the pair to the citron group) is avoided. Table 5.1 illustrates this procedure and shows how it effectively balances the weight.

Matching on more than one variable. What happens when there is more than one important variable to balance? It is possible to match for several variables at once. However, a larger number of participants is required and the matching is more difficult. For example, we might want our groups matched on both weight and health. Although degree of health is difficult to measure, perhaps we could simply classify each prisoner as relatively healthy or unhealthy. For each category we would list the weights of those participants classified as belonging to it. Then, we would simply follow the steps outlined above of pairing up adjacent weights and randomly assigning one to each treatment group. As long as weight and health are not correlated with each other we will have achieved balance for both. If

TABLE 5-1	Creating Groups Matched by Weight	
Rank Order	Weight	Assigned Group
1	210	C
2	197	NC
3	193	NC
4	188	C
5	172	NC
6	168	C
7	159	C
8	146	NC
9	132	NC
10	125	C

Average of C = (210+188+168+159+125)/5 = 170
Average of NC = (197+193+172+146+132)/5 = 168

they are correlated, as seems likely, balancing both variables would be much more difficult and would require a large initial sample from which only a small proportion could be used.

From the above discussion it should be clear that a major limitation of the matched groups design is that only a small number of the potentially relevant variables can be controlled in this way. However, since the matching process also includes randomized assignment we can expect that other variables will be at least roughly balanced. Matching designs are frequently used when we investigate individual difference variables, such as gender, age, or personality characteristics. In hypnosis research, for example, a critically important individual difference variable is susceptibility—that is, individual differences in responsiveness to hypnotic procedures. Most investigators begin by screening potential participants on a hypnotic susceptibility scale so that they can be classified as high, medium, or low in responsiveness. From each of these groupings participants are assigned in equal proportions to the various experimental treatment conditions. This sort of matching procedure is usually termed **blocking**, and the resulting design is called a **randomized blocks design**.[2]

Participant loss. The reason we take such pains to create balanced groups is to prevent any confounds that might threaten internal validity. One such threat, which may be initially unforeseen, occurs through **participant loss** after initial group assignment has been made. Almost every research project experiences such loss. Often prospective participants will put their name on an experimental sign-up sheet, or agree when a recruitment request is made over the phone, but then fail to show up. Some experiments involve repeated sessions, or long-term follow-ups, and those who participate in the initial sessions may fail to return for the later ones. Failures to complete the experiment are not only frustrating for the researcher but also, and more seriously, may undermine internal validity. This unfortunate situation arises if the loss is somehow related to particular treatment conditions. If participants are just as likely to drop out of one condition as another, the only problem caused is the time and effort needed to recruit replacements. However, if many more participants drop out of one condition than another, a serious problem is created. The initial balancing of treatment groups has now been disrupted. Not only do we have fewer participants in one group but, in all likelihood, those who remain are very different from those who started.

To understand this, consider how an experiment in pain might be conducted. We ask one group of participants to undergo a series of painful immersions of the forearm in circulating ice water—often called the cold-pressor test. The treatment involves repeated 30-second immersions during which physiological recordings are taken and subjective pain ratings are made. The control (no-pain) group is tested while their forearms are in lukewarm water. To meet accepted ethical standards researchers must inform participants accurately about the nature of the treatment they will receive, especially when it involves discomfort, and also must remind them of their right to discontinue at any time for any reason (see Chapter 9). Suppose, then, that some of the participants assigned to the pain group decide to leave after learning about the level of pain involved, and that still more walk out after being subjected to the first few cold-pressor treatments. In contrast, all of the participants in the control group remain. What has happened is that groups that were initially balanced through random assignment, or matching, are now no longer balanced. Participants who remain in the pain group are likely to have special characteristics—perhaps a higher-than-usual pain tolerance or an idealistic desire to sacrifice themselves for the sake of science. These characteristics may well influence participants' ratings and, unfortunately, are now confounded with the independent variable. Unless some means can be found of disentangling the influences of the confounded variables the internal validity of the study has been hopelessly compromised.

Since the effects of participant loss can devastate internal validity, safeguards should be set up in advance. Sometimes it is possible to identify (through appropriate interview techniques or some form of pretesting) those individuals who are likely to drop out. For example, all participants might be given an initial test of pain tolerance and only those with high tolerance invited to participate. Hopefully, such a procedure would reduce the overall drop-out rate and, more importantly, prevent it from being disproportionate. Alternatively, we could run all participants and every time someone from the pain group drops out we could drop a control participant with a similar score on the pain tolerance test. This, in a sense, is matching in reverse. Its aim is to continually restore balance as the study is being conducted. One disadvantage is that it is relatively wasteful of participants since it may require a large number to be discarded. This disadvantage, however, is minor compared to the loss of internal validity that would otherwise occur.

Is the Experiment Sensitive?

While internal validity is clearly the most critical feature of an experimental design, **sensitivity** ranks as a close second. If the independent variable we have chosen to study really does have an effect on our dependent variable, we hope that our experiment will clearly reveal this effect. The sensitivity of an experiment is its ability (or power) to detect whatever effect the independent variable has. In some cases—either because the effect is so small, or because the design is insensitive—the effect of the independent variable may not be evident.

An analogy may help you understand this. Think of using a metal detector to locate objects, such as coins or rings, that have been lost at the beach. If we sweep the detector over a given area and it fails to register the presence of metal we may take this as an indication that no metal is there. But is this necessarily so? It may be that there is actually metal in the area, but because the amount is so small, or buried so deep, it simply doesn't register. Or perhaps the problem lies with the detector we are using. Maybe it's a relatively cheap low-power model that is capable only of detecting a large hunk of metal directly beneath the surface. Had we used the expensive, more sensitive, model we would have been able to detect even relatively small objects buried deeper in the ground.

To complete the analogy, think of the experimental design as the detector and the metal object as the effect caused by the independent variable. A very sensitive design will detect even small effects. Conversely, if the effect is very large it may well show up, even with a relatively insensitive design. Since our purpose in conducting experiments is to detect whatever effects, large or small, actually do exist it makes sense to make the experiment as sensitive as possible. So, then, how do we create a sensitive design?

Sample size. Several factors are important in determining sensitivity, but the one most directly under the experimenter's control is the size of the sample.[3] Other things being equal, the greater the number of participants per treatment group the more sensitive the experiment will be. A question frequently asked by students doing experimental projects is how many participants they will need to test. Finding a specific answer to this question requires information that may not readily be available, or that may have to be guessed at—such as the size of the expected effect and the within-group variability. However, the answer in most cases is far larger than our students expect. For example, to have an 80% chance of detecting an average-sized effect you would need approximately 60 participants per treatment group (Keppel, 1991). Student experimenters typically plan on running about 10 participants per group. This may be fine for practice, or for pilot projects, but these studies are incapable of detecting any but the very largest effects. If you hope to be a sensitive experimenter, then, think in terms of large numbers.

Within-group variability. A second factor is **within-group variability** (also called error variability). The smaller this variability is, the more sensitive the experiment will be. Error variability reflects the influence of extraneous variables. We saw that it was important to control such variability, through constancy or balancing, in order to prevent confounding. While balancing promotes internal validity, by equalizing groups, it does not directly influence within-group variability. If there are large individual differences among our participants such differences will create a great deal of variability in the scores within each of our treatment groups. (See Appendix B for a fuller discussion of this concept.) Thus, even though random assignment guards against confounding it does not control this within-group variability. Such variability can only be reduced by the use of constancy. If we hold these individual-difference variables constant—for example, by selecting only male participants in good health between the ages of 20 and 25—we will greatly reduce the variability. Such variability can be thought of as background noise. The smaller the amount of noise the easier it is to detect the occurrence of a particular signal—such as the effect of the independent variable. Thus, the more variables that are held constant, as opposed to simply balanced, the more sensitive the experiment will be. An unfortunate side-effect, however, is that this control technique tends to reduce external validity.[4]

Choice of design. Sensitivity is also influenced by the choice of experimental design. Using a randomized-blocks design, or a factorial design (see Chapter 7) in which more than one independent variable is manipulated, will increase sensitivity. And, as will be made clear in the next chapter, within-subject designs are typically far more sensitive than between-subject designs.

Are the Results Reliable?

Having performed an experiment and obtained a particular outcome, we would like to know whether the finding is **reliable**. That is, is the particular result one we can count on finding whenever the same experimental conditions are present?

The only way to know for certain is to repeat the experiment again and again. Doing so, though, would consume enormous amounts of time and energy that might better be directed elsewhere. In fact, exact repetitions of experiments are rarely done, and usually only when there is reason for doubt. Instead, an estimate of a study's reliability is made from the data collected. There are two main ways in which this is done.

Statistical significance. One of the ways involves the use of statistical inference procedures to determine the likelihood that the outcome was simply due to chance. From your course work in statistics you may recall the logic of null hypothesis testing (reviewed in Appendix B). The **null hypothesis** states that there are no differences among treatment population means. Any differences that we observe in our sample means, according to this hypothesis, arise simply from chance. To make a case for the reliability of our results we must, therefore, show that they can't be accounted for by chance alone. By conducting statistical tests, such as a *t* test or analysis of variance, we determine how likely it is that the observed difference between means would occur if the null hypothesis were true. If the likelihood is sufficiently small (less than 5%, say) we reject the null hypothesis, asserting that the results cannot reasonably be ascribed to chance. I will elaborate on this process a bit more in a later section. The point I wish to make now is that ruling out chance is essential to establishing reliability.

Multiple measures. A second way in which reliability may be established is through taking multiple measures of the dependent variable. This can be done either by administering the same dependent measures repeatedly, or by including several different measures of the dependent variable. For example, in studying how concentration is affected by noise we could include several different measures of concentration: total number of problems solved, solution time, and number of errors made. If each of these measures is valid, then the reliability of the findings can be estimated by determining whether the pattern of the results is the same for each. Usually this is done by calculating correlation coefficients for each pair of measures in the study. If the coefficients are generally strong and positive this indicates that the various measures of the dependent variable are being similarly affected by the independent variable.

Does the Experiment Have External Validity?

A final characteristic of a sound experiment is **external validity**, the extent to which the study's findings are apt to generalize beyond the particular conditions obtaining in the original experiment. We want to know whether the results will hold for other people, other places, other times, and in other situations. In a sense, this characteristic is an extension of reliability. We judge findings reliable if they hold up under a *particular set* of conditions; that is, if they can be replicated. We judge them to have external validity if they hold up under a *wide range* of conditions.

Suppose in a laboratory experiment conducted with college students we were to find that noise interfered with concentration. It would be important to know if the same interferences would occur with people of different ages and educational backgrounds, in different settings such as schools, airports and factories, and at different times of the day, week, or year. Our usual working assumption is that our experimental findings *will* generalize.[5] Thus, when a substance is found to cause cancer in laboratory rats there is a reasonable suspicion that it will also do so with humans. Of course, there is also some uncertainty, and if the issue is an important one there is generally motivation to do further testing. It is typically the case in science that when interesting and potentially important results emerge from a study there will be a number of follow-up investigations to determine how widely they may be applied. Literally dozens of studies, for example, have been carried out to assess the generalizability of the effects of noise on concentration (Staples, 1996).

To some extent, external validity may be assessed within the bounds of a single study. We noted earlier that holding variables constant increased sensitivity, but decreased external validity. When extraneous variables are allowed to fluctuate over a wide range we are in a good position to judge whether a particular effect will survive outside the laboratory, where control is not generally possible. As we will see in a later chapter, certain types of experimental designs (factorial designs, Chapter 7) are particularly useful in assessing external validity.

When the effect of an independent variable on a dependent variable is basically the same, despite wide variations in participants and settings, we call the finding **robust**. This term conveys the notion of hardiness, sturdiness, and persistence. Ideally, then, we would like experimental research to produce findings that are not only internally valid and reliable, but robust as well.

SPECIAL DESIGNS AND CONTROL PROCEDURES

We have now presented the basic framework of the between-subjects design. The standard procedure is to manipulate an independent variable in such a way that different groups of participants are assigned to different levels. The manner in which participants are divided into groups is through some form of random assignment, occasionally combined with matching. A great deal of research in psychology fits into this basic mold. There are, however, some important variations on this theme.

Natural-Groups Design

As we have seen, creating levels of the independent variable through direct manipulation is the best way of determining the effect that variable might have on a particular dependent variable. There are many instances, however, where we would like to study the influence of an independent variable but are not able to manipulate it. This, of course, is the case for biological characteristics such as gender, race, and age, as well as personal and social characteristics such as marital status, education, intelligence, and personality. There are still other cases where it might be possible to manipulate an independent variable, but where we are prevented from doing so by ethical considerations. For example, it would not be ethical to start a fight to determine an individual's reaction to a personal attack, nor could we arrange for a person to have sex with an assigned partner in order to study aspects of sexual attraction. Ethical principles applying to treatment of participants are discussed in detail in Chapter 9.

The major alternative to experimental manipulation is the **natural-groups design**. Here, the strategy is to select levels of the independent variable from among naturally existing levels, rather than creating them through experimental manipulation. A good example is gender research where the independent variable is the biological sex of the participants, and the levels are developed by selecting comparable samples of males and females. Similarly, research on aging employs age as an independent variable and typically proceeds by comparing selected samples of participants of different ages. In hypnosis research, the usual strategy is to administer an initial screening test of hypnotic susceptibility so that participants may be selected on this basis and then compared on their responses to the experimental task.

Natural-group designs are versatile and widely used. Unfortunately, their results are easily misinterpreted. When significant differences between groups are found they may be incorrectly interpreted as showing a causal influence of the independent variable. However, the natural-groups design is not a true experimental design because the independent variable is not manipulated. On reflection, it is also clear that participants are not randomly assigned to groups. Instead, they are selected to represent groups they already belong to. Therefore, the essential conditions necessary for establishing causal explanations—changing one factor while keeping other factors the same—are lacking. The natural-groups design is really a form of correlational research. That is, it reveals the relationship between two variables, the selected levels of the independent variable and the dependent variable. Correlational studies typically meet only the covariation requirement of causal explanations. Some studies, appropriately designed, may also meet the time-order requirement. The third requirement, effectively ruling out alternative interpretations, however, requires experimental manipulation and control. Hence, this requirement is not met by natural-groups designs.

Yoked-Control Design

Special types of control procedures are called for in certain types of studies. One type of problem that occasionally arises is that the procedure used to manipulate an independent variable may, at the same time, create unanticipated changes in certain other variables. When this occurs a confound is produced that threatens internal validity. Since the confounding is due to the procedure used to produce the independent variable, rather than to some participant characteristic, the usual control procedure of balancing through random assignment is unable to correct for this. However, a solution may be found by using a **yoked-control** design. The design involves creating paired sets of participants who are exposed to exactly the same procedures and experiences, with the exception of a key detail that represents the manipulation of the independent variable.

To see how this works, consider a problem that was encountered in the study of group decision-making. Previous research had shown that group decisions were typically more extreme, or polarized, than individual ones, but the cause remained unclear. Was it due to the information and arguments produced during group discussion or to the arousal and motivation that accompany participation in a lively face-to-face discussion? The usual research strategy, of comparing groups and individuals on the same decision-making task, confounded the motivational effects of group participation with the additional new information that participants were exposed to. These effects were separated in a study employing a yoked control (St. Jean, 1970). For each group that participated in a live discussion a transcript of the discussion was made and presented to the same number of individuals working alone. That is, sets of individuals were yoked to particular groups; both received exactly the same informational content but the individual participants did not experience live participation. With this control in place it was possible to show that the live group participation contributed to the polarizing effect, over and above the effect created by new information.

Placebo Control

A conceptually similar problem is the placebo effect. In many research situations the procedures employed for manipulating an independent variable also create an expectancy that a particular effect will occur. This is especially likely when the treatment is highly visible and easily identified. Such was the case, we saw, with Mesmer's applications of animal magnetism. The patients who flocked to the baquet did so in the belief that they would experience a convulsive crisis and, thereby, secure relief from their ailments. Their expectancies were undoubtedly heightened by the atmosphere of the baquet and the sight of fellow patients swooning as the magnetism coursed through them. Our problem, then, is to find a way of separating genuine treatment effects from those that arise due to participants' expectancies.

The ideal control for such effects is essentially the one employed by the Franklin Commission. Recall that in some of their trials they blindfolded their participants, keeping them unaware of when the treatment was being administered. This procedure of keeping the person unaware of (or unable to identify) the treatment is called a **placebo control**. It is so called because it was developed in research on drug effects where it was found necessary to compare participants given the experimental drug with participants given a placebo, an identical-looking and -tasting substance that contained no active ingredients. Participants would not know ahead of time whether they were receiving the drug or the placebo.

The way in which a placebo control is employed in psychological research is through attempts to disguise the identity of the treatment that is being administered. This is sometimes accomplished through the use of a cover story that draws attention away from the nature of the treatment, or even misinforms the person as to the purpose of the study. The objective of such manoeuvres is to hold expectancy constant, to prevent participants in one treatment condition from having information or beliefs about the study that are different from those who are in a comparison condition.

Experimenter Controls

Expectations for particular outcomes may be held by experimenters as well as by participants. If the person who is collecting the data is also the one who designed the study—perhaps with the intention of testing a particular hunch or hypothesis—it would not be surprising to find that he or she has a strong expectancy about what the outcome will be. A problem occurs only when there is a possibility that this expectancy could influence the actual outcome. That such influences can, and do, occur has been shown by Rosenthal (1966) in a series of interesting studies.

In one such study undergraduate experimenters were asked to carry out a laboratory exercise that involved running rats through a maze. The purpose of the exercise, they were told, was to replicate earlier work in behavioural genetics showing that rats could be bred to be maze bright or maze dull. Each student was assigned a rat said to come from either the "bright" or "dull" litter, but in fact all rats came from the same litter. However, those who had been assigned the rats from the "bright" litter reported significantly better maze performance than those whose rats came from the "dull" litter. Questionnaires filled out by the experimenters revealed that those with the "bright" rats not only expected better performance but also liked their rats better and spent more time handling, petting and talking to their animals. The difference in the rats' performance, then, could reasonably be attributed to differences in stress hormones and arousal levels created by differential handling. Had the experimenters not been aware of the identity of their rats there could have been no systematic differences in their treatment of the two groups.

This experimenter expectancy effect has been demonstrated with human as well as animal participants. In fact, it would seem more likely to occur with human participants since the desire to be helpful may predispose experimental volunteers to pick up and interpret a wide assortment of verbal and nonverbal cues. Based on facial expressions, or tone of voice, participants may come to sense something of what it is that the experimenter expects. To prevent these expectations from becoming confounded with treatments requires special control procedures.

It may be possible, in some cases, to prevent participants from having any direct interactions with the experimenter, perhaps by delivering the experimental instructions and manipulations over a computer monitor. In cases where this is not possible or desirable, the best available control is to keep the **experimenter blind** to the participant's treatment condition. In a drug study, for example, the experimenter who hands out capsules, or later evaluates reactions, should not know whether a particular individual has received an active drug or a placebo. And, as we indicated in the previous section, participants should also not be able to identify the treatment condition they are being run in. Experiments in which both participants and experimenters are unable to identify a particular treatment condition are called **double-blind.** The double-blind control has become the accepted standard in drug research and is now beginning to find wide applications in psychology as well.

ANALYSIS OF BETWEEN-SUBJECTS DATA

The reason for doing experiments, of course, is to find answers to questions. Unfortunately, the answers don't just leap out at us from the mounds of collected data. In order to uncover these answers we must first process the data in a way that produces the comparisons that are critical to the original research questions. These critical comparisons may take the form of contrasting percentages (or frequencies) in the case of categorical data, or contrasting means (or medians) if the data are quantitative. In addition to formulating these comparisons we also need to conduct further analyses to determine whether the comparison differences are statistically significant. Recall that this step is necessary to establish reliability, to rule out chance as a plausible explanation.

Table 5.2 presents actual raw data from a basic two-group experiment. These data were collected in a study that investigated the interesting phenomenon that hypnotic participants tend to substantially underestimate the amount of time spent in hypnosis (St. Jean, 1988). The question was whether the shortened time experience was a result of actual participation in hypnosis or simply due to experiencing an interesting and novel series of events. Student volunteers were randomly assigned to either a participant condition, in which they were individually hypnotized, or to an observer condition, in which they viewed a videotape of a standard hypnosis session. At the conclusion of the period all participants (both the active participants and the passive observers) were asked to estimate the duration of the hypnosis session. Because the actual duration varied somewhat, each time estimate was divided by the actual time to produce an estimation ratio; the smaller the ratio, the greater the tendency to underestimate the actual duration. The estimation ratios for the 20 participants and 20 observers are presented in Table 5.2.

To answer the question of whether active participation makes a difference we must find some way of summarizing the data that allows us to make a critical comparison between the two conditions. Since the data are quantitative we can compute the mean estimation ratio (along with the corresponding standard deviation) in each condition. Contrasting the participant mean (.46) with the observer mean (.88) produces the critical comparison needed. The standard deviations are also included because they provide important information about the variability of the estimates in each group.

TABLE 5-2	Time Estimation Ratios
Participants	Observers
.60	.74
1.02	.81
.31	1.03
.79	.44
.24	.59
.75	1.11
.26	.94
.56	1.06
.20	.78
.48	.91
.28	1.11
.41	.67
.24	1.25
.20	1.41
.32	.78
.29	.86
.94	.47
.47	.59
.50	.76
.29	1.29
M = .46	.88
SD = .25	.27

What answer, then, have we come up with? The comparison of the two means indicates that the active participants, on average, underestimated the actual duration to a much greater extent than did the passive observers. While this difference in means appears substantial we need to determine whether it is, in fact, a reliable difference. Could a difference this size have occurred simply as a result of chance?

Analysis of Variance

The most widely used technique of analyzing experimental data is **analysis of variance**. This is a series of statistical computations that produces an index called the *F* **ratio**. This ratio is then used to determine the likelihood that the differences among group means could have arisen solely due to chance.

It is particularly important for beginning researchers to understand the logic underlying analysis of variance. The *F* ratio that we calculate consists of two components. The numerator of the ratio represents the variation (or differences) among the treatment group means. In the between-subjects design this component is called **between-groups variance**. In our hypnosis experiment it is the difference between the two estimation ratios (.88 and .46) that forms the basic ingredient in the calculation of between-groups variance. The denominator of the *F* ratio represents the extent to which the scores within each of the treatment groups differ from one another; this is the **within-groups variance**. The within-groups variance is calculated from the variation within the 20 scores contained in each treatment group; in fact it is closely related to the group standard deviations. The logic of the analysis rests on an understanding of the factors contributing to each type of variance.

$$F = \frac{\text{Between-groups variance}}{\text{Within-groups variance}}$$

Between-groups variance occurs for two reasons. One of these is the effect of the independent variable. If the different treatments really do result in different responses then this effect should be reflected in our dependent variable measurements, and should show up as differences among the means in our treatment groups. This is called **systematic variation**, since it is due to an identifiable source, the independent variable. The second reason that means may be different is simply due to chance or error, and this source is called **error variation**. Our measurements are never perfectly reliable and errors in measurement may result in somewhat different mean scores. There is also the possibility of random error in the assignment of participants to groups. To some extent, then, differences in our group means may simply be due to the uncertainties inherent in the random assignment process.

Within-groups variance is due to only one source: error variation. Such variation occurs for the reasons mentioned above—individual differences in response and errors of measurement. Since all of the participants assigned to a particular group receive the same treatment there is, by definition, no systematic variation. Thus, the calculation of within-groups variance gives us a direct estimate of experimental error.

Let's consider, then, how we can make use of the F ratio. If the null hypothesis is true— if there really are no differences due to the independent variable—then there is no systematic variation at all. Instead, only error variation would contribute to both the numerator and the denominator. Our F ratio, then, would be error variation (in the numerator) divided by error variation (in the denominator) and the result should be approximately one. On the other hand, if the null hypothesis were false—if the independent variable really did have an effect—then we do have at least some systematic variation. This systematic variation is added to the error variation in the numerator, but not to the denominator, resulting in a ratio that should be substantially larger than one.

$$F = \frac{\text{Systematic variance} + \text{Error variance}}{\text{Error variance}}$$

In making the decision of whether to retain or reject the null hypothesis we are guided by the size of the F ratio. If the F ratio is one (or less) we would have no grounds for rejecting the null hypothesis since there is no evidence of systematic variation. If the F ratio is substantially larger than one this is indicative of systematic variation and we can confidently reject the null hypothesis. The word "substantially," however, is rather ambiguous. How much larger than one does the F ratio have to be? The answer is that it must be large enough for us to be able to say that it is very unlikely to have occurred by chance. How likely is unlikely? By convention, most researchers agree that 5 times in 100 or less ($p < .05$) is sufficiently unlikely. The F ratio calculated for the data in Table 5.2 is 26.59. An F ratio this size (or larger) does, in fact, occur less than 5% of the time when the null hypothesis is true. (In fact, much less. The actual probability is less than 1 in 10,000.) Therefore, the null hypothesis is rejected, allowing us to conclude that the difference between the two means cannot reasonably be attributed to chance. The finding, then, that the participation condition resulted in shorter time estimates than the observation condition is said to be statistically significant. Whether it is significant in the larger sense of being meaningful or important depends on its theoretical and practical implications.

Experiments With More Than Two Levels

We have focussed on a two-group example because this represents the simplest form of a between-subjects experiment. Many experiments, however, will employ independent variables with more than two levels and, hence, require more than two groups. The time estimation study, for example might have added a third treatment group—perhaps a participation group that spent the period engaged in nonhypnotic activities. Regardless of the number of levels, the F ratio takes the same form. Between-groups variance in the numerator represents the variation among the treatment group means, no matter how many there are. Within-group variance in the denominator represents an average of all the separate group variances. If the computed F is statistically significant this is an indication that there is systematic variance caused by the different levels of the independent variable. However, if we have three or more levels we are uncertain where the significant differences are. It may be that there are significant differences among all conditions, or perhaps only between two of the conditions. To locate the source of the effect an analysis of variance procedure called **analytical comparisons** (Keppel, 1991) may be used to pinpoint the differences.

The most common form of analytical comparison involves testing a selected pair of treatment means to determine if they are significantly different. If the experiment included three treatment conditions there would be three pairs of means that could be tested. If the number of treatment conditions were four or more, the number of possible comparisons would be quite large. Usually, only those comparisons that are directly relevant to the study's aims (planned comparisons) would be carried out. When a number of such comparisons are carried out there is an increased risk that one, or more, may be significant due to chance alone. This is not a great concern if the comparisons really have been planned in advance and if there are only a few of them. However, if there are a large number of such comparisons, and especially if some or all are unplanned, then specialized statistical procedures must be used to reduce the risk of error. The procedures for doing these are typically taught in upper-level statistics or methodology classes and are presented in advanced statistical texts (e.g., Keppel, 1991).

SUMMARY

Due to its unique ability to establish cause and effect, the experiment is the most powerful tool in science. The origin of experimental research can be traced back to antiquity. The essence of an experiment is the manipulation of an independent variable, involving the creation of two or more observational conditions, and the measurement of a dependent variable. In addition, the influences of other, extraneous, variables must be controlled. Two major control techniques are holding variables constant (typically applied to procedural variables) and balancing variables across treatment conditions (typically applied to individual difference variables). This chapter focusses on between-subject experiments in which different groups of participants are tested at each level of the independent variable.

The four hallmarks of a sound experiment are internal validity, sensitivity, reliability, and external validity. Internal validity is the extent to which the experiment shows the true relationship between the independent and dependent variables. Achieving internal validity requires the application of appropriate controls to prevent confounding between the independent variable and one, or more, extraneous variables. A critical control procedure, balancing extraneous variables across conditions, is usually accomplished through some form of randomized assignment (which ensures that every participant has the same chance of being assigned to a particular treatment group). Block randomization ensures the allocation of equal numbers of participants to the various treatment conditions and also helps to balance variables such as time and place of testing and the use of different experimenters and different participant populations. Extraneous variables may also be balanced by matching sets of participants on a variable of particular importance and assigning equal numbers from each set to the various treatment conditions. Participant loss, if related to treatment conditions, threatens internal validity by undoing the balance created by random assignment or matching.

Sensitivity, the second characteristic of a sound experiment, is the ability to detect whatever effect the independent variable may have. Sensitivity is enhanced by large sample sizes, by reduction in error variability and by the choice of experimental design. The use of randomized-blocks designs and/or within-subject designs (see Chapter 6) will usually increase sensitivity beyond that of the basic randomized-groups design.

The third characteristic of a sound experiment is reliability. The most direct way of establishing reliability, repeating the experiment, tends to be wasteful of time and effort. Testing the null hypothesis helps to assess reliability by determining whether the results can reasonably be ascribed to chance. Reliability may also be established by taking multiple measures of the dependent variable.

External validity, the extent to which the findings are apt to generalize beyond the particular conditions studied, is the fourth characteristic of a sound experiment. Our general working assumption is that results will generalize, but this can only be established by conducting additional studies in different settings, under different conditions, and with different participant populations. A robust finding is one which holds up well despite wide variations in extraneous variables.

Special designs and control procedures are sometimes used as adjuncts, or alternatives, to the basic between-subjects design. An alternative to experimental manipulation is the natural groups design in which levels of the independent variable are selected from among naturally existing levels. While this design is able to reveal relationships that may exist between independent and dependent variables the absence of experimental manipulation renders it unable to establish causal influence. The yoked-control design controls for unanticipated effects of the manipulation procedure by exposing paired sets of participants to the same treatment procedures and consequences, with the exception of the key experience or event that constitutes the independent variable. A placebo-control design controls for different expectancies that may accompany different treatments by disguising the identity of the treatments. Experimenter controls, such as keeping the researcher unaware of the identity of a particular treatment, are used to control for possible experimenter bias. The double-blind design keeps both the participant and the researcher unaware of the identity of particular treatments.

Experimental data must be analyzed in some fashion before we are able to state results and draw conclusions. The first step is to provide a descriptive summary of the data, for example by calculating means and standard deviations. Next, statistical procedures such as analysis of variance are applied in order to determine whether the observed differences between groups are significant. The F ratio, the ratio of between-group variance to within-group variance, provides an index that can be used to determine whether the independent variable has created systematic variation in the treatment group means. In experiments with more than two levels a significant F simply indicates that the independent variable has had some effect. The particular nature of this effect must be determined through analytical comparisons that focus on particular combinations of treatment means.

KEY TERMS

analytical comparisons: An analysis of variance procedure used when the experiment has three or more levels in order to pinpoint the location of significant differences; the most common form involves testing a selected pair of treatment means to determine if they are significantly different.

between-groups variance: A measure of the extent to which treatment group means vary from each other; the numerator of the F ratio in analysis of variance.

between-subjects experiment: An experiment in which a different group of participants is tested at each level of the independent variable.

block randomization: A method of random assignment in which the total number of treatment conditions in the experiment are randomly ordered to form a block. The first participant is tested in the treatment appearing first in the block, the second in the treatment appearing second, and so on until one participant has been tested in each of the treatment conditions. A second set of participants is then tested in a second block of treatments that have been independently randomized, and this sequence continues for as many blocks as are needed to accommodate all the participants in the experiment.

blocking: A matching procedure that blocks participants together based on their similarity on an individual difference variable. The participants in each block are then randomly assigned to the various treatment conditions.

confounded: A term describing a condition that occurs when the level of an extraneous variables changes systematically with the level of an independent variable. This is a serious flaw that threatens the internal validity of an experiment.

constancy: A basic control technique that involves holding the levels of one or more variables at a fixed level.

dependent variable: Some measurable aspect of the behaviour being observed; its observed level is thought to depend on the level of the independent variable; the outcome variable.

double blind: Experiments in which neither participants nor experimenters are able to identify a particular treatment condition.

error variation: Variation in scores not caused by the independent variable. Individual differences among participants and random errors in measurement are the main sources of error variation.

experimenter blind: A control for experimenter bias that keeps the experimenter unaware of (blind to) the identity of particular treatment conditions.

***F* ratio:** The ratio of between-groups variance to within-groups variance in between-subjects analysis of variance; used to determine the likelihood that differences among treatment group means could occur simply due to chance.

independent variable: A variable whose potential effect on the behaviour of interest is being investigated; levels of the independent variable can be either manipulated or selected.

internal validity: The extent to which the data in a study reveal the true relationship between the independent and dependent variables.

matched-groups design: A balancing procedure in which participants are matched according to their scores on a particular variable and the members of each matched set are then randomly assigned to the various treatment conditions.

natural-groups design: A study in which levels of the independent variable are selected from among naturally existing levels, rather than creating them through experimental manipulation.

null hypothesis: The statistical hypothesis of no difference among population means.

participant loss: The loss of participants, through drop-out or failure to keep appointments, that occurs after assignment to conditions has been made. Such loss threatens internal validity when it occurs disproportionately in particular treatment groups.

placebo control: A control for participant expectancy that involves disguising the identity of the treatment being administered.

randomized assignment: A balancing procedure in which participants are assigned to particular treatment conditions entirely on the basis of chance.

randomized-blocks design: An experimental design in which participants are first blocked (or grouped) according to similarities on some individual difference variable and then randomly assigned to the various treatment conditions. (See also **blocking.**)

randomized-groups design: A between-subjects experiment that employs the technique of randomized assignment to balance extraneous variables across treatment conditions.

robust: A term used to characterize the effect of an independent variable on a dependent variable which remains basically the same despite wide variations in settings and participant populations. A robust effect indicates an externally valid finding.

sensitivity: The ability (or power) of an experiment to detect the effect of the independent variable on the dependent variable.

systematic variation: Variation in scores caused by the independent variable. Systematic variation contributes to observed differences among treatment group means.

within-group variance: A measure of the extent to which scores within each treatment group vary from one another. This measure forms the denominator of the F ratio in between-subjects analysis of variance.

within-subjects experiment: An experiment in which each participant is tested at every level of the independent variable; contrasts with between-subjects experiments in which each participant is tested at only one level.

yoked control: A specialized control that applies to the situation where the procedure used to manipulate an independent variable also produces changes in other variables, the nature of which cannot be completely anticipated ahead of time. The control involves forming pairs of participants who are then exposed to the same set of procedures and corresponding experiences, with the exception of a key detail that represents the manipulation of the independent variable.

ENDNOTES

1. The latest edition of the *Publication Manual of the American Psychological Association* (1994) urges authors to avoid using the term "subjects," and instead to employ more descriptive terms such as students, children, patients, prisoners, or simply participants. I have chosen to retain the headings "between-subjects" and "within-subjects" to describe experimental designs since these continue to be the most widely used designations in methods and statistics texts.

2. Be careful not to confuse the randomized blocks design with block randomization. In the former, the blocks are constructed on the basis of similarity in some personal characteristic—for example, age, gender or hypnotic susceptibility. (The randomized blocks design is one example of a larger class of designs, factorial designs, covered in Chapter 7.) In the latter, the blocks are constructed by grouping the different experimental conditions together, such that each complete set of conditions forms a single block.

3. The issue of sensitivity is basically the same as that of statistical power, discussed in Chapter 2.

4. This occurs because we can only generalize to conditions, or participant characteristics, that have been included in the study. Holding variables constant (as opposed to balancing them) sharply restricts the range of conditions included.

5. There are some situations, however, in which we don't expect generalization to occur. For example, a researcher may predict that a drug will relieve headache pain, but not muscle pain, or that the drug will be effective with children, but not adults. This reflects the concept of interaction which is dealt with in Chapter 7. At that point, I further consider the issue of generalization.

chapter six

WITHIN-SUBJECTS EXPERIMENTS

In the between-subjects designs discussed in the previous chapter the basic strategy was to randomly assign participants to different groups and to test each group with a different level of the independent variable. It may have occurred to you that there is a simpler, more straightforward way of doing experiments. Instead of going to all the trouble of forming different treatment groups, why not just have one group where each participant is tested under all the different treatment conditions? This strategy of making repeated observations on the same participant is known as a **within-subjects design**.[1]

In an earlier chapter we discussed ways of assessing the effects of noise on concentration. One approach, using natural groups, involved comparing students in a noisy school with those in a quiet school. A second approach, using randomized groups, involved assigning participants to either a high-noise or a low-noise treatment and comparing their performances on a concentration task. A third approach, using the within-subjects design, would have each participant tested twice, once in the high-noise condition and once in the low-noise condition. What do you think of this third approach? Is it a better or a worse way to do the experiment?

ADVANTAGES OF WITHIN-SUBJECTS DESIGNS

There are some clear advantages to using the within-subjects approach. For one thing we wouldn't have to worry about whether our different groups of participants were balanced with respect to important individual characteristics such as intelligence, distractability, or hearing acuity. For another, we could get by with fewer participants since the same number of observations could be obtained with half the number of participants. There are also some other, less obvious, advantages. We will examine each in turn.

Economy

When students begin conducting their own research projects they frequently experience concern over how many participants they will need. These concerns are understandable. After all, a substantial part of the work effort is recruiting, scheduling, testing, and debriefing the participants. And, as noted earlier, students are often dismayed to learn that conducting an experiment with sufficient power to detect an average-sized treatment effect may require 50 or more participants per treatment group. Any means by which the required number of participants can be reduced is, therefore, quite attractive.

The substantial savings in participants afforded by the within-subjects design derives from several factors. The first is the straightforward fact that by testing each person repeatedly the same number of observations can be obtained with fewer participants than would be the case if each participant were tested only once. If the independent variable has two levels, then 30 participants, tested twice, yields 60 observations; if it has three levels the same 30 participants will produce 90 observations. Thus, the number of participants required decreases proportionately with the number of treatment conditions. In fact, the required number relative to the between-subjects design decreases even more if it is possible to test participants more than once in each treatment condition. With certain types of research problems, such as determining sensitivity to physical stimuli, it is possible to make hundreds of observations on each participant. In such cases a very sensitive experiment can be conducted using only a handful of participants.

The second feature that contributes to economy is the fact that a major source of error (individual differences) has been removed from error variance. When error variance is reduced, the same amount of systematic variance (the treatment effect) will produce a larger F ratio. A major reason why a large number of participants is typically required in the between-subjects design is to magnify the systematic variance sufficiently so that it can be detected against the background of a large within-group variance. With the much smaller error variance of the within-subjects design such sample size magnification is not necessary.

Increased Sensitivity

The reduction in error variance brings a related advantage that is often more important than economy. The within-subjects design is far more sensitive than its between-subjects counterpart. This is an especially important consideration when trying to detect treatment effects that may be relatively small. For example, changing the typeface (font) of a printed page (without changing the size of the letters) may result in a small increase, or decrease, in legibility. **(Does this make a difference?)** Detecting even a small increase in legibility may well be important for the contribution it makes to reading speed and comprehension. Perhaps you have noticed that the pages of some textbooks are easier to read than others. If you have to read hundreds of pages, such small effects can turn out to be quite meaningful. The point is that even small effects can be important and that the within-subjects design has a much greater ability to detect them.

Elimination of Potential Confounds

As we stressed in Chapter 5, the most important characteristic of an experimental design is its internal validity. This validity is achieved when the influences of potentially confounding variables are controlled. In the between-subjects design, differences in participant characteristics are a source of potential confounds. These differences are usually controlled by the random assignment of participants to treatment groups. The expectation is that this procedure will effectively balance these differences across levels of the independent variable. However, random assignment may not succeed in balancing all relevant participant characteristics and, as noted earlier, this is a special concern when the groups are small. For example, in the citron experiment (Chapter 5) it may well turn out that the two groups of prisoners are balanced for health and weight, but not for age. The problem is that if our groups are unbalanced on any characteristic we have a potential confound. (It becomes an actual confound if the unbalanced characteristic has a systematic effect on the dependent variable.)

This problem is completely eliminated in the within-subjects design. Since each participant is tested under all treatment conditions individual differences are perfectly balanced across levels of the independent variable. By eliminating this important source of potential confounding, the use of a within-subjects design helps to ensure internal validity.

DISADVANTAGES

At this point, within-subjects designs may appear to possess such an overwhelming set of advantages that you may wonder why they are not routinely employed in all psychological experiments. A little reflection should reveal why this is impossible. Consider the citron experiment again. Could it have been done using a within-subjects design? Not unless the ancient Egyptians had developed a foolproof method of resuscitating corpses! (Curiously, the mummification of pharaohs may have been aimed at achieving just such an effect— but only for pharaohs, not for commoners or prisoners.) The point, of course, is that some treatments have irreversible effects. As a less drastic example, consider a research study designed to assess the effectiveness of several different therapeutic programs for the treatment of depression. Assuming some degree of success was achieved by the first program, we would be unable to evaluate the effectiveness of the second program on the same group of patients.

Recall, as well, that many important independent variables (sex, age, IQ, race, and level of education, to name but a few) cannot, by their very nature, be manipulated. To study such variables we must select appropriate levels, employing the natural-groups design discussed in Chapter 5. Thus, for some interesting questions the within-subjects approach is simply not applicable.

Even in situations where the design can potentially be used it may not be advisable to do so. In particular, there are two major concerns that face an investigator who wishes to perform a within-subjects experiment. One involves the order in which treatments are administered and the other the possibility that the effects of certain treatments may carry over and influence the response to other treatments. The next two sections of the chapter are devoted to these concerns.

ORDER EFFECTS

Although the within-subjects design eliminates one potential source of confounding (individual differences), it is immediately confronted with a different source. Since the treatments must be given in some order, or sequence, the ordinal position of a particular treatment (whether it is the first, second, or last treatment given) immediately becomes confounded with the treatment itself. Thus, if treatment A produces a different outcome than treatment B we don't know whether that difference is due to the nature of the treatments or to the fact that treatment A was given first. An order effect occurs whenever the position a treatment is given in influences response to the treatment.

Order effects are not unusual. One common effect of order is that treatments given later may benefit from the practice on the task afforded by earlier treatments. These effects are so potent that the term "practice effects" is commonly used synonymously with the more general term, "order effects" (Keppel et al., 1992). As an illustration of practice effects consider the efforts of a middle-aged professor learning how to play the video game Tetris on his son's Game Boy. On the first attempt (trial) the professor fumbles aimlessly with the buttons trying to figure out how they affect the falling geometric figures. In 30 seconds, or less, the game ends without any points being scored. On the second trial the professor is able to rotate a few of the figures so that they manage to fit together, forming a line of blocks. When this happens he makes the critical discovery that points are scored whenever a line is formed. Again, the game ends quickly, but this time with a small score. On succeeding trials the professor begins to "get the hang of it" and his scores improve markedly. After an hour's worth of playing he returns the Game Boy to his son, proudly announcing a final score of 730. This news is met with a sadly disparaging look (a look that only young teenage boys seem to manage) and the information that any score less than 10,000 is probably indicative of feeble-mindedness!

Performance tasks such as video games typically show strong practice effects, and these are especially pronounced over the first few trials. Consider the problem that would occur if we were to use a within-subjects design to investigate the effects of an independent variable, such as level of illumination or amount of noise, on video game performance. Suppose, for example, we wanted to test the effects of three different levels of illumination and to do so we arranged for our participants to play three successive games, each under a different level. We would likely find that the the level of illumination tested first would be associated with the poorest performance and the level tested third with the best performance. In other words practice effects would swamp any illumination effect. In order to fairly test for an illumination effect we would first have to find some way of eliminating or neutralizing practice effects.

Can you think of a solution for this? One possibility that may have occurred to you is to give each person a great deal of practice on the video game before the experiment starts. In this way, the participant could be brought to such a high level of proficiency that running the experimental trials is unlikely to further increase this level. This solution is certainly employed in experiments where it is feasible. However, it may not handle other effects associated with order of treatments. Warm-up, familiarity, boredom, and fatigue are also likely to change over a series of trials. Warm-up and familiarity could, perhaps, be controlled by some initial practice trials, but fatigue and boredom could not.

Fortunately, several techniques have been developed that enable the researcher to control for a wide variety of effects associated with order. Collectively, these techniques are called **counterbalancing**. The main strategy is to balance order effects across levels of the independent variable. These techniques fall into two general categories: within-subject balancing and cross-subject balancing.

Within-Subject Counterbalancing

In this approach order effects are balanced for each individual participant in the experiment. This is accomplished by testing each participant several times at each level of the independent variable.[2] There are two different ways of accomplishing this. We'll start with the easier of the two.

ABBA counterbalancing. Let's assume we have two levels of the independent variable—that is, two treatment conditions—that we label A and B. Each participant is tested twice under the A level and twice under the B level. In this arrangement A is given first, then B, then B again, and finally A—hence the name **ABBA** (not to be confused with the Swedish pop group popular in the late 70's!). The logic is that the average ordinal position of A ((1 + 4)/ 2 = 2.5) is the same as the average ordinal position of B ((2 + 3)/ 2 = 2.5). This design can be extended to any number of levels. If we have three treatment conditions it becomes ABCCBA, and for four, ABCDDCBA.

The advantage of this method is its basic simplicity. The disadvantage is that it works only when order effects can be assumed to be linear. By linear we mean that the effect of order is a constant increase (or decrease) in scores with each successive trial. Returning to the example of the video game a linear order effect would occur if each game played resulted in, say, a 50-point increase over the previous score. Thus, the first B treatment would have a +50 practice effect and the second B treatment a +100 practice effect (the increase is calculated cumulatively from the first trial). The final A treatment would have a +150 effect. We can see that the total practice effect for the B's would be 150, as would the total practice effect for the A's. (The first A treatment does not benefit from a practice effect.) Unfortunately, linear order effects are likely to be the exception rather than the rule. If we just consider practice effects, the largest effect of practice will show up on the second trial, reflecting the participant's increased familiarity with and understanding of the task. Effects on later trials are likely to be progressively smaller. What happens, then, is that the B treatments benefit more from practice than do the A treatments. Other order effects, such as fatigue and boredom, are also likely to be nonlinear. One way of dealing with this is to test only half the participants using the ABBA order and to test the other half using a BAAB order. Although this is a practical solution we no longer have order effects balanced within each individual participant. Instead, they are balanced across participants.

Block randomization. We discussed **block randomization** in the previous chapter—as a way of randomly assigning participants to treatment groups so that the sample sizes are equal. We can also use block randomization to prevent order effects from being confounded with treatment conditions. To see how this works, let's consider an actual experiment in which it was applied.

A classic experiment on short-term memory was carried out by Peterson and Peterson (1959). They wanted to find out how quickly information would be lost from memory if it were not rehearsed. Participants were presented three-letter combinations, called trigrams (for example, BXJ), that they were later asked to recall. To prevent rehearsal of the letters, participants were asked to do an arithmetic task out loud. Thus, on each trial a participant was presented with the trigram, followed by a three-digit number (e.g., 427). The participant's task was to vocally repeat the trigram and the number, and then to subtract by three's until the experimenter said to stop. At this point the participant would attempt to recall the letters. The independent variable was the length of the retention interval—the number of seconds that elapsed until the experimenter said stop. Six levels of the independent variable were tested: 3, 6, 9, 12, 15, and 18 seconds. Each participant was tested eight different times at each retention interval, for a total of 48 trials in all. A different letter trigram was used on each trial.

Block randomization was used to arrange the order in which the six retention intervals were tested. Eight blocks, each containing a random order of the six intervals, were constructed. For example, the first block might be [6, 15, 9, 3, 12, 18], indicating that the participant's first trial is 6 sec., the second trial 15 sec. and so on. Thus, the participant is tested once at every retention interval before any of the intervals are repeated. By the time the eighth, and final, block of trials was administered, the participant had been tested exactly eight times at each interval. Order effects are balanced because the average order for each retention interval works out to approximately the same value. Any repeated testing effects, such as practice, fatigue, or boredom, would be spread evenly across the six treatment intervals.

The advantage of this technique is that even nonlinear order effects are likely to balanced. If, for example, performance improves over the first few trials due to practice and familiarity, and then later declines due to fatigue and boredom, there is little possibility that particular changes will coincide more frequently with some test intervals than with others. The disadvantage is that block randomization requires a fairly large number of trials to be run with each participant. A sufficient number of blocks must be used since it is unlikely that order effects will balance out with only one or two replications. Thus, it is only applicable in situations in which the treatments are of brief duration.

Cross-Subject Balancing

In many cases it is not feasible, or practical, to test participants more than once for each treatment condition. If the treatments are complex or time-consuming, we may decide that we can only administer each condition once to each participant. For example, in testing the effects of noise on concentration, time constraints may dictate that participants only be tested twice—once with noise and once without. The problem is that for any particular participant the noise treatment will be confounded with ordinal position. A participant who is tested first with noise, and then later without, may perform better on the second test. Is this change in performance due to the reduction of noise or to familiarity and practice? For any one participant we can't answer this question. The best we can do is to balance order effects across participants by arranging for different participants to be administered the treatments in different orders. By testing half the participants in the noise, no-noise order and the other half in the reverse order we can eliminate the confounding.

The trick, then, is to arrange different orders for different participants. But how many different orders will we need? If, as in the noise example, there are only two levels of the independent variable, there can only be two orders – AB and BA. We can simply test half the participants with each order. If there are three levels, though, there are six possible orders (ABC, ACB, BAC, BCA, CAB, and CBA). When there are four treatment levels the number of possible orders is 24 and with five it is 120. We can determine the number of possible orders by letting N stand for the number of treatments and calculating N! (N factorial). N! is N $\times$ (N-1) $\times$ (N-2) $\times$ (N-3).... Can you determine the number of possible orders for six treatments? It is $6 \times 5 \times 4 \times 3 \times 2 \times 1 = 720$. The point is that even though it is desirable to select **all possible orders** this is only feasible when there is a small number of treatments (usually four or fewer).

All possible orders. Consider an experiment that I conducted to investigate the factors that influence the amount of risk people are willing to take in various life situations (St. Jean, 1979). Two relevant factors are the potential gain attached to a possible course of action and the possible loss that could be incurred. Participants were asked to answer a set of choice-dilemma items that presented a central character faced with making a choice between two courses of action. One course of action involved an element of risk, but had an attractive payoff if the action proved successful. The other course involved a safer action, but no attractive payoff. For example, one of the items described a young engineer, married and with two children, who currently was employed in a rather routine position that paid a modest but adequate salary. At a convention he is offered a job with a new company that promises an exciting line of work, a higher salary and opportunities for rapid advancement. The problem is that the new company is a somewhat risky business venture and if the company should fail the engineer would then be unemployed. Participants are asked to indicate the minimum odds of success they would demand before recommending that the new job offer be accepted. The possible alternatives range from a very risky 1 in 10 chance to a very conservative 10 in 10 chance (meaning that the new job should not be taken unless success was completely certain).

To investigate the effects of gain and loss I wrote four versions of each item. Each version represented a different combination of gain (high or low) and loss (high or low). On the engineer item the high gain was a much higher salary and a possibility of a share in the ownership; the low gain was a slightly higher salary and somewhat more interesting work. The high loss was the threat of being out of work for a long time if the company failed; the low loss was returning to his original job at a lower salary. The four versions, then, were (a) high gain/high loss, (b) high gain/low loss, (c) low gain/high loss, and (d) low gain/low loss. These four conditions were tested in a within-subjects design with each participant being asked to respond to four choice dilemma items, with each item presented with a different gain-loss combination. (The other three items involved an investment decision, a tournament chess game, and a potential medical emergency.)

For ease of discussion we can refer to the four gain/loss treatment combinations as treatments A, B, C, and D. The best possible balancing could be achieved by using all possible orders. With four treatments this requires 4! (24) orders. Since there are 24 orders we

TABLE 6-1	All Possible Orders of Four Treatments						
First	Second	Third	Fourth	First	Second	Third	Fourth
A	B	C	D	C	A	B	D
A	B	D	C	C	A	D	B
A	C	B	D	C	B	A	D
A	C	D	B	C	B	D	A
A	D	B	C	C	D	A	B
A	D	C	B	C	D	B	A
B	A	C	D	D	A	B	C
B	A	D	C	D	A	C	B
B	C	D	A	D	B	C	A
B	C	A	D	D	B	A	C
B	D	C	A	D	C	A	B
B	D	A	C	D	C	B	A

must have a minimum of 24 participants, at least one per order. If more participants are to be run the number should be some multiple of the number of orders, such as 48 or 72. It is important that an equal number of participants be tested with each order. The 24 possible orders are presented in Table 6.1.

Notice how using all possible orders provides three levels of balancing. First, and most important, each treatment is presented an equal number of times at each ordinal position. Treatment A occurs six times in the first position, six in the second, six in the third, and six in the fourth. The same is true of treatments B, C, and D. This effectively prevents confounding of treatments and positions. Second, each treatment follows and precedes every other treatment the same number of times. A immediately precedes B six times and immediately follows B six times. This holds for all possible pairs of treatments. Third, each treatment follows and precedes every other treatment the same number of times at each pair of ordinal positions. For example, at the first and second positions A immediately precedes B twice and immediately follows B twice. Again, the same pattern holds for all the other pairs of treatments. This sort of advanced counterbalancing becomes important if there is a possibility of differential carryover effects. (This possibility is discussed later in the chapter.)

Selected orders. It is not always possible to employ all possible orders. With more than four treatments the number of possible orders is likely to be larger than the number of available participants. Even with only three or four treatments the investigator may choose to employ a few, selected orders. One reason for selecting a smaller number of orders is that it is sometimes necessary to balance task variables as well as treatment variables. (The following section on irreversible tasks explains this.) What, then, is the minimal number of orders that will provide the basic counterbalancing necessary to prevent confounding of treatments and positions? The answer is the number of treatments in the experiment. Thus, in the four-treatment gain-loss experiment there must be at least four orders. The basic requirement is that each treatment appear once at every ordinal position. There are two ways of satisfying this requirement.

One way is to use a technique called **random starting order with rotation.** The first order simply represents any randomly constructed sequence containing the four treatments —for example, BDCA. The other three orders are constructed by sequentially rotating each treatment one position to the left. Thus, the second order becomes DCAB, the third CABD and the fourth ABDC. (These orders are presented in the left-hand panel of Table 6.2.) Assigning one person to each order, we could then run the experiment with only four participants. If additional participants are desired we would, of course, assign an equal number to each order. This arrangement accomplishes the fundamental requirement of having each treatment appear once in each ordinal position, thereby preventing confounding of treatments with positions. Notice, however, that the treatment pairs always occur in the same sequence. For example, A always follows C.

A second technique of constructing selected orders employs what is called a **Latin square** design. It is similar to random starting order with rotation in that it contains the same number of orders as treatments. The difference is that in this design each treatment precedes and follows each other an equal number of times. (An example of a Latin square is given in the right-hand panel of Table 6.2.)

As you can see, treatment A immediately precedes treatment B once and immediately follows it once. The same pattern holds for all other pairs of treatments. Thus, the Latin square provides an extra measure of balancing beyond that afforded by the random starting order with rotation method. One drawback of the Latin square is that it becomes more complicated when applied to an odd number of treatments.[3]

Irreversible Tasks

A potential concern in within-subjects designs is the nature of the task variable. The term "task variable" refers to the type of activity, or task, required of a participant in an experiment. Some types of tasks can be repeated many times without any danger of mastering them. For example, in a signal detection task participants are asked to respond whenever they detect a particular target stimulus (for example, the letter B in a changing array of letters presented on a computer screen). Participants could perform this task over hundreds of trials under different levels of various independent variables, such as distraction or level of illumination. Other tasks, however, could not be repeated in this fashion. For example, in a memory experiment we might have participants use different learning strategies for learning word lists (e.g., connecting the words to make a story versus rote rehearsal). A particular list could only be used in one of the experimental conditions, since once it is learned (or even partially learned) it could not fairly be tested with the same participants in a second experimental condition. Tasks of this sort, that can only be used once, are

TABLE 6-2	Random Starting Order				Latin Square			
First	Second	Third	Fourth		First	Second	Third	Fourth
B	D	C	A		A	B	D	C
D	C	A	B		B	C	A	D
C	A	B	D		C	D	B	A
A	B	D	C		D	A	C	B

called **irreversible tasks**. With irreversible tasks we must use different versions of the task on each trial that the participant receives. You might recall that in the Peterson and Peterson (1959) experiment, where participants were asked to recall letter trigrams after counting backwards, a different trigram was used on each of the 48 trials.

There are two reasons for alerting you to irreversible tasks. The first is the necessity of making certain that the task variable does not become confounded with the independent variable. Suppose in the memory strategy experiment we had participants learn one list of words using the story technique and a second list using rote rehearsal. If the lists of words differ in any systematic way—for example, if one list of words were easier to pronounce or to visualize—there is a potential for confounding. Confounding would occur if, for example, the easier list were always used in the story condition and the more difficult list in the rote condition. In practice, memory researchers take great pains to construct equivalent lists, but even so it is always possible that there may be some unanticipated differences. An important control measure, then, is to balance the task variable across levels of the independent variable. This prevents one possible source of confounding and helps to ensure internal validity.

There is also a second reason for doing this. It may be important to learn whether the task itself has an effect—to determine, for example, whether one list of words was in fact easier to learn than another list. In a sense, then, we may wish to treat the task as a second independent variable.

Consider again my research on potential gains and losses using choice-dilemma items. Participants responded to four different items, each associated with a different gain/loss combination. Since four different items had to be used it was important to keep the items from being confounded with the levels of the independent variable. (For example, we would not want the high-gain/low-loss combination to always be associated with the engineer item.) And, since the four items presented very different choice-dilemma situations, it was of interest to learn whether these different situations would affect risk-taking. How can both the independent variable and the task variable be balanced in the same experiment? The solution is to first balance order effects for the levels of the independent variable using one of the selected order methods. For simplicity we'll select the random starting order with rotation method as illustrated in the left-hand panel of Table 6.2. This square matrix is then repeated three more times, giving us four squares. Each square is assigned to one of four different orders of the task variable, giving us 4 × 4, or 16 orders in all. The resulting design is illustrated in Table 6.3; the letters represent the four gain-loss treatments and the Roman numerals the four choice-dilemma items.

This balancing enables us to separate the effects of order, treatment, and task from each other and to analyze the unique effects of each.[4]

CARRYOVER EFFECTS

As we have just seen, one of the problems that affects within-subjects designs, order effects, can be handled by various counterbalancing techniques. The other major problem, **carryover effects**, unfortunately has no simple solution. Carryover effects occur whenever one, or more, of the treatments given to participants affects how they respond to other treatments. The term "carryover" implies that a treatment's effect does not vanish after it is given, but instead carries over to other treatments. Some textbooks discuss this problem

TABLE 6-3	Balancing Order Effects for Treatment and Task Variables						
First	Second	Third	Fourth	First	Second	Third	Fourth
I	II	III	IV	III	IV	I	II
A	B	C	D	A	B	C	D
B	C	D	A	B	C	D	A
C	D	A	B	C	D	A	B
D	A	B	C	D	A	B	C
II	III	IV	I	IV	I	II	III
A	B	C	D	A	B	C	D
B	C	D	A	B	C	D	A
C	D	A	B	C	D	A	B
D	A	B	C	D	A	B	C

under the heading of differential transfer, to indicate that the transfer (or carryover) is specific to some treatments, but not to others. In many experiments a control, or no-treatment, condition is compared to a specific treatment. The treatment, when given first, may carry over and influence the response to the control condition, but when the control condition is given first there is no carryover to the treatment condition. This is common in drug research where, typically, an experimental drug is compared with a placebo. The placebo, which is inert, does not influence response to the experimental drug, but the experimental drug, if its effect persists, may well influence response to the placebo.

Students sometimes have difficulty understanding the difference between order effects and carryover effects. Order effects are due entirely to the particular position in a sequence of treatments. They are not specific to any particular treatment; instead they are assumed to affect all treatments equally. Carryover effects, however, are specific to particular treatments. Different treatments will have different sorts of carryover effects, and some will have no carryover effects at all.

The problem of carryover effects is serious. If they are present they seriously compromise the internal validity of an experiment. Obviously, we cannot draw valid conclusions about a treatment's effects if the response to that treatment has been influenced by a different treatment. For example, if we treat depression with drugs and then switch to psychotherapy, some or all of the improvement that occurs may be due to changes in physiology or cognitive functioning set into motion by the original drug treatment.

Researchers take different approaches to the problem of carryover effects. Some use treatments that they think (or hope) will not have such effects. Others recommend that between-subjects designs, which don't have carryover problems, be used in place of within-subjects designs. Perhaps the best appproach is to attempt to discover whether carryover effects are, in fact, present. There are several ways of doing this.

Comparing Between-Subjects and Within-Subjects Experiments

If the same treatments are included in both a between-subjects and a within-subjects experiment we can compare the results to determine whether the treatments had similar effects. This approach was used in a study by Coe, St. Jean and Burger (1981) that investigated the effects of hypnosis on vividness of imagery. Several previous studies had reported that hypnosis increased the vividness of imagery, but other studies had found no effect. The conflicting results may have been due to the fact that different studies had employed different designs. Coe et al. (1981) performed two experiments. The first, a within-subjects design, involved two administrations of an imagery test, one following a hypnotic induction and the other following a set of waking (nonhypnotic) instructions. The order of administration was counterbalanced so that half of the participants received hypnosis first and half received waking instructions first. The second experiment employed a between-subjects design with a large number of participants randomly assigned to either the hypnotic or waking treatment. The two experiments yielded different results. Hypnosis increased imagery in the within-subjects experiment, but had no effect in the between-subjects experiment. Closer examination of the within-subjects experiment revealed that the hypnosis advantage occurred only in the hypnosis-waking order. Apparently, the participants' expectations of increased hypnotic responding influenced their responses in the waking condition. The researchers concluded that there was no inherent advantage to hypnosis since it could be attributed entirely to the expectancy carryover effect.

Using all Possible Orders

We said earlier that counterbalancing using all possible orders was superior to selected orders. The reason is that it affords us the opportunity to determine whether a response to a particular treatment changes depending on the treatment that precedes it. To see how this works, look back to Table 6.1. We can select any one of the treatments, for example treatment B, and compute the average response score to it in four different situations—when it occurs first before any other treatment has been given and when it occurs immediately after treatments A, C, and D. Assuming we run one participant for each of the 24 orders, we will be able to average the scores of six participants in each of these four situations. If the response to B is different following A than it is following C, for example, this strongly suggests the presence of carryover effects. A more refined analysis would also take into account ordinal position. If the response to B following A in the second position is different than B following C in the second position, this enables us to separate a carryover effect from an order effect. (To do this reliably, though, would require more than one participant per order.) This is why the third level of counterbalancing, afforded by all possible orders, can be so important.

Dealing with Carryover Effects

Once we've detected carryover effects, what do we do about them? In some cases, for example drug effects, we can simply employ a long waiting period between treatments to be certain that the effects have worn off. This requires a great deal of knowledge about drug effects since they wear off at different rates and some may never wear off entirely. The only other alternative is to abandon the within-subjects design entirely, relying on the safer, but less sensitive, between-subjects design.

One solution to this problem is to run a within-subjects design using all possible orders and, at the same time, employing a relatively large number of participants. This enables us to test for the presence of carryover effects and, if they are absent, to have the benefit of a very sensitive design. If they are present, we can still salvage an interpretable experiment by analyzing only the data collected in the first ordinal position. By restricting our analysis to treatments in the first ordinal position we have, in effect, a between-subjects design. Let's assume, for example, that we have a total of 48 participants (two per treatment order) in our four-treatment experiment. This gives us 12 participants per treatment group. The statistical analysis will be considerably less powerful than it would be if all observations in the within-subjects design were included, but it will at least be free of confounding carryover effects.

ANALYSIS OF WITHIN-SUBJECTS DATA

Once we have conducted a within-subjects experiment it is necessary to statistically analyze the data in order to answer the questions we started with. The main goal of the analysis is to determine whether the independent variable had an effect on the dependent variable and, if so, to pinpoint the nature of the effect. In some designs it is also important to determine whether there was an effect associated with either the order variable or the task variable, or both.

Determining the Effect of the Independent Variable

As we saw in the analysis of between-subjects designs, the first step is to summarize the data. We start by arranging the data in convenient form, usually by laying out in a data table each participant's score for each of the treatment conditions. If we have used within-subjects balancing, where participants were tested more than once with each treatment, we must first find the average score for each participant for each treatment. Table 6.4 gives a sample of data collected in the experiment that examined the effects of potential gains and losses on risk-taking. Recall that there were four treatments: (a) high gain/high loss, (b) high gain/low loss, (c) low gain/high loss, and (d) low gain/low loss. These are represented in the table as treatments A, B, C, and D, respectively. The experiment used cross-subject balancing with selected orders. For simplicity, the sample given in Table 6.4 contains the scores of only four participants.

After organizing the data we calculate the means and the standard deviations of the scores in the four treatments. These summary statistics represent the main results of the experiment and would be presented as a separate table in the report. The purpose of the experiment was to determine whether the gain/loss treatments had an effect on risk-taking, and we answer this question by comparing the treatment means. We can see that there are large differences between some of these means. Are these differences due to the independent variable or could they have arisen by chance?

To determine whether the differences are reliable we carry out an analysis of variance, just as we did in the between-subjects design. The analysis of variance yields an F ratio

TABLE 6-4	Risk-Taking Scores in the Gain/Loss Experiment			
Person	A	B	C	D
1	9	3	9	4
2	8	5	9	4
3	10	5	10	5
4	7	4	8	6
Mean	8.5	4.25	9.0	4.75
SD	1.29	.96	.82	.96

and, using appropriate tables, we can determine the likelihood that an F of a particular size would occur if the null hypothesis were true. If the probability of its occurrence is less than the significance level we have set (typically .05), we reject the null hypothesis and accept the alternative hypothesis that the independent variable did, in fact, have some effect.

The logic behind using the F ratio in null-hypothesis testing was set forth in the previous chapter, and we will only briefly review it here. The numerator is based on the differences between treatment means and contains both systematic variation and error variation. The denominator is based on error variation alone. In the within-subjects design there is an important change in the calculation of error variance. Since this design removes individual differences there is much less error variation than in the between-subjects design. In the within-subjects design the error variation is called residual variance, since it is what is left over once individual differences have been removed. The F ratio then becomes treatment variance divided by residual variance.

$$F = \frac{\text{Treatment variance}}{\text{Residual variance}}$$

Given the same-size treatment effect the F ratio calculated in the within-subjects design is typically much larger than that in the between-subjects design. As a result, the within-subjects design is far more sensitive.

As we learned in Chapter 5, a significant F allows us to reject the null hypothesis of no difference in the treatment population means. We don't, however, know the location of these treatment differences until we conduct analytical comparisons. For example, analytical comparisons in the gain/loss experiment indicated that the two low-loss means were significantly different from the two high-loss means. There was no difference between the high-gain and low-gain treatments. In general, the results showed that people were more willing to take risks when the potential loss was small than when it was large. Surprisingly, the amount of potential gain had no impact on decisions. Overall, it seemed that when there was little to lose people were willing to take chances even for a small gain; conversely, when there was much to lose few chances were taken even with the prospect of a large gain.

Determining the Effect of Order and Task Variables

It is also possible, and often desirable, to determine the effects of ordinal position and task on the dependent variable. Consider, for example, the Peterson and Peterson (1959) short-term memory experiment described earlier. In addition to the effects of the independent variable (retention interval), the researchers were also interested in learning whether memory performance changed over the 48 trials in the experiment. This can easily be determined by arranging the data by trial blocks and tabulating the average number of correct responses over the six trials in each block. Examination of the means over the eight trial blocks showed, in fact, a general decline in memory performance. Just as with the independent variable, an F ratio can be calculated to determine whether the trial means are significantly different. In this case the numerator would consist of systematic variance due to trial block differences and the denominator would be the usual measure of error variance in within-subject designs—that is, residual variance.

In a similar fashion, we can also determine whether there is an effect attributable to the task variable. For example, in the gain/loss experiment we can rearrange the data to determine the average risk-taking response to each of the four choice dilemma items. Computing the appropriate F ratio of task variance divided by residual variance tells us whether there are significant differences due to the different item types. Again, analytical comparisons can be performed to pinpoint the location of these differences.[5]

SUMMARY

Within-subjects experiments are those in which each participant is tested, or observed, in every treatment condition, rather than just one as is the case in between-subjects experiments. A major advantage of the within-subjects design is economy: the same analytical power can be achieved with a far smaller number of participants. The removal of individual differences from the error variance means that the same-sized treatment effect will show up more clearly and, therefore, require fewer participants to attain the same level of power. This directly leads to a second advantage: increased sensitivity to the presence of small effects. A third advantage is the elimination of potential confounds with individual-difference variables.

There are situations in which within-subjects designs cannot be used. For example, they cannot be applied to the investigation of individual difference variables, which by their nature cannot be manipulated. Also, they are unsuited to the study of variables which may have a permanent or semipermanent effect, such as psychotherapy. Even in situations where they can be applied, within-subject designs face two major sources of concern.

One such concern is the threat of confounding produced by the order in which a treatment is given. Whenever one treatment follows another there is the possibility that it may benefit from the practice, or familiarity with the situation, afforded by the first treatment. When many treatments are given, fatigue or boredom may affect responses to the latter treatments. To prevent such confounding, order effects must be counterbalanced. Within-subject counterbalancing balances order effects for every single participant by requiring that two or more observations be made at each level of the independent variable. This may be accomplished through the use of ABBA counterbalancing or block randomization. Cross-subject counterbalancing, on the other hand, requires only a single observation per level, but achieves balance across a group of participants rather than for every single one.

The most thorough cross-subject balancing is attained by using all possible orders of treatments, but is practical only when the number of treatments is fairly small. Selected orders, such as random starting order with rotation and Latin square, achieve basic levels of balancing by using the same number of orders as the number of treatments. A further problem occurs when irreversible tasks (that can only be used once) are employed since different tasks may become confounded with treatments or orders. This double threat requires a double balancing technique that can be accomplished by rotating selected orders through both treatments and tasks.

A second major concern is the threat posed by carryover effects. The danger is that the effects of particular treatments will persist and carry over to influence responses to subsequent treatments. Carryover effects seriously compromise the internal validity of the experiment and, unfortunately, cannot be controlled in the manner that order effects can. The best the researcher can hope to do is to identify such effects when they occur and switch to a between-subjects design. Carryover effects can be identified by comparing the results with those from between-subjects experiments using the same independent variable, or by employing all possible orders and comparing results obtained from different sequences or combinations of treatments. When carryover effects are suspected, a useful strategy is to use all possible orders with a large sample size. If carryover effects are detected, the analysis of data can be restricted to treatments appearing in the first ordinal position, which constitutes a between-subjects design. If carryover effects are not present, the researcher has the benefit of increased sensitivity conferred by the full within-subject experiment.

Analysis of the within-subjects design is much like that of the between-subjects design. The first step is the calculation of summary statistics (means and standard deviations) for each treatment condition. However, the F ratio takes a somewhat different form. The numerator is treatment variance, based on differences among means. The denominator is residual variance, which is the error variance that remains once individual differences have been removed. Since residual variance is usually quite small the resulting F ratio tends to be much larger than would occur in the corresponding between-subjects design. In addition to analyzing the effects of the independent variable, the data can be rearranged to analyze effects of task and order. As in the between-subjects design, analytical comparisons are used to locate the source of significant effects.

KEY TERMS

ABBA counterbalancing: A form of within-subject counterbalancing in which the "A" treatment is given first, then the "B" treatment, the "B" treatment again, and then the "A" treatment again. If order effects are linear this procedure distributes them evenly across treatment conditions.

all possible orders: A form of cross-subject counterbalancing in which all possible orders of a set of treatments are constructed and each participant is tested with a separate order. This provides the most complete form of cross-subject counterbalancing.

block randomization: A form of within-subject counterbalancing in which the complete set of treatments is randomly arranged to form a block. A number of such treatment blocks are then admnistered to each participant.

carryover effects: Effects of a previous treatment that persist (carry over) and influence response to a later treatment.

counterbalancing: The strategy of balancing order effects across levels of an independent variable in order to prevent them from becoming confounded with treatments.

irreversible tasks: Tasks that can only be administered once since familiarity with them would prevent them from fairly being tested a second time. Thus, different versions of the task must be used on each trial the participant receives.

Latin-square design: A special arrangement of treatment sequences used as a form of cross-subject counterbalancing. A Latin square contains the same number of orders as there are treatments, with the special provision that each treatment precedes and follows every other treatment an equal number of times.

order effects: Changes in the dependent variable attributable to the ordinal position of treatment administration. Common order effects include practice, warm-up, boredom, and fatigue. Order effects must be controlled through counterbalancing to prevent the confounding of order and treatments.

random starting order with rotation: A form of cross-subject counterbalancing in which the number of orders equals the number of treatments. The first order is constructed through random arrangement of the treatments; each succeeding order is constructed by rotating each treatment one position to the left. The result is that each treatment appears in each position once; however, treatments always occur in the same sequence.

within-subjects design: A basic experimental design in which each participant is tested under all of the different treatment conditions.

ENDNOTES

1. Some texts refer to this as a *repeated-measures* design.

2. Designs in which each participant is tested more than once at each level of the independent variable are sometimes called *complete within-subject* designs.

3. In such cases, a second square must be constructed by reversing the order of treatments in each row of the first square.

4. This design would be analyzed as a factorial design. See Chapter 7.

5. Analysis of the choice-dilemma items indicated that people tended to advocate higher levels of risk in competitive games or sports, but much lower levels in situations where dependent others could be hurt by negative outcomes.

chapter seven

FACTORIAL EXPERIMENTS

Life is complex. Despite our best attempts to simplify matters and to find straightfor-ward solutions to our problems, we continually run into complicating factors. Having managed to quit smoking, for example, we may now find ourselves exposed to second-ary smoke, smog, or automobile fumes.

The problem, in general, is that many variables operate at the same time. If, by care-ful experimentation, we are able to isolate a particular causal factor we remain faced with the fact that it is only one among many interacting factors. What happens when these other factors, as is typically the case in the real world, operate simultaneously?

This poses a problem for the research scientist who is concerned with external validity. Will the same relationships hold outside the laboratory or will they be obscured, or moderated, by other interacting factors? These issues also must be faced by the theoretical scientist since most theories that attempt to explain human behaviour specify a network of interacting factors. How is complexity of this sort to be approached? Fortunately, there is a special experimental design—the factorial design—which helps us to deal with these kinds of issues.

WHAT ARE FACTORIAL DESIGNS?

A factorial design is one that incorporates two or more independent variables. People who participate in a factorial experiment are tested under particular **treatment**

combinations rather than under single treatment conditions, as is the case when only one independent variable is being studied. Each combination brings together particular levels of the separate independent variables. In a complete factorial design, all possible treatment combinations—formed by combining each level of one variable with each level of every other variable—are included. To make this concrete, let's take a simple example.

As a class project in social psychology two students decided to study the effects of personal appearance variables on impression formation. They chose two variables—hair colour and skin tan—and constructed an experiment to look at the possible effects these variables might have on personality judgments. You will recall that to qualify as an independent variable at least two levels must be included. Thus, the simplest possible factorial experiment they could carry out would include two levels of hair colour and two levels of skin tan. This, in fact, is what they did. From computer-generated images obtained at a local beauty salon they constructed photographs of the same young Caucasian female face with either blonde or brown hair, and with either pale white skin or a deep coppery tan. (Ah, the magic of computer imaging!)

How many photographs did they need to run their study? The answer, of course, is four—one for each of the possible treatment combinations: pale blonde, pale brunette, tan blonde, and tan brunette. The general rule is that the number of treatment combinations is determined by multiplying the number of levels of one independent variable by the number of levels of every other independent variable. For convenience, and as an informative designation, factorial designs are identified by arabic numerals, representing the number of levels of each variable. Thus, the students' experiment was a 2 × 2 design (read as a 2 *by* 2), employing two independent variables (hair colour and skin tone), with each variable having two levels. Had the students also included sex of the model as a third independent variable, their experiment would then have become a 2 × 2 × 2, requiring eight treatment combinations. Or, had they included three levels of hair colour—blonde, brunette, and also redhead—and combined these with the two levels of skin tone they would have produced a 3 × 2 design. As you can see, the possible variations are virtually endless.

To be certain you understand this, try to think of some other variables, along with their associated levels, that might influence impression formation and see if you can come up with the appropriate numeric designation for your design.

TYPES OF FACTORIAL DESIGNS

We have just explained one important way of classifying factorials—by the number of variables and the levels of each. Another important classification is based on whether each independent variable is manipulated as a between-subjects factor or a within-subjects factor. The example we gave in the previous section was a completely between-subjects factorial. That is, each treatment combination was applied to a separate group of participants. Since it was a 2 × 2 design there were four separate treatment groups. The completely between-subjects factorial is a very common design in psychological research, but it is not the only possibility.

The Completely Within-Subjects Factorial

With some research problems it makes more sense to employ a completely within-subjects factorial, where each participant is tested in all of the treatment combinations, rather than in only one. This is a much more economical design since it requires far fewer participants and correspondingly less time on the part of the experimenter. As an example, consider a hypothetical experiment to determine the factors that contribute to the legibility of printed text. One such factor is font size (the height of the printed letters). Another is the relative contrast between the darkness of the letters and the surrounding white space. We could easily construct a 2 × 2 factorial by arranging to present printed material in either a large (18 point) or small (10 point) font and using either boldface (**very dark**) or regular type. We would then test participants by arranging for them to read all four selections of material, with each selection representing one of the four treatment combinations: large bold, large regular, small bold and small regular. The four selections should be made equal in length and difficulty level. Our dependent variables might include reading time, comprehension, and measures of eyestrain and fatigue.

Mixed Designs

The third possibility is a design which combines at least one between-subjects variable with at least one within-subjects variable. For example, we could do a memory experiment to determine the effect of using imagery as a strategy to improve recall. Half of our participants receive instructions to form a vivid mental picture of each word in a list (high imagery condition) while the other half are asked to simply repeat each word to themselves (no imagery condition). Each participant is tested twice for recall—immediately following word presentation and after a delay of one hour. What we have, then, is a 2 × 2 mixed design with imagery as the between-subjects independent variable and time of recall (immediate versus delayed) as the within-subjects independent variable. In fact, this is a fairly common design, especially in research on memory and learning. Typically the between-subjects variable will represent a factor thought to influence the manner in which information is processed (such as rehearsal strategy), while the within-subjects variable represents a factor such as recall interval or number of learning trials.

ADVANTAGES OF FACTORIAL DESIGNS

Capturing Complexity

Factorial designs possess a number of important advantages over single factor designs. We began this chapter by commenting on the complexity of real life. Factorial designs offer us a way of capturing some of this complexity by allowing us to study the simultaneous operation of a number of variables. First impressions of people, for example, are likely to be influenced by a number of interacting factors—race, age, gender, clothing, physical features, and social context, to name but a few. When we do a single-variable study we manipulate one of these, age for example, while holding all the others constant. This tells us how age, by itself, may influence impressions but doesn't tell us how it may combine with other factors, such as gender or race.

Economy

A second advantage is that it is more economical to do a factorial experiment that incorporates several variables than it is to study each variable singly. The same number of observations per level of an independent variable in a 2×2 design can be obtained with half the number of participants that would be required for two, separate single-factor experiments. To understand this, let's return to our earlier example of the experiment involving hair colour and tan. If we were to do two separate studies—one manipulating only hair colour and the other manipulating only tan—we might decide to employ 40 participants in each, for a total requirement of 80. In the first study we would test 20 participants with the blonde photo and 20 with the brunette photo. Similarly, the second study would require 20 participants for the pale skin photo and 20 for the dark tan photo. In contrast, in the 2×2 factorial we would need only 10 participants in each of the four treatment combinations (a total requirement of 40) in order to provide 20 observations for each level of each variable. This advantage in economy grows substantially greater as additional variables and/or levels are added to the factorial. If the factorial experiment incorporates within-subject factors, as in the completely-within or mixed designs, there is an even greater savings in the number of participants needed to provide a particular number of observations. The economy provided by a factorial is especially important where participants are difficult to obtain or where the time required to make the necessary observations is lengthy. Just ask our thesis students!

Discovering Interactions

The third advantage of factorial designs, the opportunity to discover interactions, is by far the most important. In fact, it is the essential reason why many experiments are carried out. As we said earlier, variables do not operate in isolation. Indeed, the effect of any one variable may depend critically on the level of some other variable. For example, whether we perceive an older person as possessing great wisdom and knowledge or as verging on senility may depend on the social context in which we encounter that person—for example, addressing a university convocation or being cared for in a senior citizens' home. Understanding the concept of interaction is essential to understanding psychological research. Consequently, we devote a major section of the chapter to this important topic.

UNDERSTANDING INTERACTIONS

Distinguishing Main Effects from Interactions

To introduce you to these important concepts it is necessary to bring in some specialized vocabulary. A **main effect** refers to the overall effect of an independent variable, averaged across the levels of the other variables in the design. That is, we disregard the second variable completely and simply summarize the data according to the levels of the first variable.

Let's look at a concrete example to see what this means. We previously mentioned a hypothetical study of the effects of imagery and retention interval on the ability to recall words. Table 7.1 contains a possible set of results—giving for each treatment combination the average number of words recalled. To determine the main effect of imagery we need to look at the overall level of recall for both the yes and no conditions, averaged across the two levels (immediate and delayed) of retention interval. This is given by the two bold-print entries in the far right column of the table. We see that, on average, participants who used imagery recalled ten words, whereas those who did not recalled six. Similarly, the

TABLE 7-1	Main Effects of Imagery and Retention Interval		
	Retention Interval		
Imagery	Immediate	Delayed	Average
Yes	12	8	10
No	8	4	6
Average	10	6	

main effect of retention interval is given by the marginal means in the bottom row. When tested immediately, participants recalled an average of ten words, but after the waiting period they recalled an average of six. To determine our main effects, then, we ignore the interior cells (treatment combinations) of the table and instead focus on the row margins and the column margins. The main effects are the differences (10 vs. 6) and (10 vs. 6) between these marginal means. To determine whether such effects are statistically significant we would, of course, have to do the appropriate analysis of variance.

In addition to checking for a main effect for each variable we also need to determine whether there is an **interaction effect**. An interaction effect occurs whenever the effect of one independent variable changes over the levels of the second independent variable. For example, if we were to find that using imagery made a big difference in the number of words recalled when an immediate test was given, but little or no difference when the test was delayed, we would have an interaction. We can easily check for potential interactions by examining the cell entries themselves (the treatment-combination means) while ignoring the marginal means. One way to make such a check is to compare the differences between each set of row (or column) means. In the first column the difference between the two imagery levels in the immediate recall condition is 12 minus 8, or four. In the second column the difference between the two imagery levels in the delayed recall condition is 8 minus 4, or four. Since these differences are the same there is no interaction. What this means is that the use of imagery has the same effect—to raise the level of recall by an average of four words—at both levels of retention interval.

Let's look now at a different possible set of results, given in Table 7.2.

TABLE 7-2	Main Effects of Imagery and Retention Interval, with an Interaction Effect		
	Retention Interval		
Imagery	Immediate	Delayed	Average
Yes	12	8	10
No	12	4	8
Average	12	6	

Here we again appear to have two main effects, with participants recalling more words, on average, with imagery than without (10 vs. 8), and recalling more in the immediate than in the delayed condition (12 vs. 6). However, when we check for interaction using the difference method, we find that the differences are not equal. There is no difference between the imagery levels in the immediate condition (12 minus 12), but there is a large difference (8 minus 4) in the delayed condition. The fact that these differences are not the same alerts us to a potential interaction effect. To confirm the reliability of this effect we would need to conduct the appropriate statistical analysis. What is important to realize at this point is that our results indicate that the effect of imagery on the recall of words depends on whether the recall is immediate or delayed. More specifically, imagery has no effect on recall when tested immediately, but a substantial effect when the test is delayed. A widely used method of checking for main effects and interaction is to plot the means on a line graph. Figures 7.1 and 7.2 present graphic representations of the data contained in the two previous tables. Figure 7.1 (constructed from the data in Table 7.1) shows a situation where both independent variables have a main effect, but where there is no interaction. Note that the two lines are *parallel*. Parallel lines indicate a lack of interaction We can see from the graph that the size of the imagery effect is approximately the same for immediate recall as it is for delayed recall.

FIGURE 7-1	Line graphs showing two main effects and no interaction

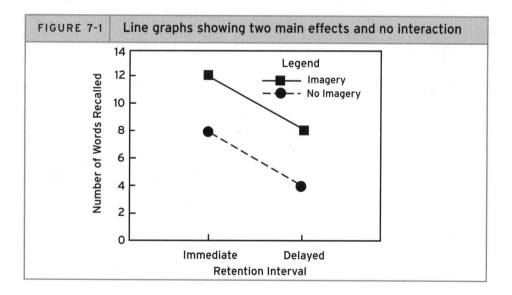

Look now at Figure 7.2. The lines clearly are not parallel, a situation that indicates the presence of an interaction. The graph shows that there is no difference between the imagery conditions when recall is immediate, but a substantial difference when it is delayed. The advantage of the graphing method is that it shows us at a glance whatever main and/or interaction effects have turned up in our study.

Consider now a third possible outcome of the study, as shown in Table 7.3. When we check for main effects by comparing overall row and column averages we find that there are none. The marginal means are exactly the same. However, clearly something is hap-

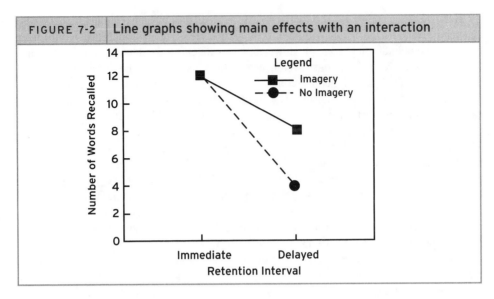

FIGURE 7-2 | Line graphs showing main effects with an interaction

pening in this experiment, and that something is an interaction. If we use the difference method we come up with 8 minus 12 (-4), compared with 12 minus 8 (+4). (It's critical to preserve the sign of the difference.) The nature of this particular interaction, however, is revealed most clearly by graphing.

In Figure 7.3 we see what appears to be a large X in the middle of the graph. This is commonly called a **crossover interaction**. It occurs because the effects of a particular independent variable reverse themselves across the levels of a second independent vari-

TABLE 7-3 | Crossover Interaction Effect

Imagery	Retention Interval		Average
	Immediate	Delayed	
Yes	8	12	10
No	12	8	10
Average	10	10	

able. In this case it appears that the use of imagery reduces the level of recall on an immediate test, but increases it on a delayed test.

We have looked at three possible patterns of data for this experiment. To be certain you understand main effects and interactions try to create table entries and corresponding graphs that would show (a) a main effect for imagery but not recall interval, (b) a main effect for recall interval but not imagery, (c) a main effect for imagery and an interaction, (d) a main effect for recall interval and an interaction, and (e) neither main effects nor interaction.

FIGURE 7-3	Line graphs showing a crossover interaction

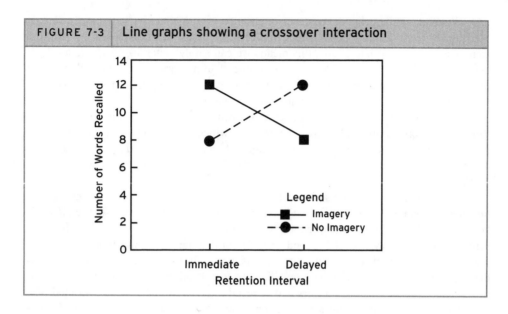

Interpreting Interactions

We have said that an interaction occurs when the effect of one variable on behaviour depends on the levels of other variables. In a simple factorial, such as a 2 × 2, it is usually fairly easy to interpret (make sense of) an interaction. With the aid of a graph we can easily see how an independent variable's effect on a dependent variable changes over different levels of a second variable. The interpretation may become a bit more difficult, however, when either variable has more than two levels.

A useful way of interpreting interactions is by breaking them into component parts called **simple effects**. A simple effect is the effect that a particular independent variable has at a single level of a second variable. An example would be the effect that imagery has only at the immediate recall interval. We find simple effects by looking at single rows (or columns) in the table, or by examining a single line on the graph. Whenever an interaction occurs we can interpret it by stating the simple effects that it is composed of. Returning to our second example above (Table 7-2) we would state that imagery has no effect on immediate recall (first simple effect), but increases delayed recall (second simple effect). There are as many simple effects as there are levels of the second variable. Each simple effect can be tested separately for statistical significance, a process that is very useful in breaking down complex interactions.

In addition to interpreting interactions by separating out simple effects it is also important to interpret the meaning of an interaction—that is, to ask what conclusions we can arrive at from a particular experiment. One reason that factorial experiments may be carried out is to assess claims for *external validity*. Recall that results of an experiment are externally valid when they extend to other people, places, situations or times. A common strategy is to choose a primary variable, such as imagery, that we expect will have a particular effect on a dependent variable and then add a secondary variable, such as recall interval, that represents various levels of some other factor that will serve as a test of generalizability. Think what the presence or absence of an interaction would mean here. If our primary variable has a main effect (imagery increases recall, say) and, in addition, there is an absence of interaction, this means we can safely generalize over the levels of the second variable. We would learn, for example, that imagery increases recall and does so to approximately the same degree regardless of the time of the recall test. An outcome such as this, then, helps to support claims for external validity.

Now consider the implications for external validity when an interaction is present. When this occurs it imposes limits on the extent to which an effect can be generalized. For example, were the interaction the one presented in Figure 7.2 we could not then claim that the imagery effect generalizes across different recall intervals. In this example, it occurred for the delayed but not the immediate test.

The extent of the limitations placed on generalizability by the presence of the interaction depends on the exact nature of the interaction. An examination of the simple effects is helpful here. It may be that the direction of the effect of the primary variable is the same across the different levels of the second variable but that the size of the effect is different. For example, we might find that imagery results in a slight increase in recall on an immediate test but a much larger increase on a delayed test. If this were the case then our ability to generalize the effect of imagery across recall intervals is not quite so restricted. The direction of the effect is still the same; it is only the size of the effect that changes. In contrast, should a crossover interaction occur (as in Figure 7.3) this prevents us from being able to generalize at all. Instead, we must state that particular effects are likely to occur only under particular conditions.

BEYOND THE 2 × 2

To this point our entire explanation of main effects and interactions has taken place in the context of a 2 × 2 factorial design. The reason for this is that the 2 × 2 design is the simplest factorial; it enables us to explain the basics of the design without adding undue complexity. Now, however, it is time to see how adding to this basic building block can bring us important new information.

Factorials can be expanded either by adding levels to existing variables or by adding new variables. We will look at both.

Adding Levels

Let's look at what happens when we add levels to one of the variables in our previous example. Of the two variables, imagery and retention interval, it is easier to add intervals to the latter. (In general it is easier, and often makes more sense, to add levels to a quantitative independent variable.)

Table 7.4 shows the imagery experiment with four levels of recall interval (a 2 × 4 design). By examining the row and column marginal means we can see that each independent variable appears to have a main effect. There is an overall higher level of recall in the imagery than in the no-imagery condition, and the level of recall steadily drops as the retention interval grows longer. Also, by using the difference method, we can see that the differences between imagery conditions are not the same for all retention intervals, thereby suggesting the presence of an interaction. These effects are easier to see when graphed. (See Figure 7.4.)

TABLE 7-4	Additional Levels of Retention Interval				
	Retention Interval				
Imagery	Immediate	1 hour	4 hours	24 hours	Average
Yes	12	10	10	8	**10**
No	12	10	6	4	**8**
Average	**12**	**10**	**8**	**6**	

What have we learned by adding additional levels to the factorial? We can see the answer to this by comparing the data in Figure 7.4 to those in Figure 7.2. Note that the immediate and 24-hour levels contain data identical to the immediate and delayed levels in the previous example. What has been added are the one-hour and four-hour levels. This enables us to give a more complete picture of both the interaction and the main effect for retention interval. We can now see that the interval main effect represents a gradual dropping off in the number of words recalled over time. With only two levels, immediate and delayed, it was impossible to tell whether the drop was gradual or abrupt.

We can also better understand the interaction. When we examine the simple effects of retention interval at each level of imagery (the two main rows in the table or lines on the graph) we see that they look somewhat similar. Both show a decline in recall over time; the only difference is that the decline is more gradual in the imagery condition. This enables us to make a more accurate generalization, allowing us to state that the impact of imagery on recall becomes more pronounced as the retention interval grows longer.

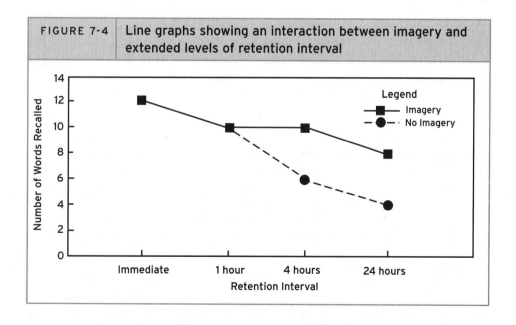

FIGURE 7-4	Line graphs showing an interaction between imagery and extended levels of retention interval

Adding Additional Variables

Factorials become considerably more complex, but potentially more informative, when additional variables are added. Our original 2×2 design, containing four treatment combinations, can easily become a $2 \times 2 \times 2$ design, with eight treatment combinations, by simply adding another two-level variable such as gender. If we were to do this we would be able to learn not only whether there is an overall difference in the recall of males and females but also whether gender interacts with imagery, with retention interval, or with a combination of both variables, thereby yielding a **three-way interaction**. To visualize a three-way interaction think of drawing two separate graphs, one for males and one for females. If the patterns of lines on the two graphs are markedly different this suggests the presence of a three-way interaction. Figure 7.5 shows what one might look like.

Here we see that the two-way (crossover) interaction between imagery and retention interval is in evidence for females but not for males. Data such as this would, of course, impose another limit on our ability to generalize. That is, we would have to further qualify the effects of imagery and retention interval based on the sex of the sample. One way of making sense of a three-way interaction is to break it down in the same manner we broke

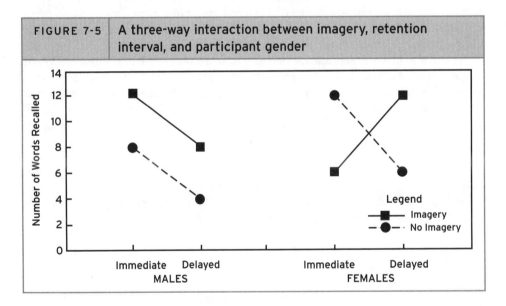

FIGURE 7-5 | **A three-way interaction between imagery, retention interval, and participant gender**

a two-way interaction into simple effects. Here, though, two steps are required. First, we examine the two-way patterns at each level of a third variable. Then each of these simple interaction effects can be further broken down into specific simple effects. In other words, we could look at the effect of each independent variable at specific treatment combinations formed by the levels of the other two variables. Information on how to do this is given in various advanced statistics and methodology texts (e.g., Keppel, 1991).

ANALYSIS OF FACTORIAL DATA

Most factorial designs are analyzed using analysis of variance procedures. The major exception to this generalization occurs when the data are qualitative rather than quantitative. Here, analyses such as chi square and log linear are used instead. We will look only at analysis of variance.

Analysis of Variance

In the two-way (two-variable) factorial design the analysis of variance yields three separate F ratios. There is an F ratio for testing the significance of each main effect and an F ratio for the interaction. The numerator of each F ratio consists of variation due to one of the three systematic sources of variance: (1) the main effect of A, (2) the main effect of B, or (3) the A × B interaction. Just as in the one-way designs each of these variances contains both treatment variance (caused by the independent variable) and error variance. The denominator, however, contains only error variance. The same logic that we outlined in Chapter 5 applies here as well—that is, if a particular independent variable had no effect then the numerator will contain only error variance and the F ratio will be approximately one. However, if an independent variable does have an effect then systematic variance will be added to error variance and the F ratio should be reliably greater than one.

In symbolic form the F ratios are usually presented as follows:

$$F_A = \frac{MS_A}{MS_e} \qquad F_B = \frac{MS_B}{MS_e} \qquad F_{A \times B} = \frac{MS_{A \times B}}{MS_e}$$

The subscript letters in the numerator indicate the particular source of variance (variable A, variable B, or the A × B interaction) that is being tested for significance. The subscript e in the denominator represents error. Note that this takes the place of within-groups error in the between-subjects design and residual error in the within-subjects design. The reason for using this general designation is that the form of MS_e will change depending on whether the factorial is completely between, completely within, or mixed.

Steps in Analysis of Factorial Designs

There is a great deal of information available in a factorial design. In order to extract this information in a logical and useful fashion it is helpful to proceed in the following manner. First, calculate means and standard deviations for each treatment combination and present them in a table. Second, calculate the three basic F ratios. (Easy-to-follow procedures are given in a variety of basic statistics textbooks—e.g., Keppel, Saufley, & Tokunaga, 1992.) Third, determine whether the interaction is statistically significant. If the interaction is *not significant* you would next check the significance of the A main effect and B main effect. If a significant main effect is found for a variable with three or more levels, analytical comparisons would be used to locate the source of the effect (see Chapter 5). However, if the interaction is *significant* the usual next step is to determine whether any of the component simple effects are significant. Rather than testing all possible simple effects most researchers would choose a particular set to analyze. The choice is between the effects of A at each of the different levels of B and the effects of B at each of the different levels of A. Which set is chosen depends, basically, on which variable is of primary interest. In our imagery experiment, for example, we would probably choose to analyze the effects of imagery at each of the different retention levels. Whenever a significant effect has more than two levels—regardless of whether it is a main effect or simple effect—the usual procedure is to follow it up with analytical comparisons in order to isolate the main source of the effect.

Let's work this out with a new example. Suppose that we want to study the effect of monetary incentive on problem solving. We give participants a series of puzzles to solve and offer them a cash reward for each correct solution. Our question is whether participants work more quickly, completing more puzzles in a given time, with a cash reward than without. Since we also wish to know whether the size of the cash reward makes a difference we decide to include three levels of monetary incentive: $0, $5, or $10 for each correct solution. We are also interested in the variable of problem difficulty (easy vs. hard), and whether it interacts with monetary incentive. Our design, then, is a 3 × 2 completely between-subjects factorial. Each participant is provided with a number of puzzles of the specified difficulty level and given a one-hour time limit. Let's assume that the results— the average number of puzzles solved in each treatment combination—are as shown in Table 7.5.

Given that a sufficient number of participants were tested, analysis of variance would, almost certainly, yield a significant Incentive × Difficulty interaction. The nature of this interaction can be most clearly seen in the form of a line graph (shown in Figure 7.6).

Since we do have an interaction our next step is to break it down into simple effects. The variable of primary interest is monetary incentive and, therefore, it makes most sense to look at its simple effects. There are two. The simple effects of monetary incentive at the

TABLE 7-5	Hypothetical Results of the Problem-Solving Experiment			
	Monetary Incentive			
Difficulty	$0.00	$5.00	$10.00	Average
Easy	4	6	8	6
Hard	2	2	2	2
Average	3	4	5	

easy level of difficulty are given by the cell means in the row labelled Easy (4, 6, and 8). Likewise, the simple effects of monetary incentive at the hard level are given by the cell means in the row labelled Hard (2, 2, and 2). Each simple effect is analyzed by conducting a one-way analysis of variance to determine whether there are significant differences among the cell means contained in that effect. We can see that this is likely to be the case for the easy simple effect since there are fairly large differences among the means. In contrast, the simple effect for the hard level is comprised of identical means. Clearly, then, what has occurred is that monetary incentive has an effect on the number of easy problems that are solved, but not on the number of difficult problems.

FIGURE 7-6	Interaction between problem difficulty and monetary incentive

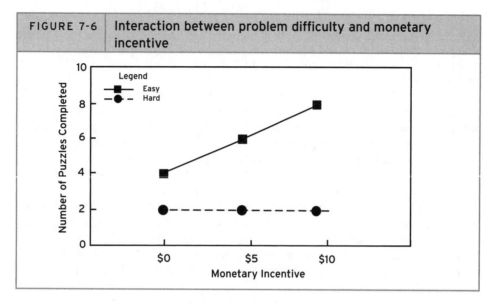

To complete our analysis we would need to state a bit more specifically the nature of this particular simple effect. It seems obvious from the pattern of the data that as monetary incentive increases so too does the number of easy problems that are solved. Since there are more than two means involved in this effect it would be appropriate to perform analytical comparisons to pinpoint the location of the significant differences. An obvious strategy would be to compare the mean of the $0 condition with that of the $5 condition and, in turn, to compare the $5 condition with the mean of the $10 condition.

A similar approach that yields some additional information is to do a particular form of analytical comparison called a **linear trend test**. This test is only appropriate for quantitative independent variables such as level of incentive. It allows us to determine whether there is a statistically significant tendency for the level of the dependent variable to change in straight line fashion with changes in the level of the independent variable. In this case, it would tell us whether the observed trend (for number of problems solved to increase as monetary incentive increased) was statistically significant. If so, we can offer the straightforward conclusion that when problems are easy, increasing the level of incentive produces corresponding increases in performance.

As you can see, the thorough analysis of a factorial design requires familiarity with a number of analytical techniques. Students who are preparing to do an honours thesis, or are planning to apply for graduate study, are generally advised (or even required) to complete a second undergraduate course in statistics. Most such courses focus extensively on analysis of variance and provide detailed coverage of the sorts of techniques introduced in this section.

SUMMARY

Behaviour is determined by the operation of many variables. Factorial designs that incorporate two or more independent variables help to capture some of this complexity. In a complete factorial design all possible treatment combinations, formed by combining every level of one independent variable with every level of at least one other independent variables, are administered. Such designs are designated by numerals representing the number of levels of each variable. For example, a 3 × 2 design indicates that there are three levels of one independent variable and two levels of a second, yielding a total of six treatment combinations.

Factorial designs may be classified as completely between-subjects, completely within-subjects, or mixed. In the completely between-subjects design a separate group of participants is assigned to each of the treatment combinations. In the completely within-subjects design the same participants are tested in all treatment combinations. A mixed design combines at least one between-subjects variable with at least one within-subjects variable. Thus, the same participants are tested under all the levels of one variable, but different participants are assigned to the different levels of the second variable.

Factorial designs possess a number of important advantages over single-factor designs. First, they allow researchers to capture some of the complexity of life through studying the simultaneous operation of a number of variables. A second advantage is that it is more economical to conduct a factorial experiment than it is to study each variable singly. The third, and most important, advantage of factorials is the opportunity to discover interactions among variables. An interaction occurs whenever the effect of one independent variable changes over the levels of a second independent variable.

A factorial design provides information about the main effects of each independent variable and also about possible interaction effects that occur through the joint operation of several variables. A main effect is identified by the differences among the overall means of the levels of one variable, averaged across the levels of other variables. Interaction effects are identified by separately examining the effects one variable has at each of the different levels of a second variable. A useful way of doing this is by graphically plotting the treatment-combination (or cell) means of one variable at each level of a second variable. If the lines connecting the sets of means for each level are parallel, no interaction is present. In contrast, if the lines are not parallel, this suggests the presence of an interaction effect.

Interactions are interpreted by examination of simple effects. A simple effect is the effect that one independent variable has at a single level of a second independent variable. Descriptive statements of the individual simple effects help to make clear the nature of particular interactions. The presence of interaction effects places limits on the extent to which the effects of each independent variable can be generalized. Conversely, the absence of interaction effects helps to establish external validity.

Factorials can be expanded by adding levels to existing variables or by adding new variables. Adding levels gives a more complete representation of the range of a particular variable and provides a better overall description of the nature of both main and interaction effects. Adding additional variables yields more information about the factors determining behaviour and permits the discovery of higher-order interactions. A three-way interaction is interpreted by examining two-way patterns at different levels of a third variable.

Most factorial designs are analyzed using analysis of variance procedures. In the two-way factorial design three separate F ratios are calculated, one for each of the two main effects and one for the interaction effect. The numerator of each F ratio contains both error variance and variance due to the systematic source (either main effect or interaction) being tested. The denominator contains error variance alone. In the usual order of testing, the F for interaction is the first to be evaluated. If the interaction is not significant each of the main effects is then evaluated. Significant main effects involving three or more levels may be followed by analytical comparisons to locate the particular sources of variance. If, however, the interaction effect is significant the usual next step is to separately evaluate the component simple effects. A significant simple effect containing three or more levels is further analyzed by analytical comparisons on the treatment combination means. A special form of analytical comparison, a linear trend test, may be performed when the levels of an independent variable are quantitative in order to determine whether levels of the dependent variable change in straight line fashion with the levels of the independent variable.

KEY TERMS

complete factorial design: A design in which all possible treatment combinations, formed by combining each level of one independent variable with each level of every other variable, are included.

completely between-subjects factorial design: A design in which each treatment combination is applied to a separate group of participants.

completely within-subjects factorial design: A design in which all treatment combinations are applied to each participant.

crossover interaction: An interaction in which the effects of a particular independent variable reverse themselves across the levels of a second independent variable; graphically displayed as an X-shaped figure.

factorial design: A design in which the treatments are formed by combining levels from several separate independent variables.

interaction effect: An outcome in which the effect of one independent variable changes over the levels of a second independent variable.

linear trend test: An analytical comparison that is appropriate for assessing the effect of a quantitative independent variable. A linear trend test indicates whether there is a statistically significant tendency for the levels of the independent variable to change in straight line fashion with changes in the level of the independent variable.

main effect: The overall effect of an independent variable averaged across the levels of the other variables in the design.

simple effect: The effect a particular independent variable has at a single level of a second independent variable.

three-way interaction: An interaction among the levels of three independent variables. A three-way interaction occurs whenever the treatment combination outcomes of two independent variables change over the levels of a third independent variable.

treatment combinations: Treatments that represent combinations of levels from separate independent variables; the treatments administered in factorial designs.

chapter eight

QUASI-EXPERIMENTAL RESEARCH

In the last three chapters we covered basic designs of experimental research. These sophisticated methods of investigation tend to work best in laboratory situations where the researcher is able to make full use of various control procedures, such as holding conditions constant and the random assignment of participants to treatment conditions. It is often difficult, however, to apply these methods in pure fashion to the world outside the laboratory. One attempt to do so, field experiments, was covered in Chapter 2. In this chapter we cover approaches that may be used where it is impossible, or highly impractical, to employ experimental methods.

As we have seen, experimental methods tend to find their readiest application in the controlled environment of the research laboratory. In general, research of this sort is aimed at producing basic knowledge. The highest level of knowledge involves causal explanations, developed by determining the effects particular variables have on certain other variables. When causal statements are linked together in the form of basic principles they become psychological theories. Testable predictions derived from these theories are checked into order to assess the validity and range of usefulness of the theoretical concepts (see also Chapter 1). Experimental methods are particularly important in this process since it is essential to isolate the variables that are theoretically relevant. An example of this process with respect to the social role theory of hypnosis was given in Chapter 1.

APPLIED RESEARCH

In addition to seeking basic knowledge, psychologists are also concerned with questions of practical application and social relevance. Recently, for example, in the wake of the shooting deaths of 12 students and teachers in Littleton, Colorado, psychologists have focussed particular attention on school violence (Volz, 1999). Can we point to factors that would help us understand such incidents and, even more important, can we do anything that would help to reduce the likelihood of this occurring in the future? If, as now seems likely, experiences of bullying and social rejection are linked to such violent events (Greenfield & Juvonen, 1999), would the implementation of programs aimed at reducing such victimization also reduce the likelihood of future violence?

Indeed, there are a great many socially relevant questions that researchers would like to find answers to. Are women as likely as men to receive management promotions? Do warning labels on tobacco or alcohol products help to deter usage? Does one type of diet plan work better than another? Will a new government program really create more jobs or reduce unemployment? What type of therapy works best for a particular type of phobia? Finding answers to practical questions of this sort usually requires doing research outside the laboratory, in natural settings.

Problems in Applying the Experimental Method

Although such questions are often causal in nature it may not be possible, or practical, to apply experimental methods. In the first place, doing an experiment requires manipulating an independent variable. Such manipulation may not be possible since, in many cases, the variable of interest is outside the experimenter's range of control. For example, a school board may have implemented an anti-bullying program in the local school district, or a federal health agency may have stipulated that warning labels be attached to certain products. In the above examples the critical independent variables have already been manipulated and the job of the researcher is to try to determine what effect they may have had. This job is complicated by lack of control over how the critical variable is implemented, who is chosen to receive the treatment, and the possible influence of a wide range of extraneous variables.

A second, and related, problem is that random assignment to treatment conditions is frequently impossible. This creates a major problem in establishing internal validity. The problem is that when we make a comparison between a group that has received a particular treatment and a group that has not we can never be certain that the groups are similar in other ways. Often, in fact, we suspect that they are very dissimilar. People who start a particular diet in hopes of losing a few pounds are probably quite different from those who choose not to start that diet (or any diet). These differences may involve level of fitness, social support, nutritional awareness, and even basic metabolic rate. If the diet group loses weight while the comparison group does not, how can we be certain that it was due to the diet rather than to one or more of these other factors? The major dilemma, then, is that we are trying to answer important causal questions, yet are unable to use the method that is best suited to the task.

Understanding Quasi-Experimental Designs

The response to this dilemma has been the development of a group of quasi-experimental research designs. Although not genuine experimental designs, they incorporate at least some of the features of experiments. In a sense they are the next best thing. The prefix *quasi* means similar to or resembling. Thus, these designs resemble experiments, but lack at least one critical feature of a true experiment. We present these designs later in the chapter. First, though, we take a detour in order to clarify some important considerations in understanding the logic underlying quasi-experimental designs.

THREATS TO INTERNAL VALIDITY

In previous chapters I made a point of emphasizing that the most important characteristic of any research project is its internal validity. To refresh your memory, internal validity was defined as the extent, or degree to which, changes in the dependent variable could be unambiguously linked to changes in the independent variable. Chapter 5 outlined the major control procedures that are utilized to help ensure internal validity. The critical concern was to prevent confounding—that is, in setting up our experimental design we want to prevent the possibility of some extraneous variable changing along with the independent variable. The usual experimental control procedures of constancy, balancing, and randomization are used for just this purpose. The problem, then, when experimental designs cannot be used is the increased likelihood that one, or more, extraneous variables may become confounded and pose a serious threat to internal validity. Threats to internal validity may arise from a number of different sources. A researcher who uses quasi-experimental designs needs to be aware of these sources so that special steps may be taken to control those that are particularly likely to be problematic. In their classic work on quasi-experimental designs, Campbell and Stanley (1966) discuss eight major categories of threats to internal validity. A summary of these threats is presented below.

History

This category refers to the chance occurrence of unscheduled events during the course of the research project. Suppose that an anti-bullying program has been implemented in a particular school system and that a study is being conducted to determine its effect. If, during the course of the study, a major news story breaks that links bullying to extreme violence (as was the case in Littleton, Colorado), it is quite possible that the emotional reaction to this event may, in itself, change attitudes towards bullying. The problem from the perspective of the researcher, then, is knowing whether changes in students' attitudes and behaviours are due to the anti-bullying program or to the major news event. Without some control for the **history threat** posed by unanticipated events the internal validity of the study would be quite low.

Can you think of a way of controlling for this? It's extremely difficult to do anything once the study has started but, if anticipated in the planning stage, steps may be taken to reduce this threat. The most important control procedure would be to include a comparison group that doesn't receive the treatment program. Perhaps another similar school district can be found that is not implementing this program. We would need to collect before and after measures from both school systems. The history threat (the news story) would have an impact on both school systems, but only one has received the treatment program. If there is greater change in the treatment schools than in the non-treatment schools we would feel a bit more confident in asserting that the observed changes were not simply due to the news story. Can we credit the change to the treatment program, then? It's tempting to do so, but other threats have to be examined as well.

Maturation

The **maturation** category of threats includes any regular changes associated with the passage of time. These would include biological growth, mental and emotional development, the accumulation of social experiences, and increases in general knowledge. If the research project takes place over the course of weeks, or months, then these maturation factors will pose a possible threat. For example, if the anti-bullying study is carried out in high schools a plausible threat would be the students' social maturation over the course of a school year. As students gain increasing life experiences, prepare for post-secondary employment or education, and increase their level of social awareness they may gradually become less tolerant of bullying behaviour. The problem, then, is that the changes the anti-bullying program were designed to create may come about naturally as students mature. As with the history threat, maturation is best controlled through the use of a similar comparison group—perhaps another group of high-school students at the same age or grade level who don't receive the program. A greater change in the treatment group helps rule out the maturation threat.

Testing

A third type of threat occurs whenever repeated testing is used. On many types of tests, regardless of whether they measure physical skills, mental abilities, or social maturity, participants typically perform better on the second test than the first. This increased performance reflects the effects of familiarity, warm-up, and motivation. In my research methods classes students typically score better on the second quiz than the first, perhaps because they have learned what to expect. Whenever a research project involves repeated **testing**, then, there is always the threat that any increase or change from one test to another is due to a simple testing effect rather than to the treatment or program being evaluated. This could easily occur in the anti-bullying study. Suppose that questionnaires measuring acceptance and tolerance of bullying are given at the start of the school year and again at the end. Changes in response may be due to familiarity with the questions and to the opportunity to reflect on what would be a good, or socially acceptable, answer. That is, a difference in reported attitudes could occur without any underlying change taking place. Once again, the inclusion of a comparison group that receives the same repeated test, but without the intervening treatment program, would help to control for this problem.

Regression to the Mean

Another sort of testing effect may occur when subjects are tested twice. Extreme scores, very high or very low, on the first test tend to be less extreme on the second test; they move, or regress, in the direction of the mean. This occurs regularly with quiz scores. A student who gets 100% on the first quiz often scores a bit lower, 90 or 95%, on the second.

Conversely, the student who scored only 25% on the first quiz almost always does better on the second. Why do you think this occurs? If you answered that it is just luck, or chance, you are basically right. A very high score occurs partly because the student is bright, or has studied hard, but also partly due to chance factors—guessing right on some questions, or the fact that no questions were asked on material that was not read or studied. The extremely low scorer may, by mistake, have not studied the right material and perhaps also made some unlucky guesses. On a second test, the same chance factors are unlikely to recur in the same fashion and the resulting scores will be less extreme.

Regression is a threat in research studies whenever extreme groups are chosen for study. Suppose that we had selected students who had been identified as the most extreme bullies, or perhaps those who had experienced the highest levels of victimization. A program is then put into place and, at a later date, a second assessment is made. Due to regression the scores on our measures will be less extreme than they were at the first assessment and this change could be mistakenly taken as evidence that the program is working. That is, we see that our big, bad bullies are apparently doing less bullying and those who were most victimized are now being victimized less. How can we separate out real change from the apparent change due to regression? One way is to employ that old standby, the comparison group. In other words, we also need two measures on a group of high-level bullies who have not been exposed to the program. Have they changed as much? If so, it is likely regression. If not, then we can rule regression out.

A somewhat different control procedure involves taking multiple measures over time, both before and after the introduction of the treatment. This allows us to compare the change following the treatment with the natural fluctuations in behaviour that occur for a variety of reasons (including regression). This time-series design is discussed in detail later in the chapter.

Instrumentation

Measuring the dependent variable, or outcome, of the study always requires the use of some instrument. In some cases physical instruments such as video recorders, computers, or stopwatches are used. In other cases data may be gathered through the use of questionnaires, interviews, or human observers. An **instrumentation threat** occurs whenever the operation of the instrument changes during the course of the study. Obvious problems would occur if a camcorder's batteries ran down, a hard drive crashed, or a stopwatch ran fast or slow. Less obvious, but even more threatening, problems arise when changes take place in the human observers. For example, the anti-bullying study may rely on student monitors or teachers to report instances of bullying. It is possible that during the course of the study these observers may become more sensitive (or, in some cases, less sensitive) to bullying behaviour than at the start of the study. Perhaps, as time goes by, even fairly minor instances such as verbal taunts, or particular nonverbal gestures, are reported as bullying behaviours, even though the same instances may not have been noted when the study began. Thus, even if the program is working it may appear not to be since just as many, if not more, instances of bullying are reported at the end of the study. Of course, the main control is to periodically check the instruments, whether mechanical or human, to determine whether their operation has changed. With human observers, the use of good operational definitions, training, and the deployment of independent observers (as discussed in Chapter 2) can all help to ensure reliable observations. A comparison group can also help here since any systematic changes in sensitivity that are simply due to experience or practice should occur with observers in both conditions.

Mortality

In any study that extends over time it is inevitable that some participants will drop out. The term **mortality** refers to the drop-out rate due to all causes and is not meant to suggest that those who participate in psychological research may suffer lethal consequences! In most research the discontinuation of participation is simply a minor annoyance to the researcher, who must try to replace the dropouts or suffer a loss of power in the analysis (see Chapter 2). In some cases, however, mortality is a much more serious threat. If participants drop out due to some feature of the study or treatment being given then those who remain will not be representative of the starting sample. (See Chapter 5 for a previous discussion of this problem.) Imagine, for example, that the anti-bullying program involves close monitoring by teachers, or other observers, of school areas where bullying has been frequently reported—perhaps the cafeteria and the schoolyard during recess and lunch periods. Over time the instances of bullying in these locations are observed to decrease. It looks like the program is working as intended. What may be happening, however, is that some of the participants (perhaps the hard-core bullies) have moved away from the observation areas. They may, perhaps, have transferred their activities to more remote areas of the school building (the washrooms perhaps) or off the school grounds entirely. Those who remain in the observed areas, then, are not representative of those who were observed at the beginning of the study.

I have stretched the above example a little to make it fit with our bullying theme. Mortality usually refers to a complete discontinuation of participation in the study. Some bullies (and victims) may literally drop out of school, but usually there are strong restraints that prevent this. In other studies, where participation is entirely voluntary, we are likely to get a higher rate of mortality. For example, the sponsors of exercise and weight-loss programs may obtain distorted results when there are more than a few dropouts. Obviously, the finishers are not likely to be representative of the entire starting sample.

It's difficult to control adequately for mortality. A non-treatment comparison may help to assess whether the treatment group mortality is excessive. Another helpful control is to collect pretest measures on all participants and then assess whether dropouts are likely to be different from non-dropouts. If there is a comparison group available a sort of reverse matching can be performed: Every time a treatment-group participant discontinues a comparison participant with an identical pretest score can be dropped in compensation. This way the groups are kept roughly equivalent.

Selection

A **selection threat** occurs whenever the comparison group participants differ in some systematic way from the treatment group participants. The two groups may be found to differ in age, IQ, socioeconomic status, education level, family background, or in some other way. Any such differences pose a serious threat to internal validity. Suppose, for example, that the anti-bullying program is implemented in a middle-class suburban school. If the comparison school has a student-body with different characteristics—perhaps drawing on an urban population or serving neighbourhoods of a different socioeconomic status—it will be difficult to make valid comparisons. Such differences may result in aggressive behaviours being displayed more frequently, or more commonly tolerated, in one school system than another. As a result, if lower levels of aggression are reported in the school with the anti-bullying program, this may simply reflect differences in pre-existing levels of aggression.

Selection threats are easily controlled when random assignment can be used. When it can't be used, comparison groups must be selected very carefully. In our bullying study we'd like to be certain that the two schools (or school systems) being compared are reasonably equivalent in student-body characteristics. It is generally important in such studies to collect a variety of socioeconomic and demographic data. As well, it would be essential to measure initial levels of aggression, bullying, and victimization in both the comparison and treatment groups. If the two groups are roughly equivalent on all important measures, at least initially, then we can reasonably exclude a selection threat.

Interactions with Selection

Initial differences between comparison groups may interact with other factors—especially history, maturation, and instrumentation. That is, one group may mature faster than another, may have different events happen to it during the course of the study, or the test instrument may be more sensitive to changes in one group than another. For example, a high school with a large number of students enrolled in a college preparatory program may produce a faster rate of social maturation, especially in the senior year, than a comparison school with relatively few college prep students. Obviously, such an interaction could have a strong impact on acceptance of bullying. An interaction with history could occur if a particular event, such as a drive-by shooting, occurred in one school district but not another. Alternatively, observers in one school might, over the course of the study, increase in their level of sensitivity to incidents of bullying or victimization, while those in another school do not. Such differences could arise due to selection factors, such as those mentioned above, that may be linked to different levels of aggression in the two settings.

The means of controlling for such threats are basically the same as for the selection threat—that is, trying to reduce as much as possible any initial differences. In addition, simply being aware of such possibilities helps to alert the investigator to potential threats to validity that need to be checked.

Other Threats

The eight threats detailed above are those that are especially problematic whenever experimental procedures cannot be used. In addition, there are other threats that are difficult to control even when experimental procedures are used. Two such threats—*observer bias* and *reactivity*—have been covered previously in this book (see chapters 2 and 5). It is easy to see how both could be a threat in the bullying study. A researcher who expected bullying to decrease following program implementation may tend to see fewer instances, or less severe instances, even when there has been no change. Students who are observed during the study may change due to reactivity. That is, being aware of the observation they may behave in a more civilized or circumspect manner than was previously the case. As well, such awareness may lead to a responsiveness to *demand characteristics*. Information about the aims of the study, or expectations of the researchers, may be picked up, directly or indirectly, and behaviour may change to meet expectations or to create a positive image. The special controls that we previously discussed in chapters 2 and 5 (observer blind and/or placebo controls) would have to be implemented to create a valid study.

One other threat, **contamination** (Shaughnessy & Zechmeister, 1997), needs to be examined. Usually we think of contamination as being chemical or biological in nature (contaminated food, for example), and it may be difficult to see how this could apply to psychological research. In a research context, contamination occurs whenever relevant information concerning the aims of the study or procedures employed is communicated, or otherwise transmitted, from one group to another. That is, if one group informed the other about the special treatment they were being given this information would contaminate (change) the nature of the treatment the second group received. For example, if some of the students and/or teachers of the comparison school had contact with those in the treatment school they might be tempted to begin their own impromptu anti-bullying program. If so, they would be contaminated as a comparison group.

In teaching my methods classes I sometimes use the following attention-getting example. Whenever I teach two sections of the course in the same term I tell my students that this arrangement afforded me a good opportunity to do an educational experiment. "Your class," I explain, "was given the traditional closed-book set of quizzes. The other class was allowed to take their quizzes in open-book fashion—that is, they could look up the answers to any question they didn't know." I go on to state that the point of this was to see which method would promote better long-term retention of the material, which I would eventually determine by comparing the final exam scores of the two classes. Having expounded on this in serious tones, I note that some students respond with looks of anger or anguish (especially the open-mouthed "How could you do this to us?" look). I then add that I asked the open-book class to sign a pledge of silence so that this information would not be communicated to the closed-book class. Continuing the explanation, I ask whether, despite the pledge, they might nevertheless have heard something of this. Most shake their heads ruefully no. I then ask what they think their reaction would have been if they had heard? Would it have affected their studying behaviour? Most feel that it would. (They would have transferred to the other class, they claim, or, if that was not possible, given up studying entirely since they wouldn't have had much of a chance compared to the other class.) At this point, then, its easy to make the point about how contamination can threaten the validity of a study.[1]

QUASI-EXPERIMENTAL DESIGNS

The threats to internal validity that we have detailed are best controlled through the use of experimental procedures. When such procedures are not available (or feasible) we turn to the next-best substitute. The **quasi-experimental designs**, presented below, are attempts to provide at least some aspects of experimental control. Although these designs lack randomized assignment (the hallmark of the true experiment), they attempt to compensate by incorporating one, or more, benchmarks of comparison. In the remainder of the chapter we explore four widely used quasi-experimental designs. The validity of each design is assessed by examining the extent to which it controls for the various threats to internal validity covered in the preceding section.

To show how quasi-experimental designs work we examine how each would be applied to a sample problem. One particular area of application for such designs is determining the effect of a natural treatment. Such treatments include natural disasters (hurricanes, earthquakes), changes in government programs, laws or social policy (such as changes in speed limits or drunk-driving penalties, new welfare programs, and various educational reforms) and mega-building projects (urban renewal and other large-scale construction projects). An interesting example from the latter category is the recent completion of the 14-kilometre (9-mile) Confederation Bridge linking the Canadian provinces of New Brunswick and Prince Edward Island (P.E.I.). Prior to the June, 1997 opening of the bridge the main access to the Island was via ferry service. The proposal to replace the ferry service with the bridge incited a tremendous local (and even national) debate on the impact this would have on the environment, on the tourist industry, and even on the Island way of life. These are clearly important questions. How could we go about trying to find some answers?

The One Group Pretest-Post test Design

It might strike you that the simplest way to get answers would be to do a before-and-after comparison. For example, if we could find some good measure of one of the variables we're interested in (some aspect of environmental quality or tourist activity, for example) we could simply compare its magnitude at some point before the bridge was opened with its level after it was opened. Since the P.E.I. government keeps close track of several tourism-related variables, and publishes these in an annual database posted on its Web site, it's easy to make such a comparison (Prince Edward Island Department of the Provincial Treasury, 2000). For example, in 1996 tourist spending was $150.8 million, but jumped to $245.9 million in 1997, the first year the bridge was open. There was a similar increase in the number of automobile tourists—from 279,905 in 1996 to 373,896 in 1997. These comparisons certainly suggest that the bridge had a tremendous impact on tourism.

Can you think of any problems with relying on such simple comparisons? If it occurred to you that perhaps there would have been such an increase even without the bridge, then you are on the right track. The problem with such pretest-posttest comparisons is that they leave many threats to validity uncontrolled. In particular, they don't control for history, maturation, testing, regression, and reactivity. A history threat occurs when other events coincide with the treatment. The Island tourist industry may have stepped up its advertising program, world-wide attention given the event may have attracted curious visitors, or the tourist season may have been accompanied by an unusually long spell of fine summer weather. In fact, all of these seem to have occurred at about the same time, and it's difficult to tell what the effect of these combined factors may have been.

At first glance, the maturation threat sounds unlikely in this situation. Recall, though, that maturation means change over time. As time goes by, we may find more people travelling, a growth in the number of tourist attractions, and growth in various forms of tourist advertising. As well, it appears that global warming is making for longer and hotter summers, which in turn may further increase the attractiveness of ocean-based tourist destinations. In other words, the increased level of tourism may simply represent a natural growth process, a process that would occur with or without the bridge.

Threats such as regression and testing occur when people are tested on two separate occasions. Since the tourist statistics don't require any direct testing or questioning they would not seem to be a threat in this particular project. However, they are worth pointing out since in many other situations (for example, where questionnaires might be used to assess attitudes toward bullying before and after a particular event) they would be a problem. Reactivity is also a threat whenever study participants become aware of the measurement process and, especially, when they can guess a study's intent. Reactivity would occur in the bridge assessment if people were directly surveyed on how the bridge has affected them.

Nonequivalent Control Group Design

How can threats such as history, maturation, testing, and regression be eliminated? The ideal method is to use an equivalent control group, one that is alike in every way except for the specific treatment. If, in a science-fictional sense, we could create parallel universes, one in which the Confederation Bridge is built and one in which it isn't, we would have the ideal solution. Failing this, the best we can hope for is to find a comparison group, or case, which is as similar as possible to the treatment group. In this instance, it would mean finding a comparison tourist destination and examining the same statistical indices for the same time periods. Whatever effects are created by maturation, regression, and testing should be the same in both locations. Also, any general history effects—an unusually hot summer, international monetary exchange rates, the general state of the economy— should be the same in both. As a result, this design is a tremendous improvement over the one-group version. The only major factors that remain uncontrolled are interactions with selection.

We could implement this design by selecting for comparison a second Canadian province—ideally one that is in close geographical proximity, has a well-developed tourist industry, but is not directly affected by the Confederation Bridge. A province which appears to meet these criteria, and for which similar statistics are available, is Nova Scotia. Tourist spending in Nova Scotia was $905 million in 1996, increasing to $1.06 billion in 1997 (Nova Scotia Department of Tourism and Culture, 1999). Thus, there was a fairly substantial increase in both provinces, a fact that might be attributed to some of the maturation (general growth) and history factors discussed earlier. However, the percentage increase in spending was much greater in P.E.I. (63%) than it was in Nova Scotia (17%). We also find that P.E.I. experienced a much sharper increase in automobile visitors (33%) than did Nova Scotia (13%) over the same time period.

The fact that P.E.I. experienced a greater increase in tourist activity from 1996 to 1997 than did Nova Scotia is consistent with the hypothesis that the bridge had a special impact. This effect does not seem due to an overall increase in tourist activity or to general weather or climatic conditions. The main remaining threat to internal validity involves possible interactions with selection. An interaction with maturity could occur if, for some reason, tourism was increasing at a faster rate on P.E.I. than Nova Scotia. An interaction with instrumentation could occur if, during the study period, the means by which tourist data were collected or recorded changed in one province but not the other.[2] An interaction with history could occur if special or unusual events occurred in one province but not the other. This third possibility seems the most likely of the three. On P.E.I. a number of major celebrations marked the opening of the bridge and, for a period of time, national and international attention was focussed on the Island. It is entirely possible, then, that the celebrations and special media attention (whatever the occasion) could, by themselves, bring about an increase in tourism. Is there any way of separating the bridge effect from the celebration effect?

The Interrupted Time Series Design

If you were thinking that over time the special attention would diminish and that things should return to normal, you are ready to learn about the **interrupted time series design**. The special feature of this design is that measurements are taken at several points, both before and after the introduction of the treatment. An effect that is treatment-related should show up as a sharp discontinuity in the time series data. To apply this we could track the level of tourism for a number of years before the opening of the bridge and for a number of years afterwards. This would allow us to see the normal fluctuations in the data and to assess whether the change that occurred immediately after the treatment was substantially greater than the usual year-to-year changes. We could also determine whether the change was permanent or simply a one-time fluctuation, as would be the case if the change were due to special media attention. The interrupted time-series design represents a major improvement over the simple pretest-posttest design since it helps to rule out the effects of maturation, testing, and regression.

To see how such data might be interpreted, look at the graph in Figure 8.1. The plotted lines represent automobile traffic entering the province and level of tourist spending for the years 1993 to 1999.[3] As you can see, there appears to be a slow growth in tourism from 1993 to 1996. Starting in 1997, when the bridge was opened, there is a sharp upsurge in both auto traffic and tourist spending. This increase is maintained in 1998 and 1999, a fact that helps rule out temporary factors such as media attention, novelty, and special celebrations. The major threat that this design does not rule out is history. That is, any event that happened to co-occur in time with the opening of the bridge, and that could potentially have an enduring impact on tourism, remains a threat to the study's validity. This could

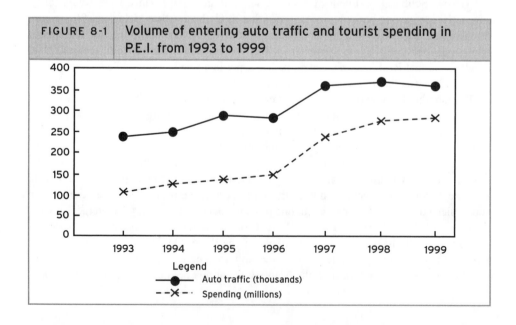

FIGURE 8-1   **Volume of entering auto traffic and tourist spending in P.E.I. from 1993 to 1999**

Legend
— ● — Auto traffic (thousands)
- - ✕ - · Spending (millions)

include both general or widespread events, such as a change in the value of Canadian currency, federal taxation rates, or climate changes, as well as fairly specific, or local, events such as the building of new resort centres, opening of a world-class golf course, or any other special attractions that could potentially draw tourists.

Time Series with Nonequivalent Control Group

A further improvement on the time series design could be made by adding a comparison group. Doing so would help eliminate the general history factors mentioned in the previous section, factors such as climate or economic changes that could be expected to affect many areas. All we need to do to implement this design is to expand our previous nonequivalent comparison group design by including time series data in the comparison.

Let's see what it looks like when we do this. In Figure 8.2 we have expanded the comparison Nova Scotia data into a time series graph.[4] The data show a steady, gradual rise in traffic and spending over the years covered. Unlike the P.E.I. data there is no sharp discontinuity between the years 1996 and 1997. This pattern helps to rule out general history factors such as changes in climate or economic conditions that just happened to coincide with the bridge. Had such factors been responsible we would see the same pattern of discontinuity in the data for both provinces. The fact that it occurs only in the P.E.I. data supports the hypothesis that it is, in fact, the presence of the bridge that is the chief cause of the increase in tourism. The only remaining threats to validity are those that could be classified as local history effects—that is, events that uniquely affected the situation on Prince Edward Island. These could include major new tourist incentives, local weather effects, or some combination of the above. While such possibilities cannot be definitively ruled out, the plausibility of such factors accounting for an effect of this magnitude seems rather low.

The preceding discussion illustrates the nature of the data interpretation process that accompanies the use of quasi-experimental designs. Unlike the case with experimental designs we cannot, through the simple expedient of random assignment, rule out a large

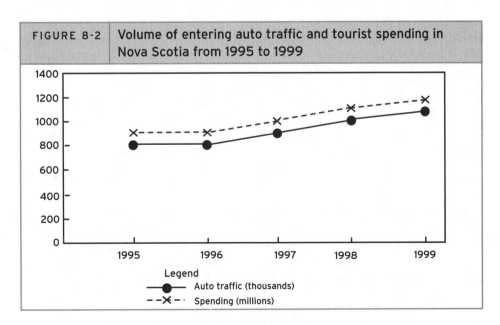

| FIGURE 8-2 | Volume of entering auto traffic and tourist spending in Nova Scotia from 1995 to 1999 |

Legend
—●— Auto traffic (thousands)
--✕-· Spending (millions)

variety of alternative interpretations. Instead, threats must be examined individually and an informed judgment made in each case regarding the design's ability to eliminate it from consideration. Even the best available design, the interrupted time-series with nonequivalent comparison, cannot completely rule out every threat to validity. There are always some extraneous events (new golf courses, flashy advertising campaigns) that remain uncontrolled and pose threats to the internal validity of any quasi-experimental study. The researchers who design and carry out such studies must live with the sobering thought that some degree of reasonable doubt will accompany any conclusions that are drawn. The best that can be done is to present reasoned arguments about the plausibility of those threats that remain uncontrolled. While this fact may be unsettling to those who like their conclusions air-tight we need to remember that science is a human enterprise. The results of scientific studies are never permanently set in stone. Rather, they are always open to further examination and reinterpretation.

SUMMARY

In addition to seeking knowledge, psychologists are also concerned with questions of practical application. Although such questions are often causal in nature it is not always possible, or practical, to apply experimental methods. Manipulation of the independent variable may be outside the researcher's control and random assignment to conditions may not be possible. In these situations quasi-experimental designs may be applied. These designs, although not true experiments, build in at least some of the features of experimental control.

The controlled procedures of experimental research are usually sufficient to rule out most of the major threats to internal validity. However, when experimentation is not possible each of these threats must be separately evaluated. A history threat occurs when unscheduled events coincide with the treatment being evaluated. Maturation threats include any changes regularly associated with the passage of time. A testing threat occurs when changes in response are induced by repeated testing. Regression to the mean poses a threat when groups are selected based on extreme scores on a pretest; such scores are likely to be less extreme on a second test. An instrumentation threat occurs when the operation of the measuring instrument, including the human observer, changes over the course of the study. A mortality threat occurs when participants drop out due to some feature of the treatment they are receiving. A selection threat occurs when the treatment group participants differ in some systematic way from the comparison group. Interactions with selection pose a threat whenever initial group difference interact with factors such as history, maturation, and instrumentation. Factors that threaten the internal validity of experimental research, especially observer bias and reactivity, likewise threaten quasi-experimental research. In addition, both forms of research may be threatened by contamination, the possibility that the treatment may affect not only the treatment group but also the comparison group.

Quasi-experimental designs are evaluated on the basis of their ability to control for the various threats to internal validity. The simplest quasi-experimental design, the one-group pretest posttest, is essentially a before-and-after comparison. It is generally considered a weak design as it fails to control for history, maturation, testing, regression, and reactivity. The nonequivalent control group design involves the comparison of a group that receives the treatment with a group that does not. The major threats uncontrolled by this design are selection, interactions with selection and, in some cases, contamination. The interrupted time series design involves taking a series of measurements, both before and after the introduction of the treatment. This design helps to rule out the effects of maturation, testing, and regression, but does not control for history. The time series with nonequivalent control group design extends the logic of the time series design to include a comparison group. This design helps rule out all major threats to internal validity, with the sole exception of local history effects.

KEY TERMS

contamination: A threat to internal validity that occurs whenever the treatment given to one group also affects the comparison group.

history threat: A threat to internal validity due to the occurrence of unscheduled events that coincide with the implementation of the independent variable.

instrumentation threat: A threat to internal validity that arises due to changes in the operation of the measuring instrument, including changes in the human observer.

interactions with selection: A threat to internal validity that occurs when initial differences among comparison groups interact with factors such as history, maturation, and instrumentation.

interrupted time series design: A design in which measurements are taken at a number of points both before and after implementation of the treatment. This design helps to rule out the effects of maturation, testing, and regression.

maturation threat: A threat to internal validity due to any regular changes associated with the passage of time, including biological growth, social and emotional development, and increases in knowledge.

mortality threat: A threat to internal validity that occurs whenever participants drop out due to some feature of the treatment they are receiving.

nonequivalent control group design: A design in which a treatment group is compared to some other group that has not received the treatment. Since the groups were not formed through random assignment they are nonequivalent and, hence, subject to threats from selection and interactions with selection.

one group pretest-posttest design: A design in which a pretest is administered to a group, followed by a treatment and a posttest. This is usually considered a low-quality design because a number of threats to internal validity are left uncontrolled.

quasi-experimental design: A research design that resembles an experimental design but lacks at least one critical feature of a true experiment.

regression to the mean: The tendency for extreme scores to become less extreme on a second test.

selection threat: A threat to internal validity that occurs whenever the comparison group differs in some systematic way from the treatment group.

testing threat: A threat to internal validity that occurs as a result of changes induced by repeated testing.

time series with nonequivalent control group: A design in which a number of measurements are taken both before and after the introduction of a treatment in the treatment group and the same time series measurements are also taken in a comparison group that does not receive the treatment. In addition to controlling for maturation, testing, and instrumentation this design also helps to rule out general history threats.

ENDNOTES

1. How do I wiggle out of this white lie? It usually happens that this class falls on, or close to, April Fool's Day, which, when I point out the date, helps to legitimate the temporary deception.

2. This does not appear to have been the case.

3. These data are based on the May 15 to October 31 tourist season.

4. At the time of writing only the data from the years 1995 to 1999 were available from the Nova Scotia government Web site. The traffic data are based on the May to October tourist season. The 1999 spending volume was not directly available; instead, it was estimated by applying the same percentage increase to the 1998 figure as pertained for traffic volume.

ETHICS IN RESEARCH

The first eight chapters of this book have focussed on the concepts necessary to an understanding of psychological research. In this concluding chapter we take a broader view that places the research enterprise within the larger context of professional activities engaged in by psychologists. These activities also include teaching, counselling, testing, administration, and the provision of therapeutic services. The common denominator among such diverse undertakings is that they represent professional behaviour of psychologists and, as such, are guided and constrained by a set of ethical principles. These principles are articulated in detail through codes of ethics developed by professional associations such as the Canadian Psychological Association (CPA) and American Psychological Association (APA).

The main purpose of the current chapter is to familiarize you with the ethical principles that apply to the conduct of psychological research and to the process of ethical decision-making that occurs before such research is initiated. Such familiarity is absolutely necessary if you plan to conduct your own research, whether in the form of a class project, undergraduate honours thesis, or graduate level masters or doctoral research. Even if you don't plan to do any research of your own it is still important to learn about ethics in order to broaden your understanding of the nature of psychological research and its potential applications in society. This point deserves special emphasis. Learning about ethics, and thinking about the relation of science to society, is part and parcel of becoming an educated person and a responsible citizen.

HUMAN RESEARCH

There are a number of ethical considerations that apply to research using human participants. In order to present the ethical standards that apply, and to highlight special ethical issues that must be resolved, I have followed the organizational structure employed in *A Canadian Code of Ethics for Psychologists* (Canadian Psychological Association, 1991).[1] The Code presents four major principles to be applied in ethical decision-making involving all professional activities of psychologists. Each principle subsumes a number of specific ethical standards that are to be applied in particular situations where they may be relevant. The Code also indicates the relative weight that should be given each of the four principles should they come into conflict in a particular decision.

Principle 1: Respect for the Dignity of Persons

The first principle, respect for the dignity of persons, is usually given the greatest weight in ethical decision-making. This principle holds that every person a psychologist has contact with should be treated with the basic respect and dignity due all human beings. As the Code states:

> ...psychologists acknowledge that all persons have a right to have their innate worth as human beings appreciated and that this worth is not enhanced or reduced by such differences as culture, ethnicity, colour, race, religion, gender, marital status, sexual preference, physical or mental abilities, age, socioeconomic status, and/or any other preference or personal characteristic, condition or status. (p. 9)

Simply put, the same basic respect and consideration are due everyone, without exception. Respect for dignity includes the right to privacy, self-determination, and equal justice. The research applications of this principle are particularly centred on the concepts of informed consent and protection of privacy.

Informed consent means that the research participant is fully informed of the nature of the research activities before consenting to take part. It is essential that explicit consent be obtained whenever the research process involves some risk to the participant or the invasion of privacy. Even when these conditions do not obtain, it is usually good practice to seek informed consent from all potential participants. A good starting point in the informed-consent process is to develop a written consent form that specifies the purpose of the research, the nature of the required activities, any benefits or risks to participation, and the option to withdraw from the research activity at any time. At most universities, students who are conducting human research must first submit a proposal, including a detailed consent form, to the relevant committee or course instructor before they are allowed to recruit participants. Securing informed consent, however, is not simply a matter of obtaining a signature on an official form. It is a process that engages active participation from individuals in decisions that involve them and reflects efforts to work towards a collaborative agreement between researcher and participant.

The process of obtaining informed consent may be particularly challenged when the potential participants are children or persons with diminished capacity to give informed consent. The CPA Code states that such participants should be used only when the research aims cannot be met by using persons of full capacity and when the proposed study has undergone a full ethical review. In such cases, informed consent must be sought from parents or those legally empowered to provide consent on behalf of the persons involved. Even when informed consent is obtained from a third party the researcher should seek the willing participation of the individual involved and not proceed without it unless the research process will provide a direct benefit to the participant. The extent to which such participation can be full and meaningful is a difficult issue that depends on considerations such as age, perceived control, family influence and various situational factors (Weithorn/Scherer, 1994).

The principle of informed consent may, at times, conflict with the need to disguise the hypothesis being tested in order to reduce reactivity and demand characteristics (see Chapter 2). This problem is discussed more fully later in the chapter in the context of integrity in relationships. It is generally agreed that it is unethical to mislead the participant about either the particular activities to be performed or the potential risks involved. In cases where reactivity would threaten the internal validity of the study if the hypothesis were obvious, the investigator may, at the start, inform the participant that particular details regarding the specific purpose of the study cannot be revealed because to do so would invalidate the experiment. Participants are further told that these details will be revealed when their participation is complete and that the need for concealment will then be explained. With this understanding made explicit the consent of participants is then sought. Investigators who choose to use this approach have a special obligation not to misuse or undermine the trust they are asking participants to place in them.

Protection of privacy means that the researcher may not observe an individual's private behaviour (unless specific consent has been obtained) and must respect the confidentiality of any information gained from the research participant. The observation of public behaviour—such as might occur in a shopping mall, city street or university cafeteria—does not require consent. On the other hand, observing people in their homes, or in motel rooms, or other locations where one might reasonably expect privacy, certainly would. The problem, of course, is that it is not always clear where the line separating public and private should be drawn. For example, psychologists have observed driving behaviour in the parking lots of shopping malls (Ruback & Juieng, 1997), and it seems clear that such behaviour falls within the public domain. But should psychologists also be free to peer in car windows, recording the activities of the passengers within and the nature of the items to be found?

In one controversial study, researchers concealed themselves in the toilet stalls of a men's public restroom and, with the aid of a hidden periscope, recorded urination times for unsuspecting male participants under several different conditions of observation (Middlemist, Knowles, & Matter, 1976). Does the fact the restrooms were public imply that the behaviour that takes place within is public rather than private? Informal polls of my psychology classes suggests that the answer in this case should be no. Should the same judgment be rendered for the hand-washing study (described in Chapter 2) where a student observer sat concealed in a toilet stall and listened for the sound of running water? In this case, my students do not usually feel that there has been an invasion of privacy, perhaps because toilet use was not directly observed. In both cases, however, there is usually some support for the minority view, indicating a lack of consensus over what should be considered public or private. Often, the final decision will be made by a research ethics commit-tee, composed of people of diverse backgrounds, who will apply the criterion of local com-munity standards in determining whether the observation procedures constitute an invasion of privacy.

One further research application of the principle of respect for the dignity of persons is the obligation of the researcher to preserve and protect the **confidentiality** of research records. In many cases this can be accomplished by not recording personally identifying information on the data sheet. Often all that is necessary to achieve the study's aims is basic demographic information such as gender and age, along with the condition of obser-vation and the record of behaviour. In cases where it is necessary to identify individuals, as when several test sessions are involved or when separate questionnaires or tests are com-pleted, special codes or participant numbers can be used in place of names. Published reports of research should present grouped data, in the form of averages or percentages, rather than individual reports. In cases where individual reports are central to the purpose of the research, as in case studies, special care must be taken to preserve the anonymity of the participants. Video and audio records of a participant's behaviour must not be made available to others without the express written consent of the participant.

Principle 2: Responsible Caring

This principle is second in weight to respect for the dignity of persons. It enjoins the psy-chologist to promote the welfare of the individuals, families, and groups with whom the psychologist has professional contact. The essence of this principle is captured in the fol-lowing excerpt from the Code:

> Responsible caring leads psychologists to "take care" to discern the potential harm and benefits involved, to predict the likelihood of their occurrence, to proceed only if the potential benefits outweigh the potential harms, to use and develop methods that will minimize harms and maxi-mize benefits, and to take responsibility for correcting any harmful effects that have occurred as a result of their activities. (p. 14)

Research applications of this principle include, first and foremost, the obligation to identify any procedures that may put the participant at **increased risk** of harm. The con-cept of harm includes any potential damage, pain or discomfort that may be caused the par-ticipant, whether physical or psychological. The notion of "increased risk" is generally understood to mean risk that is directly due to research participation and that would not normally be encountered in one's daily activities. For example, studies on the nature of pain may employ procedures such as electric shock or immersion in ice water. Quite obvi-ously the risk of pain is many times greater than one would normally encounter. Whether such a study should proceed would depend on considerations such as the potential bene-fits to be gained, whether the harm is likely to be temporary and easily removed, and on whether there is full informed consent. In some cases, certain individuals may be at greater risk of harm than others. The obligation of the researcher is to make an effort to select as potential participants those who are least likely to suffer harm.

In judging whether the degree of risk is acceptable an ethics committee will generally formulate a risk/benefit ratio. This is essentially a collective judgment of whether the potential benefits of the research, both to the participant and to society as a whole, out-weigh the risks encountered. Potential benefits include the development of important new knowledge, treatments, or programs that may be usefully applied in a social or personal context, and also any rewards, remuneration, or educational experience that may accrue to the participant. Some research studies are more likely to produce potential benefits than are others. A class research project, laboratory assignment, or independent study conducted by a student primarily as an educational exercise is less likely to produce new knowledge or beneficial application than a study conducted by a professional researcher. Consequently, much less risk should be tolerated in the former than in the latter. One criterion that should always be applied is the soundness of the research design. Other things being equal, a well-designed, internally valid study is more capable of producing an intended benefit than one which is poorly planned or carelessly executed.

The process of **debriefing** is an essential component of responsible caring. Debriefing occurs at the conclusion of the research participation and involves providing the participant with feedback about the nature of the study, the data obtained, and the overall importance of the research. This is an opportunity to provide at least one form of benefit through helping to enhance participants' knowledge and by imparting the sense that they have made a valuable contribution to science.

The debriefing process may also serve a useful methodological function since it offers the researcher an opportunity to learn more about how particular research procedures or events were interpreted by the participants. If deception was employed the debriefing offers not only the opportunity to remove and explain it but also the possibility of learning whether it worked as intended. As an example, you may recall that my posthypnotic suggestion study, discussed in Chapter 1 (St. Jean, 1978), employed the deception of a contrived emergency to remove the hypnotist from the room shortly before the buzzer sounded to cue the response. During the debriefing session I attempted to learn whether the deception was believed by the participant and also solicited suggestions for tips on making it seem even more convincing. At the same time, I explained why the deception was considered essential to the hypothesis being tested and how this particular study might help us better understand the nature of hypnosis. My sense was that participants welcomed this thorough debriefing, understood the need for the deception, felt actively involved in the scientific process, and left with the feeling that they had made an important contribution.

Despite screening all procedures for their potential to cause harm it is not always possible to predict whether, or what kind of, harm may befall a study participant. The researcher should always be alert for signs of distress or discomfort and should be prepared to discontinue the procedure when such is discovered. In addition, participants should, where feasible, be debriefed in a manner that is likely to uncover any harm that may have occurred so that appropriate steps may be taken to remedy the harm. This is particularly important where study procedures may have induced stress or anxiety. You may recall, for example, how Milgram's (1974) obedience studies (discussed in Chapter 1) produced not only a high level of destructive obedience, but also extremely high levels of agitation, nervousness, and stress. These studies were carried out at a time before ethics committees were routinely employed and it is questionable whether such stress-inducing procedures would have received approval. To Milgram's credit, however, he took special pains to consider the question of possible harm and other ethical issues raised by his studies (e.g., Milgram, 1964). In the context of an extensive debriefing session he attempted to detect signs of potential harm and, further, arranged psychiatric interviews for those who experienced high levels of stress. In addition, follow-up questionnaires were sent to participants a year later in an attempt to discover whether any lasting harm may have been produced.

Interestingly, most of the respondents indicated that they felt their participation had bene-fited rather than harmed them. In fact, many cited the experiment as a valuable educational experience that changed the way they viewed authority relationships.

Principle 3: Integrity in Relationships

The principle of integrity in relationships holds that the professional relationships formed by psychologists, whether involving clients, students, or research participants, should be characterized by directness and honesty. The Code states:

> These expectations include: accuracy and honesty; straightforwardness and openness; the max-imization of objectivity and minimization of bias; and, avoidance of conflicts of interest. (p. 19)

This principle is the third highest in weight, and may occasionally be suspended, or temporized, when it comes into conflict with the principles of respect for dignity of per-sons or responsible caring. There may be occasions, for example, where the provision of direct and honest information would produce harm or a sense of disrespect. In such cases the higher principles would take precedence.

There are several important implications for the way in which research is conducted. The most important concerns the use of **deception,** a point that I touched on earlier when discussing informed consent. The use of deception constitutes misrepresentation and, as such, is clearly in conflict with this principle. However, the use of deception is not banned; instead the Code indicates that psychologists "have a serious obligation to consider the need for, the possible consequences of, and their responsibility to correct any resulting mistrust or other harmful effects from the use of such techniques" (p. 55).

The use of deception in research has been a controversial issue for at least 30 years. On the one hand, there are those who would argue that deception should never be used since it involves dishonest communication and is likely to undermine the public trust in psy-chology (e.g., Stark, 1998). On the other hand, there are those who defend its use, claim-ing that socially important knowledge of processes underlying behaviours such as conformity, obedience, and bystander intervention would not be possible without it. Some, such as Milgram (1992), have argued that the use of deception in science is at least as defensible as other socially sanctioned uses of deception. For example, magicians produce deceptive illusions, parents actively promote treasured childhood myths such as Santa Claus and flying reindeer, and deceptive moves, such as a clever hip fake in hockey or pump fake in football, are admired by legions of sports fans. Few, if any, would feel that integrity has been undermined in such situations and so, the argument runs, why should the same sentiments not also prevail in the case of science?

In recognition of conflicting points of view the Code does not exclude deception, but does seek to restrict its use. Deception should not be used if there are alternative proce-dures available that would serve as well. Nor should it be employed if there is a reasonable possibility that its use could, in some way, produce harm to participants. Any deception used must be temporary—that is, during debriefing the researcher is obliged to remove the deception and provide a full explanation for its use. When deceptive information is pre-sented it should be in as minimal an amount as possible. It is critically important that deception not be used with respect to any information that is necessary in order for the participant to give true informed consent. Finally, the decision to use deception should not be made in the absence of an adequate ethical review procedure.

The principle of integrity in relationships also has implications for the manner in which research is reported. Procedures and results should be reported honestly and accurately. Fair credit, in proportion to their contribution, is to be accorded to those who collaborated on, or assisted with, the research project. In communicating knowledge gained from the study the researcher should make an effort to be as fair and as accurate as possible, being careful to delineate what is supported by the evidence and what remains conjectural.

Principle 4: Responsibility to Society

The principle of responsibility to society acknowledges that psychologists, like other professionals, have an obligation to serve the needs of society as a whole, as well as its individual members. The Code states these responsibilities as follows:

> Two of the legitimate expectations of psychology as a science and a profession are that it will increase knowledge and that it will conduct its affairs in such ways that it will promote the welfare of all human beings. (p. 24)

There are several important implications of this principle for research. Perhaps the most important is the responsibility to contribute to the development of psychological knowledge. Thus, there is an expectation that researchers will work to stay informed of progress in their areas of specialization and try to build upon this progress in their own work. Included in this professional trust is the obligation to carry out theoretically important and scientifically sound research. This, of course, is one of the reasons why training in research methods is so vital in a psychologist's education.

A second implication is that the researcher should strive to be sensitive to the needs of society and, where appropriate, to take these needs into account when planning and reporting research. Since research psychologists are experts in their particular areas there is a corresponding obligation to speak out on social issues related to their areas of knowledge. When psychologists become involved in planning public policy, whether as professional consultants or private citizens, they have a responsibility to communicate and apply psychological knowledge.

The principle of responsibility to society is usually accorded a lower weight than the first three principles. Thus, activities that contribute to knowledge or otherwise aid society should only be carried out if they do not conflict with respect for the dignity of persons, responsible caring, and integrity in relationships. As an example, consider a study that might be proposed on the nature and consequences of school bullying—clearly an important social problem. The researcher decides to have trained confederates act as schoolyard bullies and, with the help of other confederates, to vary the amount of social support the bully receives. These "bullies" approach isolated children on the school grounds and demand their lunch money. The level of assertiveness, as well as other responses, of the "victim" are recorded. The study promises to yield important information about social factors that maintain and support bullying. As an exercise, imagine that you are a member of an ethics committee and are charged with applying the principles of the Code to this proposed study. Do you find any violations?[2] If so, the study cannot be approved in its present form, despite its potential social value.

ANIMAL RESEARCH

You may have noticed that almost all of the research examples in this book have involved human participants. This choice is simply a reflection of my particular areas of interest and expertise. As you are probably aware, however, psychology has a long research tradition of animal study and experimentation. You may recall Pavlov's dogs, Skinner's pigeons, and Harlow's monkeys, to name but a few of the historically classic studies employing animal subjects. Animal studies continue to make up a substantial portion of modern psychological research and, just as with human research, raise important ethical issues that must be considered and addressed.

The Value of Animal Research

Students sometimes wonder why psychologists have such a fascination with rats and mazes, especially when their main goal in taking a psychology course is to better understand themselves and others. The connection is not always immediately obvious, but the key is in the meaning of the concept "to understand." You should recall from Chapter 1 that to achieve the scientific goal of understanding we must first discover factors that have a causal influence on behaviour. To understand why a friend suffers from depression, for example, we first need to know something about the causes of depression. Isolating causal factors, as we have seen, is entirely dependent on the basic control procedures of manipulation, constancy, and balancing.

What makes animal research especially valuable is that there is a much greater opportunity to control important variables and, as a result, to establish causal relationships than is typically the case with human research. Among the important variables that can be controlled in animals are heredity, environmental conditions, and history of experiences. There is simply no comparable opportunity in human research to select known genetic strains and to closely regulate the history of events and experiences throughout the life span.

Animal research is also valuable in that it helps place humans in an evolutionary context and brings a biological perspective to the understanding of behaviour. In this vein, it is especially valuable in investigating basic processes such as learning, motivation, sensation, perception, and emotion. Such studies contribute immensely to the establishment of theoretical principles that underlie the behaviour of all organisms. In this respect, the principles of classical and operant conditioning should serve as a familiar example.

Finally, it is becoming increasingly apparent that animal research can have a very direct impact on human welfare. Much of our understanding of diseases such as cancer, and the development of important drugs and medical treatments, are a direct outgrowth of such research. With respect to psychological concerns, animal research has addressed factors involved in depression, stress, anxiety, phobias, and pain. As one animal researcher has stated:

> Many of the advances made in our knowledge of the basic mechanisms of pain and advances in pain therapy would have been impossible without experiments in animals. It is universally agreed among the scientific community that animal experiments have yielded enormous benefits for both human and other animal populations, although not necessarily for the individual animals used in these experiments. (Bonica, 1992, p. 13)

Issues in Animal Research

The ethical issues raised by using animal subjects parallel to some extent those involved in human research. Animal subjects should be treated with the dignity and respect due all living creatures. However, in the case of animal research it is recognized that the animals employed are essentially captive subjects and, in a sense, are compelled to participate. Thus, issues of informed consent and invasion of privacy do not arise.

The major concerns arising in animal research are those that derive from the principle of promoting animal welfare. A critical issue is the production and control of animal pain during research procedures. Generally speaking, the same factors that produce pain in humans will also do so in animals. The Canadian Council on Animal Care (1993) has stipulated that "procedures subjecting animals to pain, suffering, privation, or death should be used only when an acceptable alternative procedure is unavailable" (p. 159). Furthermore, the investigator has the responsibility of thoroughly examining research techniques in an effort to minimize discomfort and pain. A risk/benefit analysis must also be undertaken. Before engaging in a study that would produce any negative consequences to animal subjects there must be reason to believe that the study will yield an increase in knowledge or provide direct benefits to humans or other animals.

While concerns with animal pain and suffering remain an important issue, it should be stressed that the great bulk of animal research does not involve the production of pain or discomfort. In fact, advances in animal research have greatly reduced the likelihood of this occurring, in part through the development of procedures that are sensitive to signs of animal discomfort or pain. For instance, researchers have recently developed a procedure that detects signs of stress in rat pups through analysis of the vocalizations of mother rats (Ryan, Doucette, & Tasker, 1999). Armed with the knowledge that has emerged from such studies animal researchers are increasing able to provide humane care and to detect, and ameliorate, conditions that produce pain or discomfort.

There are additional welfare issues that pertain to treatment both before and after the study is conducted. Most institutions have regulations regarding the housing and care of animals, specifying conditions such as appropriate spacing, cage size, ventilation, humidity, feeding, exercise, waste disposal, and sanitation. In addition, attention should be paid to the social and behavioural requirements of animals, including factors such as grouping, spacing, and attachments to caretakers, and checking for the development of abnormal behaviour patterns. When the study is completed it may sometimes be necessary to sacrifice the animals, either because of the need for tissue examination or because there may be no other way to end the animal's pain or suffering. In such cases, the euthanasia procedures must be simple, safe, rapid, and painless.

THE ETHICAL REVIEW PROCESS

Almost without exception, every new research study in psychology must undergo an independent ethical review before it is conducted. The few exceptions include those studies that do not directly involve living participants, such as those based on publicly accessible archives or physical traces (see Chapter 4). Although naturalistic observation studies may not entail direct contact with participants, such studies typically require a review since issues of privacy and confidentiality may be involved.

Studies Employing Human Participants

The Tri-Council Policy. Canadian research studies involving human participants are reviewed under the guidelines established by the **Tri-Council Policy Statement** (NSERC, 1999), which combines into one the policies of the Medical Research Council,[3] the Natural Sciences and Engineering Research Council, and the Social Sciences and Humanities Research Council. Every human-participant study conducted at an institution that receives funding from any of these federal granting agencies must be certified as being in compliance with these guidelines before the study is undertaken. The Tri-Council policy is similar, in many respects, to the CPA Code, but is somewhat broader in its sweep since it was developed to apply to such diverse disciplines as medicine, biology, political studies, anthropology, modern languages, and religious studies. The aspects of this policy that are most relevant to psychology are discussed below.

The guiding ethical principles of the policy include respect for human dignity, free and informed consent, vulnerable persons, privacy and confidentiality, and justice and inclusiveness. Detailed discussions of respect for dignity, informed consent, and privacy and confidentiality appeared earlier in the chapter. Respect for vulnerable persons reflects a concern for participants who may, in some way, be diminished in capacity or institutionalized, or are children under the legal age of consent. In such cases, special measures to protect against abuse or exploitation may be warranted. Respect for justice and inclusiveness reflects a concern for fairness and justice in terms of sharing benefits of research and not arbitrarily excluding particular categories of participants. In addition, the policy also includes the principle of balancing harms and benefits, the principle of minimizing harm and the principle of maximizing benefit. These last three principles, which are largely self-explanatory, were discussed earlier in the chapter under the heading of responsible caring.

Research Ethics Boards. In order to receive Tri-Council approval, human research studies must first be reviewed by a **Research Ethics Board** (REB). Institutions that sponsor and support research—such as universities, hospitals, and various public and private foundations—are required to maintain REBs that have the responsibility of approving or rejecting research studies conducted by the members of those institutions. Each REB must consist of at least five members, including both males and females, at least two experts in the areas of research covered, at least one person with special knowledge or training in ethics, and at least one person from the community served by the institution. The primary responsibility of the REB is to review the ethical acceptability of each research proposal submitted by applying the guidelines set forth in the Tri-Council policy statement. In addition, should more than minimal risk exist, the REB also has the responsibility of evaluating the proposed research design to make certain that it is capable of answering the particular research questions being asked. This may require a peer review by experts in the field. The purpose is to make certain that the study is capable of delivering the intended benefit of an increase in knowledge or practical application.

Each project submitted to an REB is subjected to one of three possible levels of review. The standard, or default, level is a full review by the entire board meeting in face-to-face session. An expedited review, carried out by a single member or subcommittee of the REB, may be approved if the research involves no more than minimal risk. A third level of review applies to undergraduate research projects carried out as part of a course requirement. Such projects may be reviewed by a departmental ethics committee, provided that the study is of **minimal risk** and that the review complies with the Tri-Council policy. When a study is approved the REB issues an ethical certificate that is good for one year and, in most cases, renewable through expedited review. If a study is not approved, investigators are informed of the reasons and given an opportunity to reapply or to appear before the committee to argue their case. A negative decision of the REB may be formally appealed. In such cases, an REB from another institution will usually adjudicate the appeal.

Studies Employing Animal Subjects

The use and care of experimental animals is regulated by a number of national and local commissions. In Canada, the use of animals for research purposes is governed by the **Canada Council on Animal Care**. This is a peer review body that has the responsibility of developing and reviewing animal care policy, as well as ensuring that existing standards are maintained. The council has a broad membership, including scientists, educators, and representatives from industry and the animal welfare movement. One of the important functions of the council is to make regular visits to animal research sites in order to inspect the facilities and review procedures in use. On occasion, these visits may be unannounced.

A substantial portion of animal research takes place within universities. Each university is required to have an **animal care committee**, charged with providing an ethical review of every study that employs animals. These committees are typically composed of several research scientists representing different areas of animal research, at least one scientist not involved in animal research, and one or more community members from outside the university. Researchers planning to undertake animal studies must make appropriate application to such committees to secure ethical approval before research can commence. These committees act to ensure that the ethical standards developed by the Canadian Council on Animal Care (1993) are properly met.

SUMMARY

The major portion of this chapter presents the ethical principles contained in *A Canadian Code of Ethics for Psychologists* and describes their application to the conduct of research. The first principle, respect for the dignity of persons, is that everyone is entitled to basic human respect and dignity, including the right to privacy, self determination, and equal justice. In accord with this principle, researchers should secure informed consent from participants before collecting data, and are required to do so whenever the research process involves more than minimal risk, an invasion of privacy, or an attempt to change behaviour. Researchers have an obligation to respect privacy and to maintain the confidentiality of data records. The second principle, responsible caring, enjoins psychologists to promote the welfare of those people they have professional contact with. Researchers should take steps to minimize harm to participants and work to maximize benefits of participation, including increased personal knowledge and the sense of having made a valued contribution. In addition, researchers have an obligation to attempt to detect and offset any harm that may have resulted from participation. The third principle, integrity in relationships, holds that the professional communications of psychologists should be characterized by honesty, directness, and fairness. The employment of deception as a research practice, which appears to contradict this principle, remains a contentious issue. The Code seeks to restrict deception by advising that its use be limited to research situations and procedures that meet certain specific guidelines. Deception may not be employed in the absence of a full ethical review. The fourth principle, responsibility to society, holds that psychology as a discipline has an obligation to increase knowledge and to promote beneficial application of psychological principles. Thus, researchers have a responsibility to conduct scientifically sound research and to use their expertise in a manner that is beneficial to society as a whole.

Animal research is an essential component of scientific psychology and, like human research, is subject to ethical guidelines. Since animal subjects are essentially captive participants, concepts such as informed consent and invasion of privacy do not directly apply. The major ethical concerns are those that derive from the principle of promoting animal welfare. Procedures that produce pain or discomfort should be used only when there is no effective alternative and there is good reason to believe that the study will produce important benefits such as an increase in knowledge or beneficial application. Every effort must be made to minimize pain or discomfort during the procedures and to alleviate it as soon as possible. In addition, ethical guidelines stipulate the provision of humane care and maintenance of all animals employed for research purposes.

All research that directly involves living participants, whether human or animal, must undergo an ethical review process. Studies involving human participants are reviewed under the guidelines established by the Tri-Council Policy Statement. This policy stipulates that proposed studies be reviewed by a Research Ethics Board. A standard, or full, review constituting a detailed examination of all procedures is carried out by the full membership in a face-to-face session. An expedited review, conducted by the board chair or designated subcommittee, may be approved if the study entails no more than minimal risk. Undergraduate research of minimal risk may be reviewed by a department committee that reports to the Research Ethics Board. Animal studies are reviewed by an animal care committee that implements policies established by the Canadian Council on Animal Care.

KEY TERMS

animal care committee: A committee within a research institution that is charged with providing an ethical review of every study that employs animals.

Canadian Council on Animal Care: A national peer review body that has the responsibility of developing animal care policy and ensuring that existing standards are met.

confidentiality: The process of restricting the collection and dissemination of personally identifying information.

debriefing: The process of providing information to the participant regarding the purpose of the study, the reason for particular procedures, and the importance of the research. Debriefing must always be carried out when deception is employed.

deception: The use of misleading or false information in order to disguise the aims of the study or to mask the meaning of a particular procedure.

informed consent: The process of informing participants about all salient features of the research project to be undertaken, including the nature of the study, the procedures involved, the risks attached, and the benefits of participation, and obtaining their consent before starting the study. Informed consent includes the right to discontinue at any time.

increased risk: Risk of harm to the participants that is beyond what would normally be encountered in their daily activities.

integrity in relationships: The third major principle of the Canadian Psychological Association code of ethics; holds that psychologists have an obligation to be honest, fair, and straightforward in their professional relationships.

minimal risk: A situation where the risk of harm is not beyond what participants would normally encounter in their daily activities.

protection of privacy: The principle that an individual's private behaviour and affairs may not be observed, or investigated, unless the individual's consent has first been obtained.

Research Ethics Board: An institutional review committee charged with approving or rejecting research studies conducted by members of that institution.

respect for the dignity of persons: The first major principle of the Canadian Psychological Association code of ethics; holds that everyone is entitled to basic human respect, including the right to privacy and autonomy.

responsible caring: The second major principle of the Canadian Psychological Association code of ethics; holds that psychologists have an obligation to promote the welfare of those they have professional contact with.

responsibility to society: The fourth major principle of the Canadian Psychological Association code of ethics; holds that psychologists have an obligation to serve society as a whole by working to increase knowledge and promoting responsible application of knowledge.

Tri-Council Policy Statement: Statement of ethical principles adopted by the three major federal granting agencies: Canada Council, Medical Research Council (now the Canadian Institutes of Health Research), and Social Sciences and Humanities Research Council.

ENDNOTES

1. The following excerpts from *The Canadian Code of Ethics for Psychologists* (1991) are reprinted courtesy of the Canadian Psychological Association.

2. The proposed study violates the principle of respect for dignity of persons since the act of bullying threatens autonomy and communicates a lack of respect to the "victim." The possibility of harm to the targeted child's sense of safety, and the potential for inducing a feeling of powerlessness and inferiority, conflict with the principle of responsible caring. The use of confederates and an elaborate deceptive procedure, combined with the lack of informed consent, conflict with the principle of integrity in relationships.

3. The Medical Research Council is now known as the Canadian Institutes of Health Research.

Appendix A

WRITING RESEARCH REPORTS

I assume that most of the students using this book are enrolled in a research methods course with a laboratory component. If so, it is likely that you will be required to prepare laboratory reports as part of your course work. The purpose of this appendix is to provide you with the basic guidelines you should follow in organizing and writing these reports.

The organizational framework and writing style you will be using is called APA style. It is described in detail in the *Publication Manual of the American Psychological Association*, 4th ed. (APA, 1994). This style is routinely used for all research papers in psychology, including the articles that are submitted for publication in professional journals. It includes the organizing structure of the paper, conventions used for citing sources and preparing references, and guidelines for preparing tables and graphs. The first rule of APA style is to double-space everything, from the title page at the beginning to the references at the end. Also, set the margins to one inch all the way around and use only left justification.

The sections that follow correspond to the major sections of the research paper, as specified by the APA manual. At the end of the appendix is a sample paper. As you read through the sections below it will be helpful to refer to the corresponding section of this paper.

TITLE PAGE

The first page of the report is called the title page. It contains the title of the report along with the name(s) of the author(s) and each author's affiliation (usually an institution such as a university, hospital or government department). The title is usually a phrase, or short sentence, that identifies the nature of the research being reported. A good way to generate the title is to form a phrase that links the major variables being investigated. Examples of possible titles would be "The effects of distraction on a short-term memory task," "Reaction time as a function of caffeine dosage," and "Observed walking speeds of pedestrians in malls and city streets."

The first line on the title page is, surprisingly, not the full title, but instead an abbreviated title called the running head. Type the words "Running head:" flush to the left margin, followed by an abbreviated title of not more than 50 upper-case characters, including spaces. Below the running head centre the full title of the paper. On the next double-spaced line, centre your name and the names of any co-authors. The name of your university or institution should be placed on the next line below. Finally, in the upper right-hand corner place a short header (the first two or three words of the title) and the page number. The header and page number should appear on every page of your report, a feat that is easily managed with the page numbering function of most word-processing programs.

ABSTRACT

The second page of the report is devoted to the abstract—a brief summary of the report that is limited to 960 characters (about 120 words). The word "Abstract" is centred on the first line and, starting on the next line, the abstract is written as a single paragraph without indentation. Although it appears at the front of the report, the abstract is usually the last section to be written. The purpose is to offer the reader a brief summary that conveys the main points of the paper. In published articles the abstract becomes part of a large collection of abstracts contained in databases such as PsycLIT or PsycINFO. Students sometimes find it difficult to write the abstract. One way of approaching the task is to write one sentence for each of the four major sections of the report: introduction, method, results, and discussion. Or, put in somewhat different words, the abstract should state the research question, the method used to answer this question, the answer found, and what it means or why it is important.

INTRODUCTION

The introduction begins on the third page of the report. Unlike the other major sections, there is no heading called "introduction." Instead, the title of the report is repeated, centred at the top of the page. The introduction, as the name suggests, introduces the reader to the nature of the particular research and indicates why it was done. Usually, the introduction begins by posing a question or problem that has been of interest to psychologists. For example, you might start a report on short-term memory by indicating that cognitive psychologists have long been interested in factors that affect the duration and content of short-term storage. Next, some of the research in this area would be reviewed, especially focussing on those studies that bear a close relation to your investigation or laboratory exercise. This, in turn, should lead into a statement of the purpose of your particular study. How does your study add to, or fit with, past research? Is your study aimed at answering questions that have not yet been satisfactorily answered? Was it done to extend previous research findings to new populations or settings? Perhaps there have been inconsistencies in previous findings and your study is attempting to resolve them. Often, research is carried out in order to evaluate theories, by deriving hypotheses and testing them (see Chapter 1). Or, in the case of a laboratory report, you may simply be attempting to replicate well-established findings. Towards the end of the introduction you should clearly state the specific question you are asking or hypothesis you are testing. You should also make sure that you clearly identify the independent and dependent variables, if your study is an experiment, or the set of variables being investigated, if you have a correlational study. There is no standard length for an introduction. Most journal articles have introductions in the range of 1000 to 2000 words. For a standard lab report the introduction should be much shorter, perhaps 300 to 500 words.

METHOD

This section begins immediately after the introduction, on the same page. Centre the word "Method" on the next double-spaced line following the last line of the introduction. The method section is very detailed, specifying who the participants were, the materials or apparatus used, and the procedure followed. The method section is typically divided into a number of subsections, with each subsection heading typed flush with the left margin.

Participants

Here you specify the number of participants used, along with relevant demographic information such as age, sex, and other special identifying characteristics that may be particularly relevant to your study. The method of recruitment and any special incentives offered should also be noted. If animals were used you should indicate the species, as well as sex, age, and number tested. You may have noticed that some older journal articles used the subheading "subjects" rather than "participants." However, current APA style prefers the latter.

Materials/Apparatus

The heading for this section may be written as "materials," "apparatus," or "materials and apparatus," whatever best fits the nature of the study. Included here is a description of any materials, such as questionnaires or psychological tests, that were used. Be sure to include a reference to any published materials that were used. If you made up your own test or questionnaire you should briefly describe it here and include a complete copy in an appendix at the end of your report. Whereas "materials" refers to software or replenishable supplies, "apparatus" refers to hardware or equipment. You should include a description of any standard laboratory equipment you used, such as a stopwatch, reaction timer, event recorder, computer, or Skinner box. If possible, provide the company name and model number. If you constructed the apparatus yourself, be sure to provide a description of construction materials and dimensions. It is often helpful to include a schematic diagram or photograph.

Procedure

In this section you should give a step-by-step account of everything that was done in the study. Often the starting point is the instructions given the participants, including a description of the informed-consent procedure. Typically this is followed by an explanation of the tasks the participants were asked to undertake and the different conditions under which they may have performed these tasks. If participants were assigned to different conditions (as in a between-subjects experiment) you should indicate how these assignments were made. If different treatments were administered to the same participants (as in a within-subjects experiment) you should report the order of administration. Be certain to give a complete description of the manner in which the variables were operationalized. In other words, give a full account of how the independent variable(s) was (were) manipulated and the dependent variable(s) measured. If, along with their other tasks, participants were asked to complete questionnaires and/or tests, it is important to note at exactly what point in the proceedings this occurred. (Any questionnaires or tests used should, of course, be fully described in the materials section.) Usually the procedure section closes with a description of the follow-up sessions, if any, and the manner in which participants were debriefed.

Design

The design subsection is optional and may be skipped if the study is fairly simple and straightforward. However, if the design if moderately complex—with two or more independent variables, for example—it is usually a good idea to include it. Here, you should indicate the number of independent variables and the number of levels of each. It is also helpful to indicate whether the design is completely between, completely within, or mixed.

If mixed, you should identify for each of the variables whether it is between or within. If more than one dependent variable was included, each should be named.

RESULTS

The results section begins immediately after the method, on the same page. Centre the word "Results" on the next double-spaced line following the last line of the method. The main objective in this section is to provide a factual report of your data and analyses. Much of this information will be presented in the form of tables or graphs. Each table or graph should be constructed on a separate page and included at the end of the report. The results section also contains a written description of the analyses and findings. Perhaps because there is such a strong emphasis on data presentation, students often feel uncertain as to what they should actually put down in words. As a guide to the nus and bolts writing, I suggest the following four-step process:

1. First, and even though it may seem obvious, tell the reader exactly what data are being presented. For example, if the study is a reaction time experiment, indicate that the data reported are reaction times measured in milliseconds.

2. Next, refer the reader to a summary of the data. This is usually done with a sentence such as the following: "The mean reaction times in milliseconds for each of the experimental conditions are presented in Table 1." You will note that a sentence such as this effectively combines steps 1 and 2.

3. Describe the statistical analyses performed on the data. If, for example, you have done an analysis of variance you can indicate this with a sentence such as the following: "A mixed-model analysis of variance was performed on the reaction time data." Along with this, of course, you would report the outcome of the analyses. For example: "A significant main effect was obtained for caffeine condition, $\underline{F}$ (2, 27) = 4.20, $\underline{p}$ < .05, but not for time of day, $\underline{F}$ (1, 27) = 0.23, ns. The caffeine by time of day interaction did not reach significance, $\underline{F}$ (2, 27) = 2.19, $\underline{p}$ > .05." Note that statistical symbols, such as $\underline{F}$, $\underline{t}$, and $\underline{p}$, should be underlined. Any follow-up tests would be reported next. In this example the significant main effect for caffeine, since it has three levels, would be followed by analytical comparisons to pinpoint where the significant differences occur.

4. Finally, state the results in words. For example, "Participants in the high caffeine condition had faster reaction times ($\underline{M}$ = 341.2) than those in either the moderate ($\underline{M}$ = 424.5) or no ($\underline{M}$ = 465.3) caffeine conditions." If the relevant means are presented in a table it may not be necessary to include them in the sentence report as I have done. Instead you could simply preface the sentence with the phrase "As can be seen in Table 1, ..."

If there are several dependent variables, or data sets, to be analyzed, this four-step process can be followed for each. For the sake of clarity it is often helpful to present each set of analyses in a separate subsection with an appropriate heading. In the sample paper, for example, you will note separate subsections with the headings "manipulation checks" and "time-estimation data."

Table Preparation

Tables present data concisely and economically. They are usually the choice method of data presentation for written reports. Each table must be referred to in the text and presented on a separately numbered page that is placed at the end of the report (after the references but before the figures, if any). The table number (e.g., Table 1) is typed flush left on the first line of the page and the table title, also flush left, is typed on the next double-spaced line. Tables are horizontally ruled; they contain no vertical lines. It is helpful to look at examples of tables in journal articles to get a sense of the layout. Detailed information on table construction—including headings, specific types of data, and table notes—are given in the *Publication Manual* (APA, 1994) and in *Presenting Your Findings: A Practical Guide for Creating Tables* (Nicol & Pexman, 1999).

Figure Preparation

Figures include graphs, charts, photographs, drawings, and diagrams. The style of figure you are most likely to encounter in research reports, and may be required to construct for your own reports, is, of course, the graph. Graphs are particularly helpful when you want to create a pictorial representation of your findings or to reveal trends in your data. Bar graphs are the best choice when your independent variable is qualitative. An example of a bar graph—showing how time estimation changes with variations in the demands of a cognitive task—can be found in the sample paper at the end of the appendix. Line graphs are the best choice when the independent variable is quantitative. Chapter 8 contains two line graphs—showing changes in the level of tourist activity over a certain number of years for two Canadian provinces.

It is sometimes difficult to determine whether you should present your data in a table or a graph. For live presentations—a class report, thesis defence, conference talk or poster, for example—graphs are usually the better choice as they enable the audience to immediately grasp the central features of your data. Written reports are usually better served by tables since they are economical in use of space, can easily contain large quantities of data, and present precise values. Line graphs are included in written reports when it is essential to show trends or functions.

Like tables, each figure must be referred to in the text and prepared on a separately numbered page. Figures are placed at the very end of the report, following the tables. For journal submission, figure captions (the figure numbers and titles) are placed on a separate page that comes just before the figure pages. The words "Figure Caption(s)" should be centred at the top of the page. On the next double-spaced line type the label Figure 1. and the figure title. Continue listing any other figure captions on the same page, placing each on a separate double-spaced line. Note that the figure caption page is numbered but the figure pages are not.

In constructing graphs the accepted convention is to place the dependent variable on the vertical (Y) axis and the independent variable on the horizontal (X) axis. The vertical axis should be approximately two-thirds the length of the horizontal axis. Each axis must have a label specifying the identity of the variable and the units of measurement. Many word-processing programs, as well as spread-sheet programs, have a graph or chart function that simplifies preparation. More detailed information on styles of graphs and graph construction may be found in the *Publication Manual* (APA, 1994).

DISCUSSION

The discussion section begins immediately after the results, on the same page. Centre the word "Discussion" on the next double-spaced line following the last line of the results. In this section you want to tell the reader what you think the results mean. The usual starting place is to revisit the question(s) you posed in the introduction and to state the answer(s) that may now be given. In other words, tell the reader what conclusions may be fairly drawn from your study. You should also step outside the framework of your study and consider what the results may mean in terms of other work done in this area. Do your findings support the conclusions drawn from other studies, thereby contributing to external validity? Or, do they fail to replicate, or otherwise call into question, results from previous studies? If there is an inconsistency between your results and those from other studies you will probably want to speculate about possible causes for the discrepancy. You should also consider the implications of your findings for any theories that may be relevant, especially if you have discussed these theories in the introduction. It is important, as well, to consider whether there may be flaws or shortcomings in your study. If so, you should point these out and consider how they may have affected your results. Near the end of the discussion it is often a good idea to consider the implications of your study for future research (or applied practice) and to suggest some directions that such research (or application) might take. Overall, the discussion is the least structured of the major report sections and you should feel relatively free to comment on any matters you consider important.

TEXT CITATIONS AND REFERENCES

Throughout your paper, but especially in the introduction and discussion, you will have (or, at least, you should have) made reference to various sources of information that are relevant to your work. In the last major section of your paper, the "References," you must provide a list of these sources, giving complete bibliographic information. Before turning to the reference section itself it's necessary to first consider the matter of text citations.

Text Citations

Whenever you refer to someone else's work—whether a book, journal article, thesis, unpublished report, or Web document—you must provide an appropriate citation within the particular sentence that makes the reference. There are numerous examples of such citations throughout this book. In Chapter 1, for example, I referred to a theory of hypnosis developed by Sarbin and Coe (1972) and a study of posthypnotic suggestion (St. Jean, 1978) that was carried out to test this theory. The previous sentence illustrates the two major styles of citation. In the first style the authors' surnames are given in the text and the year of publication in parentheses. In the second style both the surname and publication year are enclosed in parentheses. The choice of style simply depends on whatever form best fits the flow of the sentence. Occasionally the source of information is not a published work—as in a letter, e-mail, or personal conversation. Such sources are cited in the text as dated personal communications. For example, Maxwell Gwynn (personal communication, May 9 2000) kindly referred me to a very useful Web site that provides excellent examples of how to reference a variety of electronic communications including e-mails, listservs, Web documents, and CD-ROMs **www.apsu.edu/~lesterj/cyber4.htm**. The *Publication Manual* (APA, 1994) should be consulted for more detailed information on styles of text citation. There are a number of specific rules that deal with cases such as multiple and repeated author citations, multiple publication by the same author(s) in the same year, and the order in which multiple citations should be given.

References

Centre the word "References" at the top of the next page following the discussion. Here you will provide a complete bibliographic listing of all sources cited in the text, with the exception of personal communications. The format for each bibliographic entry varies somewhat depending on the type of source cited. Journal articles and books are the most common type of source and are covered below. Examples are provided in the sample paper.

References are given in alphabetical order by author surname, with single-author entries listed ahead of those with multiple authors. Each reference entry begins on a separate line that is indented five to seven spaces. Successive lines in the same entry are not indented. For a journal article, list the surname of each author with initials, followed by the year of publication in parentheses. The title of the article is listed next. Note that only the first letter of the first word is capitalized. Next comes the title of the journal, which is capitalized and underlined. After the journal title place the volume number (underlined) and the pages inclusive that the article appears on.

For a book entry, begin with the authors and year of publication in the same fashion as for a journal article. The title of the book, underlined and with only the initial letter of the first word capitalized, appears next. This is followed by the place of publication, ending with a colon punctuation, and the name of the publisher.

For other forms of bibliographic entry—including works without authors, chapters or articles within a book, conference presentations, and unpublished papers—consult the *APA Publication Manual* (1994). The referencing of electronic sources is covered in detail by the Web site I mentioned when discussing text citations **www.apsu.edu/~lesterj/cyber4.htm**.

SAMPLE PAPER

A sample paper illustrating many of the points covered in this appendix is presented on the following pages. It is written in the style and format you should use for your laboratory reports.

Running Head: Hypnotic Task Processing and Time Estimation

Hypnotic Task Processing, Cognitive Demands,

and Time Estimation

Richard St. Jean

University of Prince Edward Island

Karen Chipman

University of Western Ontario

Abstract

This study was performed in order to determine how variations in the cognitive demands of hypnotic task processing affect retrospective time estimates. Two high-cognitive-load conditions--including a divided-attention task and a single-attention task -- were compared with a low-cognitive - load condition. Sixty undergraduate participants completed one of the three task conditions, embedded within the administration of the Stanford Hypnotic Susceptibility Scale, Form C. Following the 28 min. task all participants provided retrospective verbal estimates of the duration. Estimates in the low-cognitive-load task were significantly higher than those in the two high-load tasks, which did not differ from each other. The results are inconsistent with a dissociation account, but provide additional support for the busy beaver hypothesis.

Hypnotic Task Processing, Cognitive Demands,

and Time Estimation

For more than 200 years the nature of hypnosis has been the subject of intense scrutiny and scientific debate. Theoretical positions have tended to polarize over the pivotal issue of whether hypnosis involves a fundamental shift away from normal information process- ing (Kirsch & Lynn, 1998). Accordingly, a great deal of effort has been invested in locating some physiological or psychological index of this shift. Although many such indices have been proposed -- from eye rolls to hidden observers, and from alpha density to depth reports -- none has gone unchallenged. Physiological indicators have suffered from low reliability or lack of speci- ficity. Psychological indicators have suffered from reactivity owing to subjects' awareness of what is being measured.

It is possible, however, that a simple, reliable, and nonreactive index has been overlooked. This index is an easily obtained verbal estimate of the amount of time that has passed in the preceding interval. A num- ber of studies (reviewed by St. Jean, McInnis, Campbell-

Mayne & Swainson, 1994) have collected time estimates
from hypnotic participants, following the administration of standardized hypnotic susceptibility scales or
the completion of particular types of experimental
tasks. In nearly all of these studies the participants
have substantially underestimated the actual durations,
by margins ranging from 35 to 65%. The magnitude of
this effect appears to be related both to the actual
duration (St. Jean, Macleod, Coe & Howard, 1982) and to
the nature of the task subjects are asked to perform
(St. Jean & Robertson, 1986). Several studies have
shown that comparison nonhypnotic intervals are more
accurately estimated than are hypnotic intervals
(Bowers & Brenneman, 1979; St. Jean, 1988). However, it
seems likely that the construction of the comparison
interval is critical in this regard.

   What can time estimates tell us about the nature of
hypnosis? The answer to this question is tied to recent
developments in the area of time cognition. Several
principles now appear to be well established. One is
that filled, or well segmented intervals, appear longer
in retrospect than do unfilled or nonsegmented intervals

(Poynter, 1989). A second is that task processors and temporal information processors both require cognitive resources and compete for available capacity (Zakay, 1989). Since task processing usually has priority, any increase in task demands will reduce the residual capacity available to the temporal processor. When this residual capacity is small relatively few temporal seg- mentation markers are encoded, with the consequence that the interval appears undifferentiated and is judged to be of short duration. In other words, the busier we are the less attention we pay to indicators of passing time, leading us to later wonder where all the time has gone.

What this suggests, then, is that time estimates should prove informative regarding information process- ing during hypnosis. The more effortful, and attention demanding, hypnotic processing is the shorter such estimates should be. If, as some theories suggest (e.g., Spanos, 1991), hypnosis involves active attempts to decode and interpret hypnotic suggestions, to con- struct a self-presentational strategy and to enact behaviours in accordance with this strategy, then the effortful nature of these attempts should be reflected by attenuated time estimates. Conversely, if hypnosis is a relaxed state, characterized by an experience of effortlessness and efficient automatic processing, then few demands should be made on attentional resources and the experience of time should be lengthened.

We have addressed these issues in a variety of studies. In one, we compared participants given individual administrations of the Stanford Hypnotic Susceptibility Scale: Form C (SHSS:C; Weitzenhoffer & Hilgard, 1962) with a control sample of observers who watched a videotape of someone being administered the same scale (St. Jean, 1988). At the end of the session all participants received an unexpected request to estimate the duration of the experiment. The hypnotic participants underestimated this duration by a large margin, typically judging the 45-minute session to be 20 minutes or less. In contrast, our observers were relatively accurate, giving an average estimate of about 40 minutes. Of interest as well was the fact that the magnitude of the time estimates was not related to hypnotic susceptibility.

Based on the time cognition literature we hypothesized

that this large difference between participants and
observers occurred because the participants faced a
more cognitively demanding task than the observers. We
wondered what would happen if we were to change the
level of cognitive demands placed on both our hypnotic
and waking participants. In a subsequent study (St.
Jean et al., 1994) we manipulated cognitive load by
giving participants either a nondemanding task (relax
and listen to a pleasant story) or a very demanding
task that required the simultaneous performance of several effortful activities (count the times a particular
name occurred in the story while playing a challenging
number game presented on the computer). All participants underestimated the actual duration of the task,
but those in the high-load condition did so to a substantially greater extent. Whether participants were
tested in a hypnotic context, having first received a
hypnotic induction, or in a waking context made no
difference at all. Again, there was no relationship
with hypnotic susceptibility. We interpreted these
results as consistent with a "busy-beaver" hypothesis
that portrays hypnosis as a cognitively challenging

task that engages the participant in an effortful problem-solving activity.

However, an alternative interpretation of these
results remains open. Since our high-cognitive-load
manipulation involved a divided-attention format it
could be argued that the results were task-dependent.
Not only was it difficult, but it also required rapid
switches in the focus of attention. Perhaps, then, it
was the shifting of attention rather than the workload
per se that mediated the effect. Conceivably, one possible mechanism for this might be the triggering of a
dissociation in the cognitive controls system (Hilgard,
1977) such that the output of the temporal processor is
not available to the executive. This explanation, by
positing that dissociations elicited by the induction
procedure functionally isolate the temporal processing
system, could extend itself to hypnotic underestimation
in general.

The current study was designed to assess this
interpretation by comparing divided and undivided
attentional tasks, equated for processing load. The
cognitive load was created by playing a demanding computer game, set at a high level of difficulty. For

participants in the undivided condition this was the sole task required. Those in the divided condition simultaneously listened to an engaging story narration presented on audiotape. As a control condition we included a low-cognitive-load task in which the sole task was to listen passively to the story, the same control that we had utilized in our previous study. We hypothesized that both the divided and undivided high-load tasks would result in the production of shorter time estimates than the low-load control task. We did not expect to find a time-estimation difference between the divided and undivided high-load tasks.

Method

Participants

    Sixty undergraduate students (14 males and 56 females), previously assessed on the Harvard Group Scale of Hypnotic Susceptibility: Form A (Shor & Orne, 1962) served as participants. All were recruited from introductory psychology classes and received extra course credit for their participation.

Materials

    Each participant was assessed on the full 12-item

SHSS:C. Other materials included a tape-recorded short story, <u>The Veldt</u> (Bradbury, 1951), and a brief postexperimental rating form containing 10-point scales to measure interest, involvement, and concentration level.

<u>Procedure</u>

Each participant was tested individually by the second author. All participants were informed that the purpose of the study was to investigate the relationship between hypnosis and attention. They were then asked to read an informed-consent form (which was also read aloud by the experimenter) that specified the nature of the tasks they would be asked to undertake -- responding to an individually administered hypnosis scale and participating in an information processing task. After obtaining the participant's signed consent the SHSS:C was administered up through item number 5. At that point participants were randomly assigned to one of three treatment conditions: (a) passive story listening, (b) computer problem solving, or (c) a combined computer problem solving and listening task. Following the experimental task period -- a constant duration of 28 minutes -- all participants were asked to close their eyes and provide a verbal estimate, to the nearest minute, of the task duration. The remaining items of the SHSS:C were then administered in standard fashion. Participants were then asked to complete a postexperimental questionnaire containing a second time measure and scales for rating interest, involvement, task difficulty and concentration level. Finally, participants were debriefed, given an opportunity to ask questions, and thanked for their time.

Results

Manipulation checks

Since both of the high-cognitive-load conditions were designed to be overloading -- that is, to fully utilize attentional resources -- it was important to compare concentration ratings and computer task performance. All analyses were performed using an alpha level of .05. Although participants attempted a larger number of trials in the undivided ($\underline{M}$ = 394.5) than the divided ($\underline{M}$ = 354.05) condition, $\underline{F}$ (1,38) = 4.84, $\underline{p}$ <.05, there was no difference in percentage of errors, $\underline{F}$ (1,38) = .84, ratings of concentration, $\underline{F}$ (1,38) = .38, or perceived task difficulty, $\underline{F}$ (1,38) = .01.

Both conditions were rated as moderately difficult and requiring a high level of concentration.

<u>Time estimates</u>

The critical data of interest, the mean time estimates, are presented in Table 1. These data are also shown as proportionate underestimates in Figure 1, indicating that participants in all three conditions substantially underestimated the actual 28 min. duration. An overall analysis of variance on these data, using an alpha level of .05, did not yield a significant effect due to task conditions, F (2,57) = 2.64, P = .078. However, planned comparisons based on the overload hypothesis showed that the combined overload conditions resulted in significantly shorter time estimates than passive listening, F (1,57)= 4,99, p <.05; but did not differ from each other, F (1,57) = .30. Within each condition, as can be seen in Table 1, correlations between time estimates and scores on the SHSS:C were low and insignificant.

Discussion

This pattern of data is inconsistent with the dissociation account. If reduced time estimation in hypnosis were due to dissociation initiated by a

divided-attention task then time estimates should have
been substantially shorter in this condition than in
either the single-attention task or the passive-listen-
ing task. Instead, the extent of underestimation in the
divided-attention task was little different from that
in the single-attention task, a result that suggests
attentional processing as the common denominator. In
addition, a dissociated controls account implies that
time estimation should be strongly tied to hypnotic
susceptibility, with highs who are presumably better
able to dissociate producing shorter estimates than
lows. Again, however, we found no relation with hypnotic susceptibility as measured by either the HGSHS:A
or the SHSS:C. We view these results as providing additional support for our busy beaver hypothesis. When
attentional resources are fully occupied by the demands
of the hypnotic task there is minimal processing capacity to spare for extraneous information, including
time-related cues.

   Our busy beaver account of hypnotic time estimation
fits better with some theoretical accounts than with
others. Views of the hypnotic process as active, goal-
oriented, challenging and skill demanding (Coe & Sarbin,

1991; Spanos, 1991) are particularly compatible with the underestimation effect. Other accounts, especially those that view hypnotic responding as effortless (Bowers, 1992) or automatic (Dixon, Brunet, & Laurence, 1990) or equate hypnosis with relaxation (Edmonston, 1991) appear inconsistent with these findings.

References

Bowers, K. S. (1992). Imagination and dissociative control in hypnotic responding. <u>International Journal of Clinical and Experimental Hypnosis, 40</u>, 253-275.

Bowers, K. S., & Brenneman, H. A. (1979). Hypnosis and the perception of time. <u>International Journal of Clinical and Experimental Hypnosis, 27</u>, 29-41.

Bradbury, R. (1951). The veldt. In R. Bradbury (Ed.), <u>The illustrated man</u> (pp. 7-18). New York: Bantam Books.

Coe, W. C., & Sarbin, T. R. (1991). Role theory: Hypnosis from a dramaturgical and narrational perspective. In S. J. Lynn & J. W. Rhue (Eds.), <u>Theories of hypnosis: Current models and perspectives</u> (pp. 303-323). New York: Guilford.

Dixon, M., Brunet, A., & Laurence, J. (1990). Hypnotizabilty and automaticity: Toward a parallel distributed processing model of hypnotic responding. <u>Journal of Abnormal Psychology, 99</u>, 336-343.

Edmonston, W. E. (1991). Anesis. In S. J. Lynn & J. W. Rhue (Eds.), <u>Theories of hypnosis: Current models and perspectives</u> (pp. 197-237). New York: Guilford.

Hilgard, E. R. (1977). <u>Divided consciousness:</u> <u>Multiple controls in human thought and action</u>. New York: Wiley.

Kirsch, I., & Lynn, S. J. (1998). Social-cognitive alternatives to dissociation theories of hypnosis. <u>Review of General Psychology, 2</u>, 66-80.

Poynter, D. (1989). Judging the duration of time intervals: A process of remembering segments of experience. In I. Levin & D. Zakay (Eds.),<u> Time and human cognition: A lifespan perspective</u> (pp. 333-363). Amsterdam: Elsevier Science Publishers.

St. Jean, R. (1988). Hypnotic underestimation of time: Fact or artifact. <u>British Journal of Experimental and Clinical Hypnosis, 5</u>, 83-85.

St. Jean, R., MacLeod, C., Coe, W. C., & Howard, M. L. (1982). Amnesia and hynotic time estimation. <u>International Journal of Clinical and Experimental Hypnosis, 30</u>, 127-137.

St. Jean, R., McInnis, K., Campbell-Mayne, L., & Swainson, P. (1994). Hypnotic underestimation of time: The busy beaver hypothesis. <u>Journal of Abnormal Psychology, 103</u>, 565-569.

St. Jean, R., & Robertson, L. (1986). Attentional versus absorptive processing in hypnotic time estimation. <u>Journal of Abnormal Psychology,</u> <u>95</u>, 40-42.

Shor, R. E., & Orne, E. C. (1962). <u>The Harvard Group Scale of Hypnotic Susceptibility</u>. Palo Alto, CA: Consulting Psychologists Press.

Spanos, N.P. (1991). A sociocognitive approach to hypnosis. In S. J. Lynn & J. W. Rhue (Eds.), <u>Theories of hypnosis: Current models and perspectives</u> (pp. 324-361). New York: Guilford.

Weitzenhoffer, A. M., & Hilgard, E. R. (1962). <u>Stanford Hypnotic Susceptibility Scale, Form C</u>. Palo Alto, CA: Consulting Psychologists Press.

Zakay, D. (1989). Subjective time and attentional resource allocation: An integrated model of time estimation. In I. Levin & D. Zakay (Eds.), <u>Time and human cognition: A lifespan perspective</u> (pp. 365-397). Amsterdam: Elsevier Science Publishers.

Table 1

Mean Time Estimates and Correlations with

Susceptibility in Three Hypnotic Task Conditions

Hypnotic Task	M	SD	r
Passive	21.8	8.78	.01
Divided	17.3	8.28	-.01
Undivided	15.9	8.07	-.27

Figure Caption

<u>Figure 1</u>. Underestimation of task intervals.

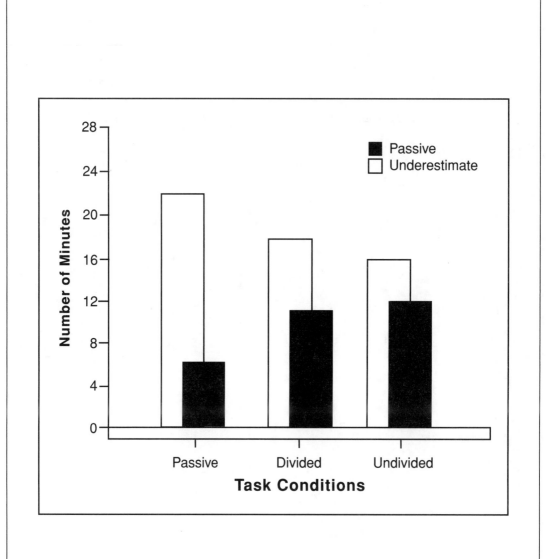

Appendix B

A Rudimentary Guide To Statistics

(Or, How Not to Be Bowled Over)

by Daniel J. Wiener

This guide has been prepared to assist you in understanding some basic concepts in statistics. Students sometimes feel helpless, over-awed, or even terrified at the prospect of learning anything so mathematical and technical as statistics. This attitude is unfortunate, and it is also unnecessary. While it is true that statistics is an applied branch of higher mathematics, the basic concepts and operations used by psychologists are simple and straightforward. There are no graphs or formulas in what follows; just a few numbers and some simple arithmetic. In order to keep things clear, all the examples are drawn from what is hoped will be a universally familiar activity—the sport of bowling.

DESCRIPTIVE STATISTICS

To begin with, there are two different branches of statistics, **descriptive** and **inferential**. Descriptive statistics are numbers used to summarize or abbreviate information. For example, rather than say that John's bowling scores in his last five games were 150, 153, 156, 146, and 160, we might summarize his performance by saying that John averaged 153 over his last five games. An average is a descriptive statistic (or index) that represents a whole set of scores (or observations) using a single number. The most frequently employed average (in psychology) is the descriptive statistic known as the **mean**. To compute the mean we simply add up all the scores and then divide by the number of scores. For example:

$$150 + 153 + 156 + 146 + 160 = 765;$$

$$765 \text{ divided by } 5 = 153.$$

One advantage of using averages such as the mean is that they allow us to draw comparisons more clearly. Suppose that another bowler, Paul, made the following scores in his last seven games: 149, 138, 128, 153, 131, 179, and 143. It is difficult to know who performed better just by looking at the two sets of scores. But if we compare John's average of 153 with Paul's average of 143, it is evident that John has been bowling better than Paul lately, since he has averaged 10 pins better.

Another useful descriptive statistic is some index of variability. Clearly, John seems to throw a fairly steady game, while Paul is much more variable and unpredictable. One way of obtaining an index of variability would be to consider first how spread out the scores are around the mean. We can see that John's scores are fairly close to his average of 153, while Paul's scores are more widely scattered around his own average of 143. If we found the distances between each player's scores and his mean score, and then averaged these distances, we would know his average variability. Thus, for John, whose mean score is 153, we would first find these distances:

$$153 - 150 = 3; 153 - 153 = 0; 156 - 153 = 3;$$

$$153 - 146 = 0; 160 - 153 = 7$$

The average, or mean, distance is computed by adding up the distances and dividing by the number of scores:

$$3 + 0 + 3 + 7 + 7 = 20; 20 \text{ divided by } 5 = 4.$$

Thus, on the average, John is four pins away from his average of 153. To say it another way, John's index of variability is 4. When computed in the same way, Paul's index of variability is 12; on the average, Paul is 12 pins away from his average of 143. Paul is thus three times as variable as John, since his index of 12 is three times as great as John's index of 4.

If you have already taken a course in statistics you may be familiar with the **standard deviation** as an index of variability. To calculate the standard deviation you begin, as before, by finding the distance, or deviation, of each score from its mean. Each deviation is squared and the sum of these squared deviations is divided by the degrees of freedom (the total number of scores minus one). Taking the square root of this result gives the standard deviation. This procedure is a bit more complicated than finding the average variability; however, the standard deviation is more mathematically sound and plays an important role in statistical theory and analyses. For comparison, the standard deviation of John's scores is 5.38 and for Paul it is 17.17.

Besides the average and an index of variability many other descriptive statistics have been developed. Suppose that we are interested in describing the relationship between John's and Paul's scores when they bowl together every Saturday night. Let us consider three possible situations:

Situation A: We might find no relationship between John's scores and Paul's—i.e., whether John does well or poorly has no bearing on Paul's performance, and vice versa. This might result from each player concentrating on his own game while ignoring the other's performance.

Situation B: We might find that their scores vary together. That is, both score high in the same game, or both score low. This might result from John, say, throwing two or three strikes in the early frames, and Paul trying harder to keep up. The competition would be keen and each would do better than his own average. Similarly, the pressure might dwindle if one or both got off to a poor start; then each would tend to bowl worse than his own average.

Situation C: We might find that their scores vary oppositely (or inversely). That is, when Paul does well, John does poorly, and vice versa. This might result from one player "giving up" if the other got off to a strong start, or "pouring it on" if the other started off poorly.

One descriptive index of the relationship between John's scores and Paul's is called correlation. A correlation is a number between minus one (-1.0) and plus one (+1.0). A correlation of zero (0.0) would describe Situation A, where there is "no relationship" between John's and Paul's scores. Situation B would be described by a positive correlation (between 0.0 and +1.0), and the specific value of the correlation would indicate how strongly this tendency to vary together is. Thus, if John bowled his best score in the same game that Paul bowled his own best, and if their next-best, third-best, and so forth down to their worst scores, also occurred in the same games, this would be a perfect relationship, represented by a correlation of +1.0. If there were a slight change from this pattern, such that John's third-best and fourth-best scores were bowled in the same games as Paul's fourth-best and third-best scores, respectively, there would still be a strong, though not perfect, tendency for their scores to vary together. This situation might be represented by a correlation of +0.9. If the tendency to vary together were still weaker, the correlation describing it would be still smaller, say +0.3.

Situation C, where John and Paul's scores tend to vary oppositely, would be described by a negative correlation (between -1.0 and 0.0). As with a positive correlation, the stronger the negative relationship is, the closer to -1.0 the correlation would be; the weaker the tendency, the closer the correlation would be to 0.0.

To make what has been said regarding correlation still clearer, let us suppose that John and Paul bowled six games together. Let us represent a player's best score with the number 1, his next-best score with a 2, and so forth down to his worst score, designated by the number 6. If the order of the games is rearranged so that John's scores are always in an order going from his best score (1) to his worst (6), we can represent the different correlations described above by different possible orders of Paul's scores. This has been done below. In each case, the number representing Paul's score in any one game appears directly under John's number for that same game:

John: 1 2 3 4 5 6	This represents a perfect
Paul: 1 2 3 4 5 6	positive (+1.0) correlation.
John: 1 2 3 4 5 6	Strongly positive
Paul: 1 2 4 3 5 6	(+0.94) correlation.
John: 1 2 3 4 5 6	Weakly positive
Paul: 3 1 4 2 6 5	(+0.26) correlation
John: 1 2 3 4 5 6	Virtually zero
Paul: 4 3 5 1 6 2	(-0.09) correlation
John: 1 2 3 4 5 6	Weakly negative
Paul: 5 6 2 1 4 3	(-0.26) correlation
John: 1 2 3 4 5 6	Strongly negative
Paul: 6 5 3 4 2 1	(-0.94) correlation
John: 1 2 3 4 5 6	Perfect negative
Paul: 6 5 4 3 2 1	(-1.0) correlation

INFERENTIAL STATISTICS

Whereas descriptive statistics are numbers used to clarify our understanding by summarizing or abbreviating information, inferential statistics are procedures used to make guesses beyond what information we already possess. For example, we would use inferential statistics to answer questions such as how well Paul would do if John scored 158 one Saturday night, or whether taking bowling lessons improves one's game. In order to understand how we attempt to answer these questions, it will first be necessary to discuss the concepts of **probability** and **sampling**.

A probability is a number from 0 to 1 which represents how likely it is that a particular event will occur. If an event will not occur at all, for instance the event of John's bowling ball remaining suspended in mid-air when it is released, we assign it a probability of zero. The more likely an event is to happen, the larger the probability we assign. Thus, the event of John bowling a 180 or better in his next game has a smaller probability (say, .17) than the event of his bowling a 153 or better (say, .52). If an event is certain to happen, for example the event of John's ball falling to the floor when it is released in mid-air, we give it a probability of 1.

One way of estimating the probability of an event is to observe how often the event has occurred in the past, relative to the number of opportunities the event had in which to occur. The ratio of occurrences divided by opportunities gives us the probability; thus, a probability is the proportion of occurrences in the total number of opportunities. Suppose that we have seen John release his ball in mid-air 10 times and that it fell every time. Based on this, the probability of the event "ball-remains-suspended-in-mid-air" is zero (occurrences) divided by 10 (opportunities), or 0. Similarly, the probability of the event "ball-falls-to-floor" is 10 (occurrences) divided by 10 (opportunities), or 1. If we were to watch John bowl 100 games on Saturday nights during July and August and notice that he scored 153 or better in 52 games while scoring 180 or better in 17 games, we would assign the former event a probability of 52 (occurrences) divided by 100 (opportunities), or .52, and the latter event a probability of .17.

The 100 games that we watched John bowl in the previous example is one possible sample of John's bowling. A sample is some fraction of the total number of opportunities for an event to occur. A more common term for this total number of opportunities for an event to occur is **population.** Thus, the process of selecting from the population which opportunities to observe is called sampling. To make this clearer, consider John's bowling 153, or better, as the event we are interested in and consider the population as all the opportunities for this event to occur. Clearly, every game John bowls is an opportunity for the event to occur. But perhaps John has already bowled thousands of games, and examining all these scores would be very tedious. Worse yet, he will in the future bowl some undetermined number of games, and there is no way of observing these events now. We could wait for John to die and then examine the complete data set of all his bowling scores but, for practical reasons, we want to extend our knowledge in the present, and to do so within reasonable effort and cost. Inferential statistics, then, uses sampling in place of complete observation of the population.

As we said above, the 100 games John bowled on Saturday nights during July and August is only one possible sample. We might take as our sample the 41 games he bowled on Wednesday and Saturday nights between March 25th and April 18th, or the 76-game set formed by selecting his first and last games bowled on each of 38 randomly chosen nights. What determines which opportunities we sample depends upon our purpose. If we are interested only in John's performance on Saturday night, we should prefer to include only games bowled an Saturday night in our sample. In general, we want our sample to be **representative** of the population we are concerned with. A representative sample is a sample which accurately reflects the characteristics of the population. If, we knew, for example, that John is tired on Wednesday nights and refreshed on Saturday nights we would suspect that he might do worse on Wednesdays. A sample which included only Saturday night scores would not be representative of John's overall performance. Conversely, a sample which included both Saturday and Wednesday night scores would not be representative of his Saturday night skill. The greatest obstacle in obtaining a representative sample is that there may be factors unknown to us that affect the scores. For instance, we might think that John's scores on the last Saturday of every month for a year constitute a representative sample of his Saturday bowling skill. But, perhaps unknown to us, John often quarrels with his wife on Saturday afternoon about the money he spends on bowling. Now, if these quarrels affect his game and if they are more frequent at the end of the month, when the family finances are strained, our sample would be unrepresentative, or biassed.

The only way we have to protect ourselves from the biassing effects of such unknown factors is to use a sampling procedure that gives each event opportunity an equal chance (or probability) to be included in the sample. A method which does this is called random sampling, and a sample so selected is termed a **random sample**. By way of illustration, suppose we learn that John bowls one game every weekday during his lunch hour and we want to know his average score this week. If we could observe John on all five days, we could average his five scores (150, 148, 154, 146, and 152) and state this average as exactly what we desired to know. Here, the five scores comprise the population of event opportunities; all five possible event opportunities are included in our observation. Suppose, however, that we can arrange our own lunch time to coincide with John's on only two days, and not all five. In this case, we are sampling two observed scores out of the population of five scores. We hope to use this sample as a substitute for full observation of the population. In order to assure random sampling, we would have to make any day's game just as likely as any other day's game to be included in our sample. This might be done by writing the five weekday names on individual slips of paper, putting the slips into a hat, and pulling out two slips. The days named on the slips would be the ones included in the sample. We would observe John's scores on these two days and use the sample average as an estimate of the population average.

Notice that even though our sample is both representative and random, it might not have the same mean as the population mean of 150. If the two scores of our sample are 152 and 148, our sample mean is 150, but if the two scores are 146 and 150, the sample mean is not 150, but 148. Our sample mean could be as high as 153 (for the sample of 152 and 154) or as low as 147 (for the sample of 146 and 148). This phenomenon is called sample fluctuation or error. That is, the mean (or any other descriptive statistic) of a sample fluctuates around the true mean of the population. For this reason, samples do not give us exact information about populations, but only approximate estimates. For most purposes it is not necessary to know the exact mean; here, for instance, we get an adequate impression of John as a 150 bowler, regardless of his particular sample average. What is important, though, is knowing something about how far our sample mean is from the population mean. We could also get a sample mean of 150 for another bowler, Bill, whose five-game average is not 150 but 180. (Bill's scores are 140, 160, 180, 200, and 220).

Clearly, this would be a misleading impression of Bill's performance. If we look at the reasons for this, we see that Bill's scores, like Paul's, are much more variable than John's. Consequently, Bill's extreme scores are much farther from his average than are John's. If only the highest or lowest extreme scores appear in the sample, Bill's sample mean will be much farther from his own population mean than will John's. By calculating an index of variability for the sample, we obtain some idea of how far the sample mean may be from its true population mean.

In our last example, we supposed that we could only observe two of John's lunch-hour games. In most situations, however, we are able to increase the sample size, being governed only (as noted previously) by considerations of cost and effort. The effect of increasing the size of our sample is to lower the probability of including only extreme high or extreme low scores in our sample. This means that the larger our sample is, the closer the sample mean is likely to be to the true population mean. By way of illustration, suppose our population is the 500 games John bowled last year, and that his average was 150. If we took 100 random samples of two games each (replacing the two we drew each time before sampling again) we might find 30 samples with means under 140, 40 samples with means between 140 and 160, and 30 samples with averages over 160. Since a total of 60 out of 100 samples had means that were more than 10 points from the population average of 150, we can say that the probability of the sample mean differing at least 10 points from the population average is .60. Now, suppose that we obtain 100 random samples of four games each, instead of two games each. We might find only five samples with averages under 140, 90 with averages between 140 and 160, and 5 with averages over 160. The probability here of obtaining a sample with an average more than 10 points from the population average is thus only .10, since a total of only 10 out of 100 sample averages are more than 10 points from 150. If the sample size were further increased to 16 games, this probability might drop to .02—that is, 98 sample averages would be between 140 and 160. So only 2 out of 100 sample averages would be more than 10 points from the population average.

Thus, we see that an increase in sample size gives us a more accurate estimate of the population average. With a sample of 2 games, the probability of being more than 10 points off in our estimate of the population average is .60; that is, 60% of the time our sample average will be greater than 160 or less than 140. With a sample of 4 games, this probability drops to .10; 10% of the time we will estimate the population average as less than 140 or greater than 160. And with a sample of 16 games the probability drops to .02 that our estimate will be more than 10 points from the true population mean. Surprisingly, it makes very little difference how large the population we sample from is. Had the population been 100,000 games instead of 500, we would have obtained the same probabilities. Provided that we sample representatively and randomly, we can reduce sampling fluctuation as much as we desire by increasing the size of our sample sufficiently, without regard to the population size.

At long last, we are ready to use these concepts to answer some interesting questions. Suppose that John is tired of being a 150 bowler and wants to improve his game. Accordingly, he takes lessons during April from a bowling expert. How might he (or we) tell whether the lessons did, in fact, help? Well, if John's average score improves following the lessons, say during May, we may think that the lessons have produced or caused this effect. However, it may be that John simply feels more confident for having had some lessons or, perhaps, his health improved after April. Either of these possibilities, rather than the lessons, could be the real cause. On the other hand, suppose that John's average score does not improve following the lessons. Does this mean that the lessons were not effective? Perhaps John had some bad habits that the expert corrected, but John still is not used to the correction. Or, perhaps as a result of the lessons, John sees how hard it will be to become a 180 bowler and, thus, loses his enthusiasm.

In the absence of knowledge about the existence and specific effects of these factors, we will be unable to answer the question of whether bowling lessons improved John's game. The only thing our knowledge of inferential statistics can provide us with is the probability of a certain amount of improvement in John's average due to sample fluctuation. Specifically, we compare the average score of a random sample of games bowled after his April lessons with his 150 average (of last year) from before the lessons. Let us say our sample is 16 games randomly sampled during May, June, and July and that the average score of these 16 games is 161. As previously noted, the probability that the average score of a random sample of 16 games will differ more than 10 points from the population average of 150 is .02. Since our sample average is 11 points greater than the population average, the probability that this sample has been drawn from John's population average of 150 last year is no larger than .02. If we reject the conclusion that this unusually high average of 161 came from a 150 bowler, we also reject the conclusion that John is still a 150 bowler. Since our sample average is greater than 150, we conclude that John has improved. To determine whether the cause of this improvement is the lessons John took, rather than some other factor such as increased confidence or health, requires the implementation of proper controls (as discussed in chapters 5 and 8).

Notice that in concluding that John has improved, we run a 2% risk that we may be wrong. Our sample might just have been one of the two times in 100 that a sample randomly drawn from a population with a true mean of 150 had a mean less than 140 or greater than 160. In psychological research we usually conclude that we are sampling from a population with a different mean when the probability that our sample could be drawn from the original population average is less than .05. In the parlance of statistical decision-making, this is called the probability of making a **type 1 error**—that is, of incorrectly concluding that a sample did not come from a given population (or, in somewhat different words, of incorrectly rejecting the null hypothesis). This probability, also called the significance level and symbolized by the Greek letter alpha (α), is set ahead of time by the investigator.

If, instead of John's average being 161 after the lessons, we find it to still be 150, what might we conclude? Since there has been no improvement in John's average it is tempting to conclude that the lessons have had no effect on his game. But, it is also possible that John's average has improved (or worsened) and that the sample mean of 150 is simply a sample fluctuation. If we mistakenly conclude that there has been no change, when in fact a change has occurred, we have made a **type 2 error**—incorrectly concluding that the sample came from the original population (or, incorrectly retaining the null hypothesis). How could such an error happen? Just as the 161 average could have been a sample fluctuation from a population mean of 150, so a 150 sample mean could be a chance fluctuation from a population with a higher (or lower) mean. Here, unfortunately, we cannot give the probability of our sample mean of 150 being a fluctuation from a population with a mean other than 150, because we do not know how different from 150 the true population mean is. If the true population mean were 155, the probability of drawing a random sample of 16 games averaging 150 might be .30 (or 30%), while if the true mean were 161, the probability might be .01 or (1%). Of course, if we knew for sure what the true population mean was, we would hardly need inferential statistics. We could simply compare the 150 population mean from before the lessons with the true population mean from after the lessons. However, in reality, we have no way of knowing what the true population mean is (since we could never observe all the relevant cases) and, thus, we have to live with the possibility of making an incorrect decision. Unlike a type 1 error, the probability of a type 2 error cannot be specified since, not knowing the true population mean, we can't compute the likelihood of drawing a particular sample mean from that population. We do know, however, that the probability of such an error is affected by a number of factors, including sample size, variability, and the actual value of the true population mean. One such factor is the value of alpha, the probability of a type 1 error. If we lower the value of alpha, from .05 to .01, say, we produce an increase in the probability of a type 2 error. This is the reason, by the way, why we do not set alpha as close to zero as possible. Doing so would increase type 2 error to such an extent that we would never be able to conclude that a change has taken place.

Let us end this example by summarizing both of the possible outcomes (improvement in John's bowling or no improvement) and both possible decisions (yes, improvement has occurred, or no, it has not occurred). Table B-1 presents in diagrammatic form the two possible outcomes and two possible decisions, and shows how statistical decision making may lead to either correct or incorrect conclusions. In reading the table, it is important to note that only one real situation can exist, but that we are never certain which situation it is. Given that only one situation can exist, it is only possible to make one of the two possible types of error—either type 1 or type 2. Thus, not knowing ahead of time which error is possible, it makes sense to attempt to exert some control over both possibilities—by setting alpha at a reasonable level and by restraining type 2 error through the size of the sample selected and controls employed to reduce variability.

This appendix is intended to serve only as a brief, and non-technical, introduction to the use of statistics in psychology. To further your understanding you should (if you haven't already done so) take a course in statistics or consult one of the excellent introductory texts available (e.g., Keppel, Saufley, & Tokunaga, 1992).

TABLE B-1	Statistical Decision Making	
OUR DECISION:	**REAL SITUATION:**	
	John's game has actually improved	John's game has not actually improved
Yes, John's game has improved.	Correct decision	Incorrect decision (Type 1 error)
No, John's game has not improved.	Incorrect decision (Type 2 error)	Correct decision

Appendix C

Table Of Random Numbers

10351 73663 04577 26447 05457 86191 31958 06369 66059 35870 24531
38849 21775 10338 31609 46071 67661 86595 98832 14740 32703 11644
96674 28293 36738 79896 26256 30992 22568 86008 45127 97933 43860
35813 26070 28059 61385 05156 60541 73458 50279 46669 44994 67558
49193 57935 43142 17250 88587 40957 10600 79549 19860 02508 95445

52104 29620 67681 61212 68658 64139 04823 58482 05521 07850 89063
01185 73189 56735 63767 88414 02564 94487 67797 96358 97137 48385
98097 39909 97057 73585 55555 53794 99007 97552 78961 94831 63138
11351 81064 06446 87859 57500 11977 55566 43194 93171 90421 73035
91829 57575 15976 74895 27087 32663 52165 41201 35264 49630 74969

81476 46143 60216 14297 21469 69931 61437 76963 04591 31510 35120
28882 13192 03582 39505 31483 79813 09136 69175 72749 76596 10668
81703 06829 42222 28642 74672 17814 30083 34939 53086 38819 48356
74638 29522 16918 18722 59229 01893 16781 23767 38232 96951 10454
18623 80719 58991 69185 71672 29182 23063 52023 92433 88764 30571

44857 07278 80159 28643 40644 66990 47740 49430 53969 76521 30974
48432 18682 21779 26812 91951 26045 30879 93494 22959 22604 48013
72098 01928 02003 16927 31153 14609 92963 67990 71765 62250 66874
77921 65975 01429 62766 24464 39432 80454 54843 89659 50968 27183
68353 66295 79171 83253 77887 70809 11190 51931 49751 17334 07475

97211 89534 58687 46438 49910 61395 72020 14149 31431 15010 42211
39512 86169 70378 34895 48894 20968 83860 56268 70828 14414 46845
66425 82482 17470 81033 85714 78717 78737 85060 09513 61880 92597
56016 25804 95841 86549 56395 12061 41358 35241 22119 73236 91492
13010 10473 70973 55590 74201 68172 85716 98256 81091 59227 47996

25773 82928 29885 72917 26589 92690 80420 05575 84693 76622 98619
34588 28197 86811 21974 95217 33287 15263 39949 28198 43455 29004
95793 23601 88280 73026 70990 47134 17480 02662 73491 31218 22196
71744 06396 03331 90161 20997 40773 06262 14943 82275 41355 50187
81119 38605 97102 24821 77020 57419 89949 91438 44598 44910 94553

69161 61984 53184 39424 27686 68509 08643 75578 99475 84190 20015
92658 28471 46134 67495 94488 79498 82837 70651 96083 74003 82081
32384 81378 98315 56232 75326 85870 54474 98359 40322 20187 51887
07313 25839 65322 06514 87638 70476 93472 44703 21410 30782 24185
13210 58329 80053 26230 17185 03731 03416 84128 59518 58562 17742

46701 34768 92722 76292 16471 38766 13828 27446 43368 91050 27081
84479 53999 31437 68769 29077 78549 44327 35869 15110 81442 84730
27271 61175 58989 28565 58364 20510 27514 46427 09993 95104 88823
04794 25301 84131 11782 30470 42655 64375 00681 24030 12063 50662
97095 99096 09776 66071 02265 36628 79027 08886 40752 98743 70657

08730 62408 68693 07770 83598 58065 07977 02823 73825 04708 34780
26226 23647 42000 11648 63093 78761 96124 67086 10500 69188 09243
65759 61497 50705 03251 84983 94039 85310 05057 51448 33141 51349
87270 41366 82763 87410 32961 49736 30290 90498 16094 89951 10926
08717 00219 93666 81949 91375 97224 42676 97469 85348 95189 79487

93186 95527 59828 11323 87636 59291 37513 43514 81476 20232 39556
52525 89615 24704 67192 36312 72329 06291 44626 60288 40968 67924
63547 50837 01469 19099 06660 75165 64617 76572 10079 86184 95820
90878 44830 04232 99163 18146 46259 53573 30586 16980 96786 70998
13274 13491 72243 56220 84659 44129 94923 39396 38948 55547 97548

99731 41658 13511 91461 80992 83380 48746 49689 14661 08828 46586
60896 79551 04218 69471 83802 97878 51093 86532 33298 92111 57974
72948 59261 04372 62513 33190 37003 10688 56347 96975 74313 46149
22415 34422 54197 93769 90230 37873 74744 79858 08466 21753 17910
61726 06160 99051 77584 89771 63951 03203 03940 75288 44990 37572

75876 97793 41515 51192 96227 41229 77529 59117 15525 57097 90654
48408 29171 14381 96934 36737 60232 11068 21200 79533 35442 90150
52613 53771 85543 24163 60071 81715 52767 06645 35394 96345 88015
16350 23565 91675 68235 00580 48748 45813 60522 57755 52442 52346
03609 86076 25807 46558 69723 05160 62080 66924 70190 50518 76964

49527 76688 86997 44953 13234 46727 86591 77807 56893 66719 68470
27711 56289 58893 04654 32154 18239 59370 53452 30120 21950 63853
94573 69963 53656 54683 04803 98125 19549 68423 31170 64874 04132
36655 89732 08314 26404 34352 42425 81151 34644 99959 81865 66035
72078 49232 84556 84793 40326 90923 76639 44435 85304 66552 93148

78572 31110 78792 01682 36695 91444 43419 04440 45776 95232 98283
28805 18716 73385 29455 65930 12407 66993 29453 19255 44524 33765
85389 80436 62614 49162 05893 58861 21672 21402 34852 52745 67114
65417 67260 64730 38878 09840 77909 33004 09385 43212 97175 70111

References

Allport, F. H. (1924). *Social psychology*. Boston: Houghton-Mifflin.

American Psychological Association (1994). *Publication manual of the American Psychological Association* (4th ed.). Washington, DC: Author.

Anderson, C. A., Bushman, B. J., & Groom, R. W. (1997). Hot years and serious and deadly assault: Empirical tests of the heat hypothesis. *Journal of Personality and Social Psychology, 73*, 1213-1223.

Archer, D., Iritani, B., Kimes, D. D., & Barrios, M. (1983). Face-ism: Five studies of sex differences in facial prominence. *Journal of Personality and Social Psychology, 45*, 725-735.

Asch, S. (1951). Effects of group pressure upon the modification and distortion of judgment. In H. Guetzkow (Ed.), *Groups, leadership, and men*. Pittsburgh, PA: Carnegie Press.

Bem, D. J., & McConnell, H. K. (1970). Testing the self-perception explanation of dissonance phenomena: On the salience of premanipulation attitudes. *Journal of Personality and Social Psychology, 14*, 23-31.

Bonica, J. J. (1992). Pain research and therapy: History, current status, and future goals. In C. E. Short & A. Van Poznak (Eds.), *Animal pain*. New York: Churchill Livingstone.

Campbell, D. T. & Stanley, J. C. (1966). *Experimental and quasi-experimental designs for research*. Chicago: Rand McNally.

Canadian Council on Animal Care. (1993). *Guide to the care and use of experimental animals* (2nd ed., Vol. 1). Ottawa, ON: Author.

Canadian Psychological Association. (1991). *A Canadian code of ethics for psychologists* (Rev. ed.). Ottawa, ON: Author.

Canadian Study of Health and Aging Working Group. (1994). Canadian study of health and aging: Study methods and prevalence of dementia. *Canadian Medical Health Association Journal, 150*, 899-913.

Cialdini, R. B., Borden, R. J., Thorne, A., Walker, M. R., Freeman, S., & Sloan, L. R. (1976). Basking in reflected glory: Three (football) field studies. *Journal of Personality and Social Psychology, 34*, 366-388.

Coe, W. C., St. Jean, R., & Burger, J. (1981). Hypnosis and the enhancement of visual imagery. *International Journal of Clinical and Experimental Hypnosis, 28*, 225-243.

Coe, W. C., & Sarbin, T. R. (1991). Role theory: Hypnosis from a dramaturgical and narrational perspective. In S. J. Lynn & J. W. Rhue (Eds.), *Theories of hypnosis: Current models and perspectives* (pp. 303-323). New York: Guilford.

Cottrell, N. B., Wack, D. L., Sekerak, G. J., & Rittle, R. M. (1968). Social facilitation of dominant responses by the presence of an audience and the mere presence of others. *Journal of Personality and Social Psychology, 9*, 245-250.

Davis, S. (1990). Men as success objects and women as sex objects: A study of personal advertisements. *Sex Roles, 23*, 43-50.

DeMaio, T. J. (1984). Social desirability and survey measurement: A review. In C. F. Turner & E. Martin (Eds.), *Surveying subjective phenomena* (Vol. 2, pp. 257-281). New York: Russell Sage Foundation.

Doob, A., & Gross, N. (1968). Status of frustrator as an inhibitor of horn-honking responses. *Journal of Social Psychology, 76*, 213-218.

Dutton, D. G., & Aron, A. P. (1974). Some evidence for heightened sexual attraction under conditions of high anxiety. *Journal of Personality and Social Psychology, 30*, 510-517.

Ellsworth, P. C., & Carlsmith, J. M. (1973). Eye contact and gaze aversion in aggressive encounters. *Journal of Personality and Social Psychology, 33*, 117-122.

Festinger, L., Riecken, H. W., & Schachter, S. (1956). *When prophecy fails*. New York: Harper and Row.

Franklin, B., et al. (1970). Report on animal magnetism. In M. M. Tinterow (Ed.), *Foundation of hypnosis: From Mesmer to Freud* (pp. 82-128). Springfield, IL: Thomas. (Original work published 1785.)

Gauld, A. (1992). *A history of hypnotism*. New York: Cambridge Press.

Greenfield, P. M., & Juvonen, J. (1999). A developmental look at Columbine. *American Psychological Association Monitor, 30*, 33.

Hilgard, E. R. (1977). *Divided consciousness: Multiple controls in human thought and action*. New York: Wiley-Interscience.

Hill, G. B., Forbes, W. F., & Lindsay, J. (1997). Life expectancy and dementia in Canada: The Canadian study of health and aging. *Chronic Diseases in Canada, 18*, 166-167.

Hogan, D. B., Ebly, E. M., & Fung, T. S. (1999). Disease, disability and age in cognitively intact seniors: Results from the Canadian Study of Health and Aging. *Journal of Gerontology, Series A: Biological Sciences and Medical Sciences, 54*, 77-82.

Holsti, O. R. (1969). *Content analysis for the social sciences and humanities*. Reading, MA: Addison-Wesley.

Humphreys, C. (1975). *Tearoom trade: Impersonal sex in public places*. Chicago: Aldine.

Jones, F. P. (1964). Experimental method in antiquity. *American Psychologist, 19*, 419-420.

Judd, C. M., Smith, E. R., & Kidder, L. H. (1991). *Research methods in social relations* (6th ed.). Fort Worth, TX: Holt, Rinehart and Winston.

Keppel, G. (1991). *Design and analysis: A researcher's handbook*. Englewood Cliffs, NJ: Prentice Hall.

Keppel, G., Saufley, W. H., & Tokunaga, H. (1992). *Introduction to design and analysis: A student's handbook*. New York: Freeman.

Kirsch, I. (2000). The response set theory of hypnosis. *American Journal of Clinical Hypnosis, 42*, 274-292.

Kirsch, I., & Lynn, S. J. (1998). Social-cognitive alternatives to dissociation theories of hypnotic involuntariness. *Review of General Psychology, 2*, 66-80.

LaPierre, R. T. (1934). Attitudes vs. actions. *Social Forces, 13*, 230-237.

Latané, B., & Darley, J. M. (1970). *The unresponsive bystander: Why doesn't he help?* Englewood Cliffs, NJ: Prentice Hall.

Laurence, J.-R., & Perry, C. (1988). *Hypnosis, will and memory: A psycho-legal history*. New York: Guilford.

Lavarakas, P. J. (1993). *Telephone survey methods: Sampling, selection and supervision*. Newbury Park, CA: Sage.

Levine, R. (1997). *A geography of time*. New York: Basic Books.

Levine, R. V., Lynch, K., Miyake, K., & Lucia, M. (1989). The type A city: Coronary heart disease and the pace of life. *Journal of Behavioral Medicine, 12*, 509-524.

Macaulay, D. (1979). *The motel of the mysteries*. Boston: Houghton Mifflin.

MacDonald, T. K., & Ross, M. (1999). Assessing the accuracy of predictions about dating relationships: How and why do lovers' predictions differ from those made by observers? *Personality and Social Psychology Bulletin, 25*, 1417-1429.

Masling, J. (1966). Role related behavior of the subject and psychologist and its effects upon psychological data. *Nebraska Symposium on Motivation, 14*, 67-103.

Maticka-Tyndale, E., & Herold, E. S. (1999). Condom use on spring-break vacation: The influence of intentions, prior use, and context. *Journal of Applied Social Psychology, 29*, 1010-1027.

Mazer, D. B., & Percival, E. F. (1989). Students' experiences of sexual harassment at a small university. *Sex Roles, 20*, 1-22.

McClelland, D. (1961). *The achieving society*. Princeton, NJ: Van Nostrand.

Middlemist, R. D., Knowles, E. S., & Matter, C. F. (1976). Personal space invasions in the lavatory: Suggestive evidence for arousal. *Journal of Personality and Social Psychology, 33*, 541-546.

Milgram, S. (1964). Issues in the study of obedience: A reply to Baumrind. *American Psychologist, 19*, 848-852.

Milgram, S. (1974). *Obedience to authority*. New York: Harper and Row.

Milgram, S. (1992). Subject reaction: The neglected factor in the ethics of experimentation. In S. Milgram, J. Sabini, & M. Silver (Eds.), *The individual in a social world: Essays and experiments* (2nd ed., pp. 180-190). New York: McGraw Hill.

Miller, P. (1995). Jane Goodall. *National Geographic, 188*, 102-128.

Moirier, D., & Keeports, D. (1994). Normal science and the paranormal: The effect of a scientific method course on students' beliefs. *Research in Higher Education, 35*, 443-453.

Mullen, B. (1986). Atrocity as a function of lynch mob composition: A self-attention perspective. *Personality and Social Psychology Bulletin, 12*, 187-197.

Myers, D. (1996). *Social psychology* (5th ed.). New York: McGraw-Hill.

Nicol, A. A. M., & Pexman, P. M. (1999). *Presenting your findings: A practical guide for creating tables*. Washington, DC: American Psychological Association.

Nisbett, R. E., & Wilson, T. D. (1977). Telling more than we can know: Verbal reports on mental processes. *Psychological Review, 84*, 231-259.

Nova Scotia Department of Tourism and Culture. (2000). *Tourism insights*. Retrieved April 20, 2000 from the World Wide Web: http://www.gov.ns.ca/dtc/pubs/insights.

NSERC (1999, June 18). *Tri-council policy statement: Ethical conduct for research involving humans*. Retrieved July 16, 1999 from the World Wide Web: http://www.nserc.ca/programs/ethics.

Orne, M. (1962). On the social psychology of the psychological experiment. *American Psychologist, 17*, 776-783.

Peterson, L. R., & Peterson, M. J. (1959). Short-term retention of individual verbal items. *Journal of Experimental Psychology, 58*, 193-198.

Pew Research Centre (1999). *A survey methods comparison*. Retrieved October 26, 1999 from the World Wide Web: http://www.people-press.org/onlinerpt.htm

Pezdek, C., & Banks, W. (Eds.). (1996). *The recovered memory/false memory debate*. San Diego, CA: Academic Press.

Prince Edward Island Department of the Provincial Treasury. (2000). *Twenty-sixth annual statistical review, 1999*. Retrieved July 18, 2000 from the World Wide Web: http://www.gov.pe.ca/photos/original/26annualreview.pdf

Roethlisberger, F. J., & Dickson, W. J. (1939). *Management and the worker*. Cambridge, MA: Harvard University Press.

Rosenthal, R. (1966). *Experimenter effects in behavioral research*. New York: Appleton Century crafts.

Rosenthal, R., & Jacobson, L. (1968). *Pygmalion in the classroom: Teacher expectation and student intellectual development*. New York: Holt, Rinehart and Winston.

Ross, M., McFarland, C., & Fletcher, G. J. O. (1981). The effect of attitude on recall of personal histories. *Journal of Personality and Social Psychology, 40*, 627-634.

Ruback, R. B., & Jueing, D. (1997). Territorial defense in parking lots: Retaliation against waiting drivers. *Journal of Applied Social Psychology, 27*, 821-834.

Ryan, C. L., Doucette, T. A., & Tasker, R. A. R. (1999). The behavioural significance of drug-induced changes in rat pup ultrasonic vocalizations. *Proceedings of the Society of Neuroscience, 25*, 1127.

St. Jean, R. (1970). Reformulation of the value hypothesis in group risk taking. *Proceedings of the 78th Annual Convention of the American Psychological Association, 5*, 339-340.

St. Jean, R. (1978). Posthypnotic behavior as a function of experimental surveillance. *American Journal of Clinical Hypnosis, 20*, 250-255.

St. Jean, R. (1979). Role of potential gain and losses in choice dilemma decisions. *Perceptual and Motor Skills, 49*, 617-618.

St. Jean, R. (1988). Hypnotic underestimation of time: Fact or artifact? *British Journal of Experimental and Clinical Hypnosis, 5*, 83-85.

Salant, P., & Dillman, D. A. (1994). *How to conduct your own survey*. New York: Wiley.

Sarbin, T. R., & Coe, W. C. (1972). *Hypnosis: A social psychological analysis of influence communication*. New York: Holt, Rinehart and Winston.

Schachter, D. L., Norman, K. A., & Koustall, W. (1998). The cognitive neuroscience of constructive memory. *Annual Review of Psychology, 49*, 298-318.

Schuman, H., & Presser, S. (1981). *Questions and answers in attitude surveys*. New York: Academic Press.

Schwarz, N. (1999). Self reports: How the questions shape the answers. *American Psychologist, 54*, 93-105.

Shaughnessy, J. J., & Zechmeister, E. B. (1997). *Research methods in psychology* (4th ed.). New York: McGraw-Hill.

Sigall, H., Aronson, E., & Van Hoose, T. (1970). The cooperative subject: Myth or reality? *Journal of Experimental Social Psychology, 6*, 1-10.

Staples, S. L. (1996). Human response to environmental noise: Psychological research and public policy. *American Psychologist, 51*, 143-150.

Stark, C. (1998). Ethics in the research context: Misinterpretations and misplaced meanings. *Canadian Psychology, 39*, 202-211.

Sudman, S. & Bradburn, N.M. (1982). *Asking questions*. San Francisco: Jossey Bass.

Sudman, S, Bradburn, N.M., & Schwarz, N. (1996). *Thinking about answers: the application of cognitive processes to survey methodology*. San Francisco: Jossey Bass.

Turner, C. W., Layton, J. F., & Simons, L. (1975) Naturalistic studies of aggressive behaviour: Aggressive stimuli, victim visibility, and horn honking. *Journal of Personality and Social Psychology, 31*, 1098-1107.

Van Til, L., MacMillan, H., & Poulin, C. (1998). *Prince Edward Island 1998 student drug survey*. Charlottetown, PEI: Prince Edward Island Department of Health and Community Services.

Volz, J. (1999). Congress looks to APA on violence prevention. *American Psychological Association Monitor, 30*, 32.

Webb, E. J., Campbell, D. T., Schwartz, R. D., Sechrest, L., & Grove, J. B. (1981). *Nonreactive measures in the social sciences* (2nd ed.). Boston: Houghton Mifflin.

Weithorn, L. A., & Scherer, D. G. (1994). Children's involvement in research participation decisions: Psychological considerations. In M. A. Grodin & L. H. Glantz (Eds.), *Children as research subjects: Science, ethics and law*. New York: Oxford University Press.

Wolf, D. (1991). *The rebels: A brotherhood of outlaw bikers*. Toronto: University of Toronto Press.

Woody, E. Z., & Bowers, K. S. (1994). A frontal assault on dissociated control. In S. J. Lynn & J. W. Rhue (Eds.), *Dissociation: Clinical, theoretical and research perspectives* (pp. 52-79). New York: Guilford.

Ziemann, U., Corwell, B., & Cohen, J. G. (1998). Modulation of plasticity in human motor cortex after forearm ischemic nerve block. *Journal of Neuroscience, 18*, 1115-1123.

Index